# JOSHUA
FOOTSTEPS OF FAITH

Growing and Changing Commentary

GROWING AND CHANGING COMMENTARY

# JOSHUA
## FOOTSTEPS OF FAITH

OLD TESTAMENT
VOLUME 6

## MATTHEW STEVEN BLACK

PROCLAIM
PUBLISHERS

WENATCHEE, WASHINGTON

Joshua: Footsteps of Faith, Growing and Changing Commentary
Copyright © 2021 by Matthew Black
ISBN:     978-1-954858-02-2 (Print Book)
          978-1-954858-03-9 (Ebook)

Proclaim Publishers
PO Box 2082, Wenatchee, WA 98807
proclaimpublishers.com

Cover art: *The Gilgal Circle in Israel*

Notes: (1) Ancient quotations have been at times changed to the ESV as well as some archaic language updated, and additional phrases added for clarification. At times verse references (non-existent until recent times) have been interspersed as well to guide the modern reader. (2) We have done our best to be careful in footnoting. Due to the nature of the sermonic material, various items are quoted freely, and may not have proper footnoting. If any great error is noticed, please contact the publisher, and it will be remedied in whatever way is available to us.

First Printing, January 2021
Manufactured in the United States of America

Dedicated to my friend and fellow elder Jerry Soen. I praise the Lord
for your indefatigable joy in the Holy Spirit and faith
that moves mountains.

# CONTENTS

# ABBREVIATIONS

## Common

cf – Latin "conferatur", compare, or see, or see also
ff – and following (pages or verses)
i.e. – Latin "id est", that is
e.g. – Latin "exempli gratia", for example

## Books of the Bible

OLD TESTAMENT

| | | | |
|---|---|---|---|
| Genesis | Gen | 2 Chronicles | 2 Chr |
| Exodus | Exo | Ezra | Ezr |
| Leviticus | Lev | Nehemiah | Neh |
| Numbers | Num | Esther | Est |
| Deuteronomy | Deut | Job | Job |
| Joshua | Josh | Psalms | Psa |
| Judges | Jdg | Proverbs | Pro |
| Ruth | Rth | Ecclesiastes | Ecc |
| 1 Samuel | 1 Sam | Song of Solomon | Song |
| 2 Samuel | 2 Sam | Isaiah | Isa |
| 1 Kings | 1 Kgs | Jeremiah | Jer |
| 2 Kings | 2 Kgs | Lamentations | Lam |
| 1 Chronicles | 1 Chr | Ezekiel | Eze |

| | | | | |
|---|---|---|---|---|
| Daniel | Dan | | Nahum | Nah |
| Hosea | Hos | | Habakkuk | Hab |
| Joel | Joel | | Zephaniah | Zeph |
| Amos | Amos | | Haggai | Hag |
| Obadiah | Oba | | Zechariah | Zech |
| Jonah | Jonah | | Malachi | Mal |
| Micah | Mic | | | |

NEW TESTAMENT

| | | | | |
|---|---|---|---|---|
| Matthew | Mt | | Philippians | Phil |
| Mark | Mk | | Colossians | Col |
| Luke | Lk | | 1 Thessalonians | 1 Thess |
| John | Jn | | 2 Thessalonians | 2 Thess |
| Acts | Acts | | 1 Timothy | 1 Tim |
| Romans | Rom | | 2 Timothy | 2 Tim |
| 1 Corinthians | 1 Cor | | Titus | Titus |
| 2 Corinthians | 2 Cor | | Philemon | Phm |
| Galatians | Gal | | Hebrews | Heb |
| Ephesians | Eph | | James | Jas |

| | |
|---|---|
| 1 Peter | 1 Pet |
| 2 Peter | 2 Pet |
| 1 John | 1 Jn |
| 2 John | 2 Jn |
| 3 John | 3 Jn |
| Jude | Jud |
| Revelation | Rev |

# INTRODUCTION

*Not one word of all the good promises that the Lord had
made to the house of Israel had failed; all came to pass.*
JOSHUA 21:45

The book of Joshua is not merely an interesting historical record of the conquest of the Promised Land by the children of Israel through the amazing power of God. It is that, but it is so much more than that. It is a historical narrative that points the New Testament Christian to his or her inheritance.

## DATE

There are so many fascinating questions surrounding the book of Joshua. The first question is one of dates. The traditional date for the start of the conquest of Canaan is 1406 B.C. The conquest of Canaan took about seven years, and Joshua's final address and subsequent death came almost twenty years later. The book begins with the nation of Israel poised at the banks of the Jordan River, across from Jericho. It records the details of numerous military campaigns that defeated the inhabitants of the land. The book ends with Joshua's regathering of the nation for his final exhortation.

## AUTHOR

Scholars believe that Joshua himself or a scribe under his direction penned most of the book. Early chapters include firsthand experiences (the ESV uses the pronouns "we" and "us" in Joshua 5:1, 6, for example) and military details worthy of being known and recorded by a general. Joshua 24:26 refers to Joshua writing a portion of the book himself. After Joshua's death, the high priests Eleazar or Phinehas may have supplemented some material in this book that alludes to events after the conquest (15:13–19; 19:47; 24:29–33).

## MESSAGE

The message of Joshua is one of victory and warning. Joshua recounted a story of contradictions. On the one hand, God gave the land that he had promised to the nation. On the other hand, the people failed to possess the land completely, allowing some inhabitants to remain. God fulfilled his side of the bargain, but the Israelites did not finish the job. The Canaanite peoples became a damaging influence on Israel as years went by.

Joshua's message is intended not only for the Old Testament saint, but also, and even more so for the New Testament Christian. The message of the apostles is weaved with the theme of Joshua: that we are to fully take hold of our inheritance, and as believers today, we know that the inheritance of the land of Israel was merely a black and white photo of the real thing. The true inheritance of every believer is God himself. Christ gives us the down payment of our full inheritance by the promised Spirit of God (Eph 1:13-14). The New Testament is filled with inheritance language.

The push of Joshua for the Christian is that we should never live with the enemy dominating our life. "Sin will have no dominion over you..." (Rom 6:14). Christ has finally and forever defeated every enemy, just as the Lord did for Israel in the Old Testament. The similarity we have with God's ancient people is that our victory in sanctification is only secure as we walk by faith. Today we do not have physical Canaanites, but we do have enemies that war against our soul: sin, Satan, and the world. The Christian is promised victory in the measure that he walks by faith.

The book of Joshua takes forward Deuteronomy's theme of Israel as a single people worshipping Yahweh in the land God has given them. This flows out of God's covenant with Abraham (Gen 12, 15, 17) and continues to us today and into the new heavens and the new earth. We hear God's promise to Abraham to give him a land and a people that will be more than the stars of heaven and the sands of the sea, though his wife Sarah is barren. We see God, through the promised son Isaac giving the ultimate Promised Seed, Jesus, and instead of getting the Promised Land, saints of the Old and New Testament are promised to be heir of the entire cosmos (Rom 4:13). So believers of all time are "heirs of God and joint-heirs with Christ" (Rom 8:17).

Israel was promised Abraham's inheritance, and they obtained it, at least in part. But listen to the Christian's promise in Galatians: "And if you are Christ's, then you are Abraham's offspring, heirs according to promise" (Gal 3:29). So, we see that the book of Joshua has everything to do with the Christian life.

## TESTIMONY

I would like to close this introduction on a unique note of personal testimony. Normally, I would not take this space to testify in any way, but I feel compelled to the give witness to the life transforming power this book had over my life while I preached it during the dark and discouraging year of 2020, when the entire globe was taken over by a pandemic of sorts. While I write, it is Christmas Eve, and the year has almost come to an end. Yet this has been one of the most spiritually formative years of my life because of the messages given in the volume before us. It is in the message of the book of Joshua that I have found one main truth that has given me a "fullness of joy", and it is this: the Christian never has to live in defeat. I have personally learned how to live in total victory. By that I do not mean without temptation or even temporary failure in sin. What I do mean is that the normal Christian life, and the life that God intends for all Christians, young or old, to live is one of constant power and victory. This life is available to all who call upon his name, indeed it is part of the victory and inheritance that Christ gives to every one of his people when they become born again.

My challenge as you read this commentary is that you will not be satisfied until you are daily living in "all the fullness of God" with the "peace that passes understanding" and the "joy unspeakable and full of glory." This our merciful God intends for every child of God, and nothing less. Be blessed with the full happiness and Shalom that God would have you to live in. Your inheritance is the fullness of his presence. We dare not live for anything less. Indeed, I testify with the Psalmist: "In your presence is fullness of joy, and at your right hand there are pleasures forevermore" (Psa 16:11).

Matthew Steven Black
Elgin, Illinois
December 24, 2020

# 1 | JOSHUA 1:1-9

## OVERCOMERS

Every place that the sole of your foot will tread upon I have
given to you, just as I promised to Moses.

JOSHUA 1:3

Joshua is a leader from the tribe of Ephraim. They are going into the
Land of Promise to settle their inheritance. The way they go in, is
they have to go in together. It's like the Marines — they leave no
one behind. In the book of Exodus and Numbers, we get the pre-story.
Joshua is 80 years old. The last 40 years he's been in the wilderness.
But now he is chosen to take God's people into the Promised Land.
They are all overcomers in the Lord. Like the New Testament says: "we
are more than conquerors" in the power of our Lord (Rom 8:37).

The book of Joshua is one of entering in, not only to the Promised
Land, but pressing into God. My hope for this study is that we will enter
into God's presence. We will begin to see what God has for us. One of
the things I love about this passage is that the Lord speaks to Joshua. I
need God to speak to me. YHWH speaks. He speaks to us. He wants
Joshua to enter into the land. The way they enter in is stunning and
thrilling. I was there in Israel just last week where these opening chapters took place. God speaks to Joshua and God speaks to us.

The scene opens in the territory of Moab, east of the Jordan, across
from Jericho, where the people of Israel are camped (cf Num 33:48–
50; 36:13). Moses has died and his helper Joshua is now in charge. The

Lord tells Joshua to lead the people across the Jordan into Canaan. He says that he will keep the promises he made to their ancestors and give his people the whole land. But his promise to be with Joshua has a condition; Joshua must study the Law and obey all its commands, and in this way he will be assured of the Lord's help in all that he undertakes.[1]

## LISTEN TO GOD (1:1-2)

**Joshua 1:1-2** | After the death of Moses the servant of the Lord, the Lord said to Joshua the son of Nun, Moses' assistant, [2] "Moses my servant is dead. Now therefore arise, go over this Jordan, you and all this people, into the land that I am giving to them, to the people of Israel."

### Hillbillies vs Sophisticated Warriors

God had a land for Israel that was massive with a very sophisticated group of warriors. The Canaanites and the Hittites were not thugs. They were an advanced people group with iron weapons and iron chariots.

For you shall drive out the Canaanites, though they have iron chariots, and though they are strong. —Joshua 17:18

Were the Canaanites depraved? Yes. They worshipped many gods: Baal, Dagon, Asherah the "Queen of Heaven," Moloch, and many others. Most of these gods were linked to fertility and success. Some of them included human sacrifice.

The Canaanites were later known as the Phoenicians, and they were people of the sea. Their influence was far and wide, even influencing the myths of Greek polytheism. In short, these were depraved, but people with sophisticated technology for their time. Their new weapon, the chariot revolutionized warfare. They were unbeatable. Israel on the other hand had nothing as far as technology. They came to the battle with only their trust in the Lord. That's a good place to be.

God says it. You can't depend on the last generation to have faith for you. You have to have a living personal faith in the living God for yourself.

---

[1] Robert G. Bratcher and Barclay Moon Newman, *A Translator's Handbook on the Book of Joshua*, UBS Handbook Series (London; New York: United Bible Societies, 1983), 10.

**Joshua 1:2** | "Moses my servant is dead. Now therefore arise, go over this Jordan, you and all this people, into the land that I am giving to them, to the people of Israel."

Moses and all the previous generation is dead. It's time to experience God personally and uniquely for this new generation. It's not enough to listen to the stories of the past generation. Where are your stories of God breaking into the impossible? Moses may die; God's promise lives on. There is the passing of an era yet the endurance of the promise. The Lord's faithfulness does not rely on the achievements of men, however gifted they may be, nor does it evaporate in the face of funerals or rivers.[2]

The people of Joshua's day were to enter into the Promised Land. We've got a Promised Land better than Israel. Our inheritance is Christ himself. He says to us: "I will never leave thee nor forsake thee" (Heb 13:5). Have you entered into the Promised Land of Christ, or are you still in the wilderness of sin? Are you born again? Have you touched the hem of Jesus' garment? Is he the center of your universe, or just an add on?

## BELIEVE GOD (1:3-4)

**Joshua 1:3-4** | Every place that the sole of your foot will tread upon I have given to you, just as I promised to Moses. [4] From the wilderness and this Lebanon as far as the great river, the river Euphrates, all the land of the Hittites to the Great Sea toward the going down of the sun shall be your territory.

Joshua believed God. His whole life, he waited on the promises of God. God had given that promise of the Promised Land to the children of Israel. "Every place that the sole of your foot will tread upon, I have given you, just as I promised..."

This promise is identical to what God gave Moses in Deuteronomy 11:24-25. From the Jordan to the Euphrates to the Mediterranean Sea — It's all the place where God writes his name. It's the land of Israel.

God promised Joshua that "every place that the sole of your foot will tread upon I have given to you" (1:3). God later says, "I swore to give this land to your fathers" the Patriarchs (1:6). In other words, this

---

[2] Dale Ralph Davis, *Joshua: No Falling Words*, Focus on the Bible Commentary (Scotland: Christian Focus Publications, 2000), 17–18.

is about God's integrity. He has promised to be gracious and good to unworthy sinners. Let's believe him.

They were to enter crossing the "great river" — the River Jordan. The most direct route from Egypt to the land of Canaan would *not* involve crossing the Jordan River. However, the Israelites had earlier forfeited their right to enter the land directly when they embraced the spies' discouraging report about the impossibility of taking the land (Num 13–14).[3] Joshua knew that when God promises something, there's nothing impossible for God. So when they finally crossed the Jordan and set up camp at Gilgal, the very walls of their camp were formed in the shape of a footprint.

## The Footprint Camp

They believed God's promise ("every place the sole of your foot will tread...I have given you,") so much so that whenever they made their camp, which they called "Gilgal" they fashioned it in the shape of a foot. In ancient Mesopotamia, property was transferred from one person to another by the former owner lifting his foot from his property and placing the new owner's foot on it at the same time a deed was drawn up. Thus, the action with the foot symbolized a legal property transaction. The Hebrew term translated as "tread" in verse 3 relates to the setting of one's foot on territory or objects in order to take ownership.

Indeed, later God calls them to cross the Jordan on dry ground. As soon as the priests foot touches the water, the Jordan River parts. It's the same place in the Jordan where John the Baptist baptized Jesus. And they were to set up twelve stones there as a memorial. The Bible says: "those twelve stones, which they took out of the Jordan, Joshua set up at Gilgal" (4:20). Gilgal means "roll away" because God had "rolled away the reproach of Egypt" from the people. It is memorialized by the 12 stones they set up at each camp to remember God's promise.

Archeologists have found six Gilgals discovered thus far throughout the land that are in the shape of a foot or a sandal dated to the time of Joshua.[4] According to two Professors (Adam Zertal and Dror Ben-Yosef) of the University of Haifa, "The 'foot' structures that we found in

---

[3] David M. Howard Jr., *Joshua*, vol. 5, The New American Commentary (Nashville: Broadman & Holman Publishers, 1998), 76.

[4] John Black. *Footprints of Ancient Israel* (Jerusalem: International Christian Embassy Jerusalem, 2013), web article accessed 31 Jan 2018. https://int.icej.org/news/special-reports/footprints-ancient-israel.

the Jordan Valley are the first sites the people of Israel built upon entering Canaan and they testify to the biblical concept of ownership of the land with the foot."[5]

Until God's people got to Shiloh, they would use the Gilgal sites as gathering places for their national feasts, including Passover, Feast of Tabernacles, and Feast of Weeks (Pentecost, Giving of the Law). Before they set up the Tabernacle at Shiloh, they would meet in the footprint at Gilgal. There was an altar there built upon the twelve stones. That altar is there today at the first Gilgal. Another place was Mount Ebal (8:30-33). That altar was just recently discovered (2004). What I'm saying is, Joshua and God's people believed God in a profound way. What God says, he will do. Every single word. Every jot and tittle. He will do it. You can trust him!

### New Testament Promises

If we would believe God is gracious, he would pour out the heavens for us. What does this promise mean to the New Testament Christian? The Promised Land is a picture of the Christian life. We are promised everything in Christ. We are "heirs with God and co-heirs with Christ." You have everything you need for "life and godliness" "His divine power has granted to us all things that pertain to life and godliness, through the knowledge of him who called us to his own glory and excellence (2 Pet 1:3).

The children of Israel had made excuses not to enter the land 40 years earlier. But now they are ready to enter. The only way this is possible is for them to believe God. Do you believe God to sanctify you? I want you to name the hardest part of your life: the area you may have a besetting sin. Let me ask you a question: Are you living the Christian life in all the power and grace that Jesus promised? If you're married: does your marriage reflect Christ? Do your words reflect Christ? What is it that you want to get rid of, but you feel powerless? What is it that you know you need to do, but you've lost the sense of God's grace?

Married men and women, you can and must treat your spouse with kindness and grace. Your words seasoned with salt to edify the hearer. Stop living in the wilderness. Believe God for the Promised Land. It's your inheritance. We have so much more than Israel of old. We have Christ and the entire cosmos. What are you waiting for?

---

[5] Ibid.

## EXPERIENCE GOD (1:5-9)

There must be a determination to follow God in obedience. It takes courage. God says, "be strong and very courageous" (vs. 7). Where does that courage come from? It comes from fearing God and knowing him. We experience God and we trust him and fear him and fear nothing else. Listen to what God says to Joshua. What was God's secret to abiding courage? It is God's abiding presence.

### Experience God's Presence

**Joshua 1:5** | No man shall be able to stand before you all the days of your life. Just as I was with Moses, so I will be with you. I will not leave you or forsake you.

In the New Testament, these words are attributed to Jesus. He says, "I am with you always" (Mt 28:20), and "I will never leave you nor forsake you" (Heb 13:5). God's presence is the only thing that can satisfy you. "In your presence there is fullness of joy; at your right hand are pleasures forevermore" (Psa 16:11). Knowing God rips out all the idols from your heart. God satisfies where nothing and no one else can.

God says to Joshua, you are an overcomer. You are a conqueror. You will always have the victory because I am with you. "No man shall be able to stand before you all the days of your life" (1:5a). No king or warrior would ever be able to stand in victory over Joshua. We too as Christians are "more than conquerors through him who loved us". We are overcomers. Our enemies are the world, the flesh and the devil. They will not have dominion. They do not have to enslave you as a Christian. Sin will not have dominion over you. You say, "That's a great idea. What's the secret to overcoming sin?" It's the abiding presence of Jesus. Remember Jesus says in John 15:

I am the vine; you are the branches. Whoever abides in me and I in him, he it is that bears much fruit, for apart from me you can do nothing. —John 15:5

### Experience God's People

It's God's presence, but there's something else that gives us courage: God's people.

**Joshua 1:6** | Be strong and courageous, for you shall cause this people to inherit the land that I swore to their fathers to give them.

They couldn't do this alone. They had to go into the promised Land all together. That's how the Christian life is. You can't do this alone. You must not isolate. You must not escape from life. You must bring your problems and sins to your brothers and sisters.

## Experience God's Power in His Word

There is a courage that comes from the power of God's Word. You want to be an overcomer? You need to meditate on God's Word. You need to constantly counsel yourself in God's Word! You will not have success and victory without a personal commitment to the authority of God's Word in your life. Do you read the Bible? Do you memorize and meditate on it? Without it you cannot have victory. You cannot live the overcoming life without a constant meditation on the Word. You will have no courage to walk in faith unless you are saturated in God's Word.

**Joshua 1:7-8** | Only be strong and very courageous, being careful to do according to all the law that Moses my servant commanded you. Do not turn from it to the right hand or to the left, that you may have good success wherever you go. [8] This Book of the Law shall not depart from your mouth, but you shall meditate on it day and night, so that you may be careful to do according to all that is written in it. For then you will make your way prosperous, and then you will have good success.

You want power? God's Word is the Christian's power source. Look at Psalm 1.

The blessed man's "delight is in the law of the Lord, and on his law he meditates day and night. [3] He is like a tree planted by streams of water that yields its fruit in its season, and its leaf does not wither. In all that he does, he prospers." —Psalm 1:2-3

You want power? It comes through living by faith through God's Word and Spirit. Constant, careful absorbing of the Word of God leads to obedience to it. Lack of study results in lack of obedience.[6]

The Lord explicitly tied the obedience of faith to success (1:8b). The God who had promised to give the Israelites the land would not do so apart from living out their faith in obedience. The experience of their fathers forty years earlier gave grim testimony to the importance of

---

[6] Davis, *Joshua*, 19.

obedience. We will not get far in our Christian discipleship by listening
to God's Word but never acting on it. Remember the words of Pastor
James in Jerusalem.

> But be doers of the word, and not hearers only, deceiving your-
> selves. [23] For if anyone is a hearer of the word and not a doer, he is like
> a man who looks intently at his natural face in a mirror. [24] For he looks
> at himself and goes away and at once forgets what he was like. [25] But
> the one who looks into the perfect law, the law of liberty, and perse-
> veres, being no hearer who forgets but a doer who acts, he will be
> blessed in his doing. —James 1:22-25

You want power? It comes through surrender to God's Word. Meditate on God's Word. Mutter it to yourself over and over again.

## Experience God's Peace

**Joshua 1:9** | Have I not commanded you? Be strong and courageous.
Do not be frightened, and do not be dismayed, for the Lord your
God is with you wherever you go.

My daughter Ava asked me if it is safe to be a missionary. "Is it safe
to be a missionary in China?" I told her being in the center of God's will
is the safest place to be. It doesn't mean we won't suffer, but we are
right where God wants us to be. So there's nothing to fear.

Martin Luther used to define faith as saying, "Yes, this is for me."
You have to look at all the Word of God as applying to you. That is the
lesson we are being taught here, as Joshua was. We are called to say yes
to God's resources—his grace and power, his constant presence—and
appropriate them to the exact point of our conscious need.[7]

You must not let fear control you. You are called to be a courageous
overcomer. There ought to be an excitement about the life of faith. Do
be frightened or dismayed. God is with you wherever you go. That's the
fear of the Lord.

> The fear of the Lord is the beginning of wisdom, and the knowledge
> of the Holy One is insight. — Proverbs 1:9

### Conclusion

Let us take the footstep of faith in our prayers. Transformation,
power, and God's presence all begin on our knees before we take even

---

[7] David Jackman, *Joshua: People of God's Purpose*, ed. R. Kent Hughes,
Preaching the Word (Wheaton, IL: Crossway, 2014), 29–30.

one footstep of faith. God wants you to live an overcoming life. Sin should not be dominating the Christian. If it is, you have to ask first, "Am I really a Christian?" And if you are a Christian, then you need to access the presence and power of God right now in Christ.

Stop living in the wilderness. Enter in to all the promises you have right now in Christ. The way forward is in the fear of the Lord. Is Jesus Christ awesome and amazing to you? Do you tremble because of the love he has demonstrated to you? You may need to be bold and courageous for Christ. You've not been trying to reach the world, but maybe the world is reaching you. Are you evangelizing the world? We are called to do that.

> Go ye into all the world and preach the Gospel to every creature. — Mark 16:15, KJV

The Old Testament Christians were to move into the Promised Land, but for us today, Christ is our Promised Land.

> All the promises of God are Yes and Amen in Jesus. —2 Corinthians 1:20

Are you abiding in Christ? Has Christ made his home in your heart and life. Is it clear that Christ is living in you? Is there any area of your life that is unconquered by Christ? Get some help. Get some discipleship and accountability. We are not called to live the life of a "barely getting by" kind of Christian. We are overcomers!

# 2 | JOSHUA 1:10-18
## MOVING FORWARD

And they answered Joshua, "All that you have commanded
us we will do, and wherever you send us we will go. Just as
we obeyed Moses in all things, so we will obey you. Only may
the Lord your God be with you, as he was with Moses!"
JOSHUA 1:16-17

What kind of person does God use in his plan of world redemption? Moses is dead, and so God calls up Joshua. The people move forward as they obey Joshua. In the passage before us, we are going to see how Joshua is a type of Christ. The Christian moves forward in holiness through total and complete obedience to Jesus Christ. Today's study is about devotion and love to Christ, and how our devotion is seen through our total surrender and obedience to him.

All of us face impossible situations in life. Daily we ask ourselves about numbers of situations, what should I do? Or I think I know what God wants me to do, but I don't know how to do it, or I don't have the strength to do it. Joshua was facing an impossible situation — entering into the Promised Land with a very inferior army.

It seems there is a sense of fear in taking responsibility and moving forward into the Christian life. God tells Joshua to "be strong and courageous" three times in chapter 1 (1:6, 7, 9), then adds, "Do not be frightened, and do not be dismayed" (1:9). At the end of the chapter, the people tell Joshua the same thing: "Only be strong and coura-geous!" (1:18).[8]

This is the second generation from the wilderness wandering, and they had limited fighting experience. In spite of this feeling of inade-quacy, Joshua does take charge, and prepares them to trust God and to walk in victorious faith. How does Joshua build up victorious faith to move forward into the Promised Land? And how do we move forward into our life in Christ, in all the power and fullness God has for us?

## TO MOVE FORWARD YOU NEED PREPARATION (1:10-11)

Preparation! A soldier cannot go to battle without great prepara-tion. An athlete who goes to the Olympics must first prepare. How do we as Christians prepare ourselves for greatest growth in faith and Christlikeness? Let's learn from Israel. The nation of Israel is about to be on the move! Forty years in the wilderness, and finally they are on the cusp of their first battle in the Promised Land — Jericho. The people need to get ready. They need to prepare. They had never fought a battle before. Once they passed over into the land, they were going to fight. God promised to be with them.

**Joshua 1:10-11 |** And Joshua commanded the officers of the peo-ple, [11] "Pass through the midst of the camp and command the people, 'Prepare your provisions, for within three days you are to pass over this Jordan to go in to take possession of the land that the Lord your God is giving you to possess.'"

### The Mind

*Finally, Time after 40 Years.* They were no longer to have their mind on wandering in the wilderness. Life means something new now. There is a goal, a gift from God: an inheritance from God. Get ready to occupy the Promised Land! This must have been a great shift in their mind and thinking. The officers were to go throughout the camp of two million people and have them get ready to leave within three days. The people have to change their mindset. No more wandering! After all the time wandering in the wilderness, it was finally time to enter in and conquer the land. God had promised this land to Abraham (1:3-4; *cf*

---

[8] James Montgomery Boice, *Joshua* (Grand Rapids, MI: Baker Books, 2005), 19.

Gen 15:18-21). It was a gift, but they are called to conquer it through warfare, trusting God all along the way.[9]

Christian, have you changed your mindset? No more wandering. No more living in sin. You are done with the old life. Put on the Lord Jesus Christ. Be done with foul thoughts and foul words. Be done with worldly living and foolishness. Be done with anger and put on God's peace. Prepare your mind for battle. "Therefore, preparing your minds for action, and being sober-minded, set your hope fully on the grace that will be brought to you at the revelation of Jesus Christ" (1 Pet 1:13).

## The Preparations

*Prepare food, but not boats.* They prepared food, and certainly packed weapons like swords, bows, and clubs (24:12). Now understand they are told to "pass over this Jordan" (1:11) at flood stage (3:15). Few of us have seen the Jordan River, but it is normally very narrow at the crossing by the Dead Sea. Yet it's not at all narrow at flood stage (up to a mile at its widest point); it is like the raging rapids that would not be safe for anyone to cross. They are going to need a miracle.

You would have expected Joshua to say, "Prepare boats so we can cross the Jordan River." Joshua didn't try to second-guess God and work things out for himself. He knew that the God who opened the Red Sea could also open the Jordan River. He and Caleb had been present when God delivered the nation from Egypt, and they had confidence that God would work on their behalf again.[10]

## The Provisions

*Manna is still falling.* Though he trusted God for a miracle, Joshua still had to prepare for the everyday necessities of life. In modern armies the Quartermaster Corps sees to it that the soldiers have food and other necessities of life; but Israel didn't have a Quartermaster Corps. Each family and clan had to provide its own food. The manna was still falling each morning (Ex 16) and wouldn't stop until Israel was in their

[9] Robert B. Hughes and J. Carl Laney, *Tyndale Concise Bible Commentary*, The Tyndale Reference Library (Wheaton, IL: Tyndale House Publishers, 2001), 86.

[10] Warren W. Wiersbe, *Be Strong*, "Be" Commentary Series (Wheaton, IL: Victor Books, 1996), 29.

land (5:11–12). But it was important that the people stayed strong because they were about to begin a series of battles for possession of their Promised Land.[11]

## The Kingdom

*Take possession.* There was no question of the victory. The people are told to "go in to take possession of the land that the Lord your God is giving you to possess'" (1:11). The battle was not for the victory, for victory was guaranteed. The battle was for them to learn to trust God.

What were they to take possession of? Yes, the land of Promise, but more than that. They were possessing the Kingdom of God. They were growing in faith and in experiencing the presence of God. They were walking by faith, taking hold of the Kingdom of God. In other words, as they took possession of the land, they were also experiencing God taking hold of them, leading them, shepherding them. We have this in common with the believers of Joshua's day.

## The Battle

*Focus on Christ, not on the battle.* So often we want God to remove the battles in our lives. The battles are there to mature us and make us stronger and closer to the Lord. You are going to have plenty of battles. We need to be focused on Christ, not on the battle ahead.

## TO MOVE FORWARD YOU NEED A PLAN (1:12-15)

**Joshua 1:12-13** | And to the Reubenites, the Gadites, and the half-tribe of Manasseh Joshua said, **13** "Remember the word that Moses the servant of the Lord commanded you, saying, 'The Lord your God is providing you a place of rest and will give you this land.'"

## Meditate on God's Promises

The children of Israel were to remember God's promise that he would give them a "place of rest". He promised to give them this land. They believed his promises. Remember, they are inheriting the land of Israel. This is God's promise to Abraham many years before. The New Testament has so much about the Christian's inheritance. Our inheritance is Jesus Christ. Hebrews 4 talks about this very passage in Joshua.

---

[11] Ibid., 29–30.

Since therefore it remains for some to enter it, and those who formerly received the good news failed to enter because of disobedience, [7] again he appoints a certain day, "Today," saying through David so long afterward, in the words already quoted, "Today, if you hear his voice, do not harden your hearts." [8] For if Joshua had given them rest, God would not have spoken of another day later on. [9] So then, there remains a Sabbath rest for the people of God, [10] for whoever has entered God's rest has also rested from his works as God did from his. [11] Let us therefore strive to enter that rest, so that no one may fall by the same sort of disobedience. [12] For the word of God is living and active, sharper than any two-edged sword, piercing to the division of soul and of spirit, of joints and of marrow, and discerning the thoughts and intentions of the heart. [13] And no creature is hidden from his sight, but all are naked and exposed to the eyes of him to whom we must give account. [14] Since then we have a great high priest who has passed through the heavens, Jesus, the Son of God, let us hold fast our confession. [15] For we do not have a high priest who is unable to sympathize with our weaknesses, but one who in every respect has been tempted as we are, yet without sin. [16] Let us then with confidence draw near to the throne of grace, that we may receive mercy and find grace to help in time of need. — Hebrews 4:7-16

Do you see? So many in Israel failed to enter into God's rest in the Promised Land 40 years earlier. How are you going to move forward in your growth in Christ? You've got to experience Christ through his Word! He's your great high priest. How do you get to know him? His Word Remember Joshua's secret to true spiritual success?

**Joshua 1:8** | This Book of the Law shall not depart from your mouth, but you shall meditate on it day and night, so that you may be careful to do according to all that is written in it. For then you will make your way prosperous, and then you will have good success.

God's Word should constantly be on your tongue. It should never stop from being on your mouth. You should meditate: repeat, repeat, repeat, repeat, with your mind completely engaged, and your heart teachable. In modern understanding, meditation is self-counsel.

Biblical meditation is not:
- Sitting with an empty mind
- Mindlessly repeating a single word or phrase to gain some sort of altered state

Biblical meditation is:

- Engaging your mind and letting it focus our hearts on God and his glory.
- Exposing ungodly or worldly thinking by the enlightenment of God's Word.
- Getting encouragement and hope from God's very voice.
- Being educated and led by the Spirit of God through the Word to live life for God's glory.

You may want to change, but you don't know how. It's right here. Meditate on God's Word until it works on you. It will cut deep to the marrow of your soul. Do you want to be strong? Eat the strong meat of God's Word. Stop only taking in baby food and milk. Get into the Word, and let it get inside you so that you feel the presence of God the Holy Spirit in you. Set yourself apart with God or you will fall apart!

## Depend on God's People

Now we come to a second way to find protection in God. You have to always be sure to surround yourself with the people of God. Depend on God's people. That's what Israel did. Then had to enter and fight together. Do you hear: together. We live life together as God's people, like Israel.

**Joshua 1:14-15** | Your wives, your little ones, and your livestock shall remain in the land that Moses gave you beyond the Jordan, but all the men of valor among you shall pass over armed before your brothers and shall help them, [15] until the Lord gives rest to your brothers as he has to you, and they also take possession of the land that the Lord your God is giving them. Then you shall return to the land of your possession and shall possess it, the land that Moses the servant of the Lord gave you beyond the Jordan toward the sunrise."

The tribes of Reuben and Gad and half of the tribe of Manasseh settled on west side of the Jordan River. It's called the half-tribe, because the other half of Manasseh settled on the east side of the Jordan River. Each of the tribes had covenanted with the Lord while Moses was alive that they would help each other inherit the land. Joshua reminded them of Moses' words of instruction and warning (21:21–35; Deut 3:12-20) and urged them to keep the promise they had made.

In the nation of Israel it was the able men twenty years and older who went out to war (Num 1:3); and the record shows that the two and a half tribes had 136,930 men available (26:7, 18, 34). But only 40,000 men actually crossed the Jordan and fought in the Promised Land (4:13). The rest of the recruits stayed to protect the women and children in the cities the tribes had taken (32:1–5, 16-19). When the soldiers returned home, they shared the spoils of war with their brothers (22:6-8).[12]

The point is: Israel is called to inherit together. Once one tribe has conquered their land, they are to help the remaining tribes until all the tribes are settled. There is one Israel, though there are twelve tribes. They are all to settle the land together. There are no lone ranger Christians. The church is the embodiment of Jesus. Christ is our exalted head! To say you love Jesus while showing indifference toward his local church actually offends and grieves Jesus. Every local church is imperfect, and we all have our battle-scars. But we are vitally connected with Christ. You cannot be connected with Christ and *not* be connected to his Body. Are you connected? Or is church just an hour on Sunday? You will not grow until your life is enmeshed with the Body.

> We are to grow up in every way into him who is the head, into Christ, [16] from whom the whole body, joined and held together by every joint with which it is equipped, when each part is working properly, makes the body grow so that it builds itself up in love. — Ephesians 4:15-16

Consider something else. We are at massive risk when we are alone! The Bible describes Christians as sheep (Psa 95:7; Jn 10:1-18). Sheep are prey, because, frankly, they're not the sharpest tools in the shed. Jesus has blessed the church with under-shepherds—elders of local churches (Acts 20:28-32; Eph 4:11-12; 1 Pet 5:1-4)—to protect the sheep from wolves, and to protect the sheep from their own foolish curiosities and bad appetites that would lure them to wander off cliffs. Independence is no virtue in sheep, and overconfidence is no virtue in Christians. The Bible also describes Christians as members of Christ's body. Your arm will rot if it remains detached from your shoulder. Similarly, your spirit will wither if it's not connected to a visible body of Christ in a local church.

---

[12] Wiersbe. *Be Strong*, 31.

Without sound preaching applied in the context of a local church, lone rangers remain malnourished. You need faithful shepherds not only to feed the sheep at church, but in their daily lives. Lone ranger Christians set a bad example for others. Their behavior leads others to wrongly believe that the Christian life can safely be lived in isolation from other Christians. Nothing could be further from the truth. Don't be a lone ranger Christian.

We can only grow if we grow together. We have some weak among us and some strong. We are to come along side each other and enter into our inheritance (the presence of God) together. We must leave no one behind. Weak Christians and strong Christians are equal inheritors of the Kingdom of Christ. We are called to live under the headship of Jesus, building up his body in love.

## TO MOVE FORWARD YOU NEED LEADERSHIP (1:16-18)

Joshua receives the loyalty and obedience of the people. God united the people under Joshua's leadership.

**Joshua 1:16-18** | And they answered Joshua, "All that you have commanded us we will do, and wherever you send us we will go. [17] Just as we obeyed Moses in all things, so we will obey you. Only may the Lord your God be with you, as he was with Moses! [18] Whoever rebels against your commandment and disobeys your words, whatever you command him, shall be put to death. Only be strong and courageous."

When God's people unite around the core duty of obedience, they can rest assured that God will bless them in wonderful ways.[13] Why was Joshua such an effective leader?

### A Faithful Past

Joshua appears twenty-seven times in Exodus, Numbers and Deuteronomy, each time painting a picture of exemplary faithfulness. He is a type of Christ. The name Jesus in the New Testament (*Yeshua*) is a form of the Old Testament name "Joshua", which means "Jehovah saves".

---

[13] Roger Ellsworth. *Opening up Joshua*, Opening Up Commentary (Leominster: Day One Publications, 2008), 36.

Just as it was with Moses, so it needed to be with Joshua. Do you remember the very first appearance of Joshua in the Bible? It is in Exodus 17:8–16, which tells of the very first battle the tribes of Israel had after they had been led out of Egypt by Moses and crossed the desert to Rephidim. The battle was against the Amalekites, a semi-Semitic tribe that occupied the wide desert region between the southern borders of Palestine and Mount Sinai. Moses gave Joshua command of the Jewish troops in this battle.

We are told that while Joshua was leading the armies of the Lord against the Amalekites, Moses went up on a hill overlooking the battlefield and raised his hands as a sign of God's blessing. As long as his hands were up, the Israelites were winning. But when he grew tired and lowered his hands, the Amalekites would begin to defeat Israel. This became clear to Aaron and Hur, who were with Moses, so they had Moses sit on a large rock while they stood on either side of him and supported his arms. They did this until sunset, by which time the armies of the Amalekites were overcome.[14]

The importance of this victory was not Moses' arms, but two facts: (1) victory comes from the Lord, and (2) God gives victory to those who support faithful leadership. Joshua knew that the only way forward was to support Moses. He experienced Moses' God. I want to know if you are a leader, who are you leaning on? You can't do it alone! You need help! So many faithful men have fallen because they thought they could do it alone. You have to have people you are accountable to, people who encourage you. Who is encouraging you? Who is holding up your hands?

The second time we see Joshua is at Mount Sinai, to which Moses was called by God to receive the law. When Moses went up the mountain, Joshua went with him, stopping partway. He stayed at his post on the mountain during the entire forty days that Moses was meeting with God.[15] Joshua saw God on Mount Sinai.

Then Moses and Aaron, Nadab, and Abihu, and seventy of the elders of Israel went up, [10] and they saw the God of Israel. There was under his feet as it were a pavement of sapphire stone, like the very heaven for clearness. [11] And he did not lay his hand on the chief men of the

---

[14] Boice. *Joshua*, 20.
[15] Ibid., 21.

people of Israel; they beheld God, and ate and drank. — Exodus 24:11-12

As a leader, Joshua saw glories that would be impossible to describe. That's what you need if you want to lead God's people. And we are called to grow and lead in some way, because we are all called to "go into all the world and make disciples" (Mt 28:18-20). Are you experiencing the glories of God? You need to get there. We are all called to get there. It's all yours right now.

## A Faithful Savior

**Joshua 1:16, 18** | And they answered Joshua, 'All that you have commanded us we will do...Only be strong and courageous'".

Did the people fully obey Moses? No. Would they fully obey Joshua? Of course not. It is here we see Joshua as a type of Christ. He is leading the body of God's people into the Promised Land. Jesus is our Joshua. The Christian is to follow Christ in all things. He is our exalted head. Jesus told his disciples,

> If anyone would come after me, let him deny himself and take up his cross and follow me. — Matthew 16:2

> I am crucified with Christ: nevertheless I live; yet not I, but Christ lives in me: and the life which I now live in the flesh I live by the faith of the Son of God, who loved me, and gave himself for me. — Galatians 2:20, KJV

### Conclusion

This this is the same God we seek through Jesus that is faithful to all his promises. What about you? Are you moving forward in the Christian life, or do you feel like you are stuck? God is faithful. He has prepared you and given you every spiritual blessing in Christ you could ever need (Eph 1:3). You lack nothing (Psa 23:1). He's predestined you for holiness (Rom 8:29). "In him we have obtained an inheritance, having been predestined according to the purpose of him who works all things according to the counsel of his will" (Eph 1:11). So what are you waiting for? God's got the plan and he's predestined you to it. What is holding you back? Are you looking for the sin beneath the sin in your heart? Follow the anger, anxiety, despair and foolishness, and you will discover what you treasure above Christ. You will never move forward the way you want to until Christ has full control over you and is seating without competition on the throne of your heart.

Are you moving forward? If not, why not? You ought to sniff out the stench of sin in your life. Look at the emotions of your heart. Are you loving and desiring God, or are there things from this world that you hold dearer? You think the world will make you happy, but it can only offer you superficial and temporary happiness. Deep, lasting, glorified joy can only come from Jesus. Stop being stuck. Move forward through surrender. Lose your life that you may find it. Be crucified with Christ that you may life. You move forward by letting go of this life and taking hold of Christ and delighting in him above all else.

# 3 | JOSHUA 2
# THE SCARLET CORD

*Behold, when we come into the land, you shall tie this scar-*
*let cord in the window through which you let us down, and*
*you shall gather into your house your father and mother,*
*your brothers, and all your father's household.*
JOSHUA 2:18

In this second chapter of the book of Joshua is the story of a woman
who had a wonderful transformation. She started as a harlot, but she
became a saint. By all accounts, she was an important woman in Jericho. Josephus, the first century Jewish historian describes her as the
manager of an inn.[16] She likely lived and managed the homes that were
built within the walls of Jericho. These were called "casemate" walls.[17]

Jericho was not a particularly large city. But it was strongly fortified. And most important, it was one of the few entryways to the inte-
rior of Canaan. Israel had to pass this way to reach the rest of the land.[18]
Though it was good for Israel to find a friend in Rahab, the walls of
Jericho were fortified in such an amazing way that it would take a miracle to get through this city and enter Canaan.

---

[16] Josephus. *Antiquities*, Book V, chapters 1-7.
[17] Anthony J. Frendo. "Was Rahab Really a Harlot?" *Biblical Archaeology Re-*
*view* 39:5, September/October 2013.
[18] Lawrence O. Richards, *The Teacher's Commentary* (Wheaton, IL: Victor
Books, 1987), 167.

And a miracle would occur. The walls would soon fall when God's people would march around the city. I love to say that faith is the evidence of things not seen. God's given us a conscience, and the divine complexity of creation, but he's also given us vast amounts of evidence for the events of the Bible. The Bible is based on history: actual events that archeologists are still studying to this very day.

In 1930, when British archeologist John Garstang studied the site of ancient Jericho, he found collapsed walls, not walls broken down from the outside but that had fallen outward, creating a ramp of fallen bricks by which the Israelites "went up into the city" on the ramp of the walls as Joshua 6:20 records.[19] Archeologists found fallen city walls, burned stores of grain and evidence of destruction of the city by fire, all of which he dated to about 1400 BC—right in line with the Biblical chronology of the city's destruction.

Joshua and the priests of Israel are going to march around the walls of Jericho, but this great victory first begins with this somewhat controversial character: Rahab. Who was Rahab? Remember, she hides the spies of Israel in the flax. Flax is a plant that is used today to make linen fabric. It's stalks, when beaten, have a fine hair-like texture. Many have surmised that Rahab was not only an innkeeper, but she was also a trusted businesswoman in Jericho, who had a clothing business from her flax. She might have been a sort of fashionista. Certainly, she was high up in the political circle of the city, as she was well acquainted with the king. She is mentioned in the book of James as a prostitute who became a righteous woman with a living, vibrant faith.

> In the same way, was not even Rahab the prostitute considered righteous for what she did when she gave lodging to the spies and sent them off in a different direction? — James 2:25, NIV

Rahab lived down in Jericho, which is near the Dead Sea, the lowest spot on earth, and she took one of the lowest professions, that of prostitution. This woman was incredibly transformed. Remember that she was a pagan. She was living in spiritual darkness. She was also a Canaanite, destined for divine destruction, because God had said that

---

[19] John Garstang, "The Date of the Destruction of Jericho," *Palestine Exploration Fund Quarterly Statement* (*PEFQS*) 1927, pp. 96-100; "Jericho: Sir Charles Marston's Expedition of 1930," *PEFQS* 1930, pp. 123-125; "A Third Season at Jericho," *PEFQS* 1932, p. 149; "Jericho and the Biblical Story," in *Wonders of the Past*, ed. J.A. Hammerton (New York: Wise, 1937), p. 1216.

he was going to destroy the city that she lived in due to their generations of depravity.

Yet, this woman got so radically and dramatically changed, saved,
transformed, that she had a pure life. This pagan, this Canaanite, marries a man of Israel named Salmon. Some have imagined that Salmon
might have been one of the two spies that Rahab hid. At any rate, this
prostitute, this Canaanite, this pagan woman, turns to the Lord in faith
and becomes the great, great grandmother of King David, and she also
becomes a part of the genealogy of the Lord Jesus Christ (Ruth 4:21;
Mt 1:5-6). What an incredible story!

Also, in the book of Hebrews, when the list of the great heroes of
the faith is given, she's one of two women mentioned (the other is Sarah, Abraham's wife). As we begin our text in Joshua 2, she's a harlot.
She's a Canaanite. She's in a city marked for destruction. And she gets
saved! She goes from the house of shame to the Hall of Fame. She's
listed in Hebrews 11 the Hall of Faith.

> Hebrews 11:31, By faith Rahab the prostitute did not perish with
> those who were disobedient, because she had given a friendly wel-
> come to the spies.

Rahab is radically, dramatically transformed, changed for God,
changed for good, changed for eternity. I think that's worthy of study.
In our study, we're going to try to understand how this happened. What
we see is the two spies in Joshua 2 meeting Rahab and spying out the
city. When they meet, it's like two worlds colliding: pagan Rahab and
faithful spies who love the Lord.

## THE PROVIDENCE THAT CONNECTED RAHAB (2:1-7)

### An Unlikely Providence

Throughout the story of Rahab, we see that God is in control. He's
drawing people to himself. Christ said, "And I, when I am lifted up from
the earth, will draw all peoples to myself" (Jn 12:32). God is drawing
people to himself from every tribe, language, family and nation. He's in
control. Do you believe that? And often the people that he draws are
the most unlikely candidates. How did it happen?

**Joshua 2:1a** | And Joshua the son of Nun sent two men secretly from
Shittim as spies, saying, 'Go, view the land, especially Jericho.

They are getting ready for this battle to take the city of Jericho. You know the story of the incredible fall of the walls of Jericho. Before they go in, they send some men out for reconnaissance, to spy out the city and get the lay of the land. So they went into the land, and it says,

**Joshua 2:1b** | And they went and came into the house of a prostitute whose name was Rahab and lodged there.

Rahab was indeed a harlot, but she was also somewhat of a gate-keeper, a trusted person in the city. As I mentioned, she's a business-woman. She's got a clothing business. She's got a flax supply that was used to make linen and clothing.

She's likely the manager of the inn that is located within or on top of the walls of Jericho. They lodge there, spending their time there in her house, coming and going. Who would have thought that this woman would be the mother of Boaz who married Ruth, and the great, great Grandma of King David, as well as an ancestor of our Lord Jesus Christ? God chooses the most unlikely people.

Not many of you were wise according to worldly standards, not many were powerful, not many were of noble birth. [27] But God chose what is foolish in the world to shame the wise; God chose what is weak in the world to shame the strong; [28] God chose what is low and despised in the world, even things that are not, to bring to nothing things that are, [29] so that no human being might boast in the presence of God. — 1 Corinthians 1:26-29

Jesus would often praise his Father for hiding himself "from the wise and understanding" and revealing himself to the humble (Lk 10:21; Mt 11:25).

## An Unrelenting Providence

All is well until the King of Jericho gets wind of all this, and he con-fronts Rahab, and she is willing to lie. When Rahab lies, does God say, "That's it, this is over!" No, his love is unrelenting. We read:

**Joshua 2:2-7**| And it was told to the king of Jericho, "Behold, men of Israel have come here tonight to search out the land." [3] Then the king of Jericho sent to Rahab, saying, "Bring out the men who have come to you, who entered your house, for they have come to search out all the land." [4] But the woman had taken the two men and hidden them. And she said, "True, the men came to me, but I did not know where they were from. [5] And when the gate was about to be closed at dark, the men went out. I do not know where the men went. Pursue them quickly, for you will overtake them." ⁶ But she had brought them up to the roof and hid them with the stalks of flax that she had laid in order on the roof.

Here Rahab already has taken sides. She is already acting in faith by hiding the men. Did she need to lie? Should she have lied. Let's remember what the theologians teach us. God is not bound by secondary causes. In other words, whether she would lie or not lie, God had already given the victory over Jericho to his people as he promised. God's primary cause — his providential will — was never in question. Let's be clear: God did not need for Rahab to lie in order to take the city.

Another query comes as we consider the faith of Rahab. Would a truly converted person still be able to deceive? John tells us that a truly born-again person cannot continue in a life of sin.

> No one born of God makes a practice of sinning, for God's seed abides in him; and he cannot keep on sinning, because he has been born of God. ¹⁰ By this it is evident who are the children of God, and who are the children of the devil: whoever does not practice righteousness is not of God. — 1 John 3:9-10

A true child of God cannot live comfortably in sin. This is absolute truth. Jesus dismisses professing lawless Christians to hell on the day of judgment (Mt 7:21-23). A true believer cannot continue in sin. So what do we say about Rahab? She's listed in the Hebrews 11 Hall of Faith. Though she lied, she did not continue in sin, but she did continue in faith. In this situation, God (in Heb 11; Jas 2) praised Rahab, not for her lying, but for her faith and doing the best she could in such a terrible situation. She marries a Hebrews — Salmon (possibly one of the spies), gives birth to Boaz who marries Ruth, and of course you know the rest of the story as she is listed in Jesus' genealogy (Mt 1:5).

The great emphasis of Rahab is not how she began, but how great her faith was! It's very messy at first, but it is strong! Naturally, the New Testament does not fall into the trap of focusing on the lie she told, but on her life of steadfast and living faith (Heb 11:31; Jas 2:25).[20]

---

[20] Davis, *Joshua*, 26.

## A Two-Sided Providence

Now, this is very interesting. We see that God works on both sides of the equation here. God works in the heart of the sinner, and he works in the heart of the soul-winner. You know this to be true, but we see it to be true here in Joshua 2. God works in the faithful spies and in the heart of the pagan prostitute.

Think of all of the people in the city of Jericho. Here is this city, great in iniquity, great in antiquity, great in importance, and in all of the city two men go to one house. Do you think that was an accident? Do you think that it just happened by chance? No! They were divinely directed. We're going to see that this woman was already under deep spiritual conviction. We're going to come to that. It was not by mere chance that they went there. They were sent, guided by the Holy Spirit of God. It was the providence of God that confronted her.

The way the Holy Spirit of God works is this: he begins by many, many ways to work in the hearts and minds of sinful people, softening them up, getting them ready for a work of God, getting them ready to be saved. He works the heart of the sinner, softening that sinner's heart up and bringing that sinner under conviction. Then God works in the heart of the soul winner, the messenger, and he begins to get that person in the center of his will. Then by divine providence he brings them together. Here's someone under conviction, and here's a servant ready to be used, and God the Holy Spirit gets them together.

God has placed you where you are to reach out and shine the light. You may meet a few Rahabs. You have no idea how God is going to use you. The best ability is availability. God uses those who are available, like these two spies. If God is not bringing you face to face with people who need the gospel, maybe you ought to ask yourself why. Why? Why am I not having these opportunities? Might it be that you're not steerable, usable, and guidable? I heard someone say, "If you get right with God, you'll have to backslide to keep from winning souls."

## THE EVIDENCE THAT CONVICTED RAHAB (2:8-11)

God had already been working in Rahab's heart before the two spies ever got there to Jericho. Now how, how would a prostitute, a harlot, living in a Canaanite city, how would she be under the Holy Spirit's conviction? How, how did this happen? Well, let's continue to read.

**Joshua 2:8-9** | Before the men lay down, she came up to them on the roof [9] and said to the men, "I know that the Lord has given you the land, and that the fear of you has fallen upon us, and that all the inhabitants of the land melt away before you.

## Evidence in Israel's Testimony

She's already being drawn by the Lord. She says she heard of the victories of Israwl and the Red Sea crossing. Her heart melted. Everyone's heart in Jericho melted. Some turned to fear, but Rahab turned to faith. Why is it that she lined up with these men? Why is it that she hides these men? Where did a pagan get such conviction? I'll tell you. She had seen what God was doing for his people, and it brought conviction upon her. What was the evidence that convicted her? It was the moving of God in the hearts and lives and victory of his people.

### The Might of the Lord

The content of Rahab's confession justifies its central place in the story. She rehearses the might of Yahweh:

**Joshua 2:10** | For we have heard how the Lord dried up the water of the Red Sea before you when you came out of Egypt, and what you did to the two kings of the Amorites who were beyond the Jordan, to Sihon and Og, whom you devoted to destruction.

This was the basis of her faith; she had heard about the mighty acts of God. This is the normal way of coming to faith. Biblical faith is based on at least some knowledge, data, and evidence. Faith is not just a warm, cozy feeling about God. Faith grows, if at all, out of hearing what God has done for his people.[21] The author of Hebrews defines faith perfectly, by the Spirit's inspiration.

Faith shows the reality of what we hope for; it is the evidence of things we cannot see. —Hebrews 11:1, NLT

Faith is not blind. There is evidence in every particle, every law of science, every law of morality that rules our conscience. God is ruling over every particle in the universe, as Abraham Kuper famously said:

---

[21] Ibid.

There is not a square inch in the whole domain of our human existence over which Christ, who is Sovereign over all, does not cry:
"Mine!"[22]

The faith of the believer is the most honest, true and logical conclusion. Faith is not a mere wish or bashful hope, but it is an unrelenting trust in God based on the reality of nature, conscience, and his
movement and testimony in history. It is not that we must search for
this evidence. The evidence of God's fingerprints on the universe is unmistakable in every moment of time and space. To open one's eyes to
reality of God's presence in all things is the first step of faith, but true
faith must put all of one's trust in God based on all his mighty acts, both
from nature and those in the realm of the supernatural. They are all
around if one would merely open one's eyes and heart and look around.
Rahab saw the mighty acts of God and trusted in his almighty name.

### The Majesty of the Lord
Then Rahab confesses the majesty of Yahweh when she says:

**Joshua 2:11** | And as soon as we heard it, our hearts melted, and there
was no spirit left in any man because of you, for the Lord your
God, he is God in the heavens above and on the earth beneath.

That is the conviction of faith. This was to be the conclusion Israel
was to reach about her God (Deut 4:39). But here is a pagan, Canaanite
harlot with an 'Israelite' confession on her lips. She holds to the utter
supremacy of Yahweh. She comes in full trust and surrender, believing
that he is the only God functioning in heaven and upon earth.[23]

### The Mercy of the Lord
All of this leads Rahab to seek God in his mercy and grace.

**Joshua 2:12-13** | Now then, please swear to me by the Lord that, as I
have dealt kindly with you, you also will deal kindly with my father's house, and give me a sure sign [13] that you will save alive my
father and mother, my brothers and sisters, and all who belong to
them, and deliver our lives from death."

Here is the evidence of faith. Genuine faith never rests content with
being convinced of the reality of God but presses on to take refuge in

---

[22] Abraham Kuyper: *A Centennial Reader*, ed. J.D. Bratt (Eerdmans, 1998), 488.
[23] Davis, *Joshua*, 26.

God. Rahab not only must know the clear truth about God but also must escape the coming wrath of God. It isn't just a matter of correct belief but of desperate need. Saving faith is always like this. It never stops with brooding over the nature or activity of God but always runs to take refuge under his wings. Amazingly, Rahab not only trembles before the terror of the Lord but also senses that there might be mercy in this fearful God. What but the touch of Yahweh's hand could have created such faith in the heart of this pagan harlot?[24]

## Evidence in Our Personal Testimony

Not only are we to be witnesses, we ought to be part of the evidence. What is there about your life that is unexplainable? Are you opening your mouth and sharing your faith? Jesus spoke clearly and gave his marching orders to us before he ascended: "Go therefore and make disciples of all nations..." (Mt 28:19). "Go into all the world and proclaim the gospel to every creature" (Mk 16:15). Can people see Jesus in you? Are you filled with the Spirit? Living a holy life?

If the Israelites, coming across the desert, had just been like everybody else, there would have been no conviction in the heart of this pagan. But, you see, you could not deny God had opened the Red Sea for them. God had given them victory over mighty armies. God had marched before them. And Rahab said, "When we heard what your God was doing for you, our hearts did melt" (cf 3:11).

Is there enough evidence in the working of God in our lives to truly convict that person who lives next door, that person who works in the next office, that person who plays alongside you on that team? Can they see a difference? Do they see the hand of God? Brothers and sisters, the greatest argument for Christianity and the greatest argument against Christianity is the life of a Christian. You may be the only evidence of Christianity that some of your friends, loved ones and co-workers ever see. If you name the name of Jesus Christ and you're not living, walking, and talking victory, you need to stop living in your flesh and surrender. Be a vessel that God can use. If you name the name of Jesus Christ and you are surrendered, humble, then God will use you. What's your testimony of faith in Christ? Are you sharing it with others?

---

[24] Ibid.

## THE CONFIDENCE THAT CONVERTED RAHAB (2:14-24)

## Confidence Seen in the Scarlet Cord

It doesn't take long for Rahab to express her faith. She claims the LORD as her God. And now she's pleading for her loved ones. She says to the two spies:

**Joshua 2:14-21** | And the men said to her, "Our life for yours even to death! If you do not tell this business of ours, then when the Lord gives us the land we will deal kindly and faithfully with you." [15] Then she let them down by a rope through the window, for her house was built into the city wall, so that she lived in the wall. [16] And she said to them, "Go into the hills, or the pursuers will encounter you, and hide there three days until the pursuers have returned. Then afterward you may go your way." [17] The men said to her, "We will be guiltless with respect to this oath of yours that you have made us swear. [18] Behold, when we come into the land, you shall tie this scarlet cord in the window through which you let us down, and you shall gather into your house your father and mother, your brothers, and all your father's household. [19] Then if anyone goes out of the doors of your house into the street, his blood shall be on his own head, and we shall be guiltless. But if a hand is laid on anyone who is with you in the house, his blood shall be on our head. [20] But if you tell this business of ours, then we shall be guiltless with respect to your oath that you have made us swear." [21] And she said, "According to your words, so be it." Then she sent them away, and they departed. And she tied the scarlet cord in the window.

I love this scarlet cord that Rahab left in the window. It may not have meant anything to her, but indeed, her faith was pointing to another scarlet cord that runs through the Bible: the scarlet cord of redemption. The Bible tells us in the book of Hebrews that Rahab was justified by faith. Now, we're not just talking about somebody coming out of danger, not just that her physical life was spared from the invasion of Israel, but she was saved from eternal punishment by faith. She placed the scarlet rope in the window. What does that remind you of? We see a scarlet cord that runs throughout the whole Bible. Her scarlet cord would have spoken of her great wealth and affluence by a very illicit trade: prostitution. But God turned that scarlet cord into a thread of redemption that we see throughout the Bible.

## The Blood of the Passover

Remember that these spies had come out of the land of Egypt before they entered into the land of Jericho. And when they came out of Egypt, God said, "I want you to take a lamb. I want you to slay that lamb. And I want you to put the blood of that lamb upon the doorposts and the lintel of the house. And when I see that scarlet blood, "... when I see the blood," God said, "I will pass over you." You can read that in Exodus 12:13: "....when I see the blood, I will pass over you." These men said, "Hey, it's the blood that delivers. Put the scarlet thread I the window." Scarlet is the color of blood. "Let it stand for the blood of the lamb. You will come into covenant with those people who are under the blood."

## The Blood of Adam's Coat

You see, from Genesis to Revelation, there's a scarlet thread through the Bible. I mean, you see it in Adam's coat when God covered Adam with a coat in the Garden of Eden. It was a fur coat, by the way, if you don't believe in war, wearing fur. You can take it up with God. It's a fur coat. Adam wore a garment from an animal that had been slain to cover his nakedness and blood was shed.

## The Blood of Animal Sacrifices

And then, Abel offered a lamb upon an altar, the firstlings of the flock. When Noah came out of the ark, he offered a blood sacrifice. Abraham saw a ram there that took the place of Isaac there upon Mount Moriah. God instituted the Levitical priesthood in order to bring sacrifices that would point to the Lamb of God who takes away the sin of the world. That all began before the Jews came out of Egypt, there was the Passover lamb. All of the temple sacrifices were sacrifices of blood, some many of them that pointed to Calvary's cross.

## The Blood of the Revelation Song

And when you get to the book of Revelation, you see the redeemed singing, "You have redeemed us with Your blood." From Genesis to Revelation there is this scarlet thread. Why? Because Hebrews 9:22 says, "Without shedding of blood there is no forgiveness..." And every page of the divine book is stained with the scarlet blood of Jesus! What was the confidence that converted Rahab? It was confidence in the blood. Hebrews 11:31 says, "By faith, this harlot, Rahab, perished not with them that believed not." There's a fountain drawn, filled with blood drawn from Immanuel's veins. And sinners plunged beneath that flood lose all their guilty stains. Now, she was made pure. She's no longer a harlot. She's a princess in Israel. She's the great, great grandmother of King David. She's in the house and lineage of our Lord and Savior Jesus Christ. She has been changed. Remember—nature forms us, sin deforms us, education informs us, society reforms us, but Christ transforms us. It's always been salvation in Christ alone, by grace alone, through faith alone, to the glory of God alone!

## Confidence Seen in the Sovereign Lord

**Joshua 2:22-24** | They departed and went into the hills and remained there three days until the pursuers returned, and the pursuers searched all along the way and found nothing. [23] Then the two men returned. They came down from the hills and passed over and came to Joshua the son of Nun, and they told him all that had happened to them. [24] And they said to Joshua, "Truly the Lord has given all the land into our hands. And also, all the inhabitants of the land melt away because of us."

Ultimately, it is the Lord where we place our confidence. He is a God of grace and mercy and unrelenting love. This is the spies' hope. This is Rahab's hope. He is our shield and fortress! He will favor us as he did the people of Joshua's day when they testified, "all the inhabitants of the land melt away because of us" (2:24). Hallelujah!

Who is it you are praying for? God can melt the hearts of anyone. It's Christ that saves. The scarlet cord of redemption goes through the whole Bible and points us to Christ. Christ says, "I am the way, the truth, and the life, no one comes to the Father except by me" (Jn 14:6).

God is in the saving business. There's the gospel of Jesus Christ and it saves. The transforming power of the gospel. Praise God for the day you were saved. But are you seeing others saved? Are you, by God's providence, coming into contact with those Rahabs in your life? Are there those God has led you to, in order that you might share your faith? Think about it. Here was Rahab: a harlot, a Canaanite, a pagan, and becomes a great, great grandmother to King David and in the lineage of Jesus Christ. What a mighty God we serve.

### Conclusion

You know I can't help but see that scarlet cord through the whole Bible.

The Hebrews in Egypt put the blood of the Lamb on the doorposts. But let me tell you that Jesus is the "Lamb of God who takes way the sin of the world" (Jn 1:19). Has he taken away your sins?

The garments of the high priest and the curtains of the Tabernacle in the Old Testament included scarlets threads. But I want you to know, my High Priest is Jesus.

Jesus is that slain shepherd described in Zechariah 13:7. He's that good Shepherd that gets struck down and lays down his life for the sheep (Jn 10:11). Do you know him?

They laid a little baby in a manger on that first Christmas day. He was born to die. That baby would not escape death. By his blood every tribe, language, family, and nation would be redeemed.

I am redeemed by the blood of the Lamb! I have no other way to God! I'm redeemed by the blood of Jesus.

I tried works. They don't work. Works never justified a sinner. All my works never took away one stain of sin. Works and the law just made me tired and condemned me more. It takes the blood of Jesus to take away my sins.

I tried to forget my sin. I turned to the foolishness of the world when I was lost. The world left me empty. But Jesus — he makes me full and overflowing. He cleanses my heart and my conscience. He alone satisfies.

I tried to run away, like the prodigal. I wrote a note when I was 14 years old. "I'm running away." But I couldn't run from God. He pursued me! He overtook me by his love.

He brought me to Mount Calvary. It was there that I saw the most beautiful Being in the universe dying for my sins. He bound me to himself. "When I die, you die too." "When I rose from the dead, you rose with me." And just like that, my sins were taken away. Just like that I was given new life. Have you experienced that? That scarlet cord of redemption binds me to my Savior! He's so great, he can bring anyone to redemption through his blood!

# 4 | JOSHUA 3
## CROSSING THE JORDAN

*And when the soles of the feet of the priests bearing the ark of the Lord, the Lord of all the earth, shall rest in the waters of the Jordan, the waters of the Jordan shall be cut off from flowing, and the waters coming down from above shall stand in one heap.*

JOSHUA 3:13

You've heard people proclaim: It's a miracle! God is a miracle working God. One definition of a miracle is by Systematic Theologian Wayne Grudem: "A miracle is a less common kind of God's activity in which he arouses people's awe and wonder and bears witness to himself."[25] There are those everyday miracles, if you take the time to look. This morning I opened my curtains to the back yard and saw two bunnies face to face. They played, and then stood completely still. And then, like a mirror, they jumped into the air together. As they did that a third bunny wanted to get into the fun and joined the fun. I couldn't believe what I was seeing and burst out with joyful laughter.

---

[25] Wayne A. Grudem, *Systematic Theology: An Introduction to Biblical Doctrine* (Leicester, England; Grand Rapids, MI: Inter-Varsity Press; Zondervan Pub. House, 2004), 1247.

There are those unique miracles, like the birth of a baby. It seems like yesterday I was holding my youngest daughter and Ava talking with her after her birth. I told her we would be best friends, and we are. That's such a miracle.

Then there are what we are used to calling miracles: those unique acts of God. The blind see, the lame leap, and the dead are raised. We see at least some of this. People in our congregation are miraculously healed and the prayer of faith heals can heal the sick. We saw Blanca's cancer disappear. We saw Jerry's back pain of many years disappear. We see God giving visions and Jesus appearing to people in dreams throughout the Middle East and even sometimes here in the West, and eventually coming to know Christ. Augustine said: "I never have any difficulty believing in miracles, since I experienced the miracle of a change in my own heart."[26] And that's the greatest miracle: our salvation. The moment you came to know Jesus: it was a miracle.

The children of Israel needed a miracle. They had been in the wilderness for 40 year. Joshua 3 is all about getting out of the wilderness. You've got to cross the Jordan. There's a wilderness that God's people were in. That wilderness represents a place of wandering. The Israelites were in the wilderness because they disobeyed. Hebrews says the idea of "entering the Promised Land of God's rest" is akin for the Christian with entering into salvation in Christ. God doesn't want us in the wilderness. That wilderness represents death, and remember, now the second generation is hemmed in by the Jordan River at flood time. That's a mile wide at its widest point. Raging rapids. And here's the kicker. Jordan means Judgment. It's the River of Judgment.

The entire first generation with the exception of Joshua and Caleb, died in the wilderness. You can see why they wouldn't venture on through that Judgment River. It's safe in the wilderness. There are no Canaanites to fight in the wilderness. God provides in the wilderness. There's manna. And their shoes and clothing endured without rotting for 40 years. Lots of miracles: water from the rock!

---

[26] Augustine of Hippo, "The Enchiridion," in *St. Augustin: On the Holy Trinity, Doctrinal Treatises, Moral Treatises*, ed. Philip Schaff, trans. J. F. Shaw, vol. 3, A Select Library of the Nicene and Post-Nicene Fathers of the Christian Church, First Series (Buffalo, NY: Christian Literature Company, 1887), 80.

But God doesn't want us to stay in the wilderness. He wants us to leave the wilderness behind for the Promised Land. Christ is our inheritance. He is our "exceeding great reward" (Gen 15:1). He wants his "waters to break forth in the wilderness, and streams in the desert" (Isa 35:6).

Between them and that land there lay a river of difficulty. It was the river Jordan, and at this time of the year the river was swollen. Before Joshua and the people of Israel could begin their conquest of Canaan, they had to cross the Jordan River. This was no small thing as the river was at flood tide (3:15). This wasn't just a little river: it covered a great territory, and it was seemingly impossible for them to get through the flooded Jordan River and into the land. But God is a miracle working God, and this day, God performed a miracle. God got them in, even though it seemed impossible. The children of Israel came to this raging, impassible river. Their hopes were thwarted. They were so close but so far away. They were confronted with a test of faith.

Joshua needed to get two million people ready to cross the Jordan at flood level. The children of Israel have come out of Egypt; they've spent 40 years in the wilderness. Joshua was ready to go into the promised land when he was 40. Caleb was ready as well. To make this miracle all the more amazing, remember Joshua is 80.

Joshua is getting ready to lead God's people into their inheritance, into the Promise Land. This was quite different from Egypt. They are freed! But between them and this great Promised Land was the river Jordan. And it was flood time for the Jordan, like a raging rapid. It still occurs today, It's incredible. This placid little river becomes the raging

As soon as the feet of those priests touched the river Jordan, the water stopped flowing and it just started stacking up like it was held up by a plexiglass shield and the ark stopped right there in the middle of the riverbed of Jordan. God's people went right on through and came up on the other side. For twenty miles across from Adam, near Shiloh in the north, to the south at Gilgal, the Jordan River went dry during flood season.

## THE POSSIBILITY OF MIRACLES (3:1-4)

**Joshua 3:1-3** | Then Joshua rose early in the morning and they set out from Shittim. And they came to the Jordan, he and all the people of Israel, and lodged there before they passed over. [2] At the end of three days the officers went through the camp [3] and commanded the people, "As soon as you see the ark of the covenant of the Lord your God being carried by the Levitical priests, then you shall set out from your place and follow it."

## The God of Miracles

God is a miracle working God. The Christian life is one of supernatural life abiding in you. Though you struggle through the trials of this life, you are "seated in the heavenly places" ruling and reigning with Christ. The greatest miracle is for God to become flesh and dwell among us (Jn 1:14). That he would leave his throne and inhabit a human tent. And then to die in place of sinners! But oh, the transformation that has come! That's a miracle.

Dear Christian, your trials and suffering are filled with purpose. God wants to take you from the wilderness to the fullness of the Promised Land where his manifest presence fights for you. God keeps his promises to you. No matter how difficult the wilderness, he'll bring every child of God into the inheritance he has ordained. For Israel that was Canaan. For all true believers it's Jesus. It's like God promised Abraham in the Abrahamic covenant:

Fear not, Abram: I am thy shield, and thy exceeding great reward. — Genesis 15:1, KJV

## The Faith of Miracles

They were to prepare themselves to follow God. They had heard of his miracles. They had heard of the crossing of the Red Sea with the pillar of glory cloud, God's manifest presence (the Holy Spirit) fighting for them. But now they were to follow the Lord with the Ark and with the Pillar. They needed to exercise faith in the Lord in order to see these miracles.

**Joshua 3:2-3** | At the end of three days the officers went through the camp [3] and commanded the people, "As soon as you see the ark of the covenant of the Lord your God being carried by the Levitical priests, then you shall set out from your place and follow it."

God is a miracle working God. When we follow him, we must know above all that he is working on our behalf. He doesn't need our plans. We need his plans. God's people had waited 40 years. Their parents died in the wilderness. They didn't know what it was like to cross the

Red Sea. Only Caleb and Joshua knew that. Now was their time, and they had to wait three more days. Sometimes we need to wait. But follow God, and you will see miracles. God is worth the wait. The children of Israel had to wait. For forty years they had waited, while an entire generation died. The promise had been deferred because of the unbelief of the leaders. And now they would wait again, three days, with the destination in sight.

No one likes to wait. Waiting is not a strong suit for most of us. We tend to be horn honking, microwaving, FedEx mailing, fast food eating, and express lane shopping people. Yet sometimes God says wait.

Waiting is the hardest part of trusting. It is the most arduous aspect of the before principle. God's ways are not our ways. His ways are higher than our ways. God's timetable is different than our ways. His plans are much better than our plans! Amen? Too often we want God's resources, but we do not want his timing. We forget that the work God is doing in us while we wait is as important as whatever we are waiting for. Waiting means that we give God the benefit of the doubt that he knows what he is doing.

Waiting is God's way of seeing if we will trust him before we move forward. Waiting reminds me that I am not in charge. We are not just waiting around; we are growing into the image of Christ.

## A View of Miracles

**Joshua 3:4** | Yet there shall be a distance between you and it, about 2,000 cubits in length. Do not come near it, in order that you may know the way you shall go, for you have not passed this way before.

The fact that the ark would be readily visible did not mean the people could get close to it. They were called to look at it and follow it while staying a half a mile away from it! Why? The reason for the distance from the ark is in order that the people can tell where to go and can witness the cutting off of the Jordan, something they could not do if everyone was closely following the priests and the ark. But this way all could see Yahweh's great deed and all could know the path to take.[27]

Two million people needed to see the Ark at all times. They needed to see what in essence was the tangible presence of God. So they had to

---

[27] Davis, *Joshua*, 33.

stay away two thousand cubits on each side, about one-half mile. Nothing could crowd in on God's presence to block it out. What about the possibility of miracles? With God, all things are possible.

## THE PURPOSE OF MIRACLES (3:5-13)

Why did God say to Joshua—in Joshua say to the people, "tomorrow is going to be a day of miracles?" I want to give you four basic reasons.

### A New Program

First of all, God performs miracles when he wants to commence a new program. When God is about to do something new, when God is about to do something different, so many times God confirms it with a miracle.

**Joshua 3:5** | Then Joshua said to the people, "Consecrate yourselves, for tomorrow the Lord will do wonders among you."

Now, what does that word "consecrate" mean? It means to separate yourself, set yourself aside apart for a particular person or special purpose. The decision they are making is life changing, life dominating. They need to prepare their hearts and minds and not make the mistake of the previous generation. Here is God's challenge to you today. Listen to it. God brought his people to the threshold of an impossible situation, which was an opportunity. This was a re-consecration of the Red Sea redemption. This is the second generation. They have to prefer Christ for themselves. They can't just ride in on the previous generation's coattails (most of which are dead and buried in the desert anyway).

God often does miracles to commence a program, just to let people know that he is in it, that he is with them, that this is God's plan, that it has God's stamp of approval on it. God's just done some miracles for us. He's provided for us. We've seen divine healing. We've seen the salvation of people who we've been lifting to the Lord for years. God does these miracles among us to bring us to a new level of fellowship with him and power.

Are you ready for a new level of responsibility in your life? The children of Israel were going from wilderness wandering to Canaanite fighting. Now God is their warrior. He goes before them. But they still have to enter the land. Their first fight is going to be a very unusual battle. They are going to march around a city with trumpets for seven days! God may call you to do some really unusual things. That's the life of faith. It doesn't operate according to this world's mechanics.

## A New Service

This is interesting. The Scripture says God exalts Joshua.

**Joshua 3:6-8** | And Joshua said to the priests, "Take up the ark of the covenant and pass on before the people." So they took up the ark of the covenant and went before the people. [7] The Lord said to Joshua, "Today I will begin to exalt you in the sight of all Israel, that they may know that, as I was with Moses, so I will be with you. [8] And as for you, command the priests who bear the ark of the covenant, 'When you come to the brink of the waters of the Jordan, you shall stand still in the Jordan.'"

It's not exaltation, as in worship. This is exaltation as in usefulness. "God resists the proud, but he gives grace to the humble" (Jas 5:5). "Humble yourself in the sight of the Lord and he will exalt you" (Jas 4:10). Joshua must lead them through the flood of the Jordan River. Following God entails leadership. There needs to be tender courage. We need to have courageous love for those around us. We need to point the way. Joshua pointed to the ark, the symbol of God's presence. Leaders do not allow pride and panic to control them. Leaders are led by God's presence and his Word which produces humility and trust.

God exalts Joshua. Joshua can't change anything. All he has is the favor and grace and empowerment of God. But God must show up for anything to happen. Every Christian today has that empowerment by the Holy Spirit for service. You want to be used of God: be unentitled. Pick up your cross. Put on the slave's towel. That's leadership. Lead the way to the presence of Christ. Walk with God in spirit and in truth. Worship him at all times. Walk with Christ and he will exalt you for service.

## A New Success

When faith is exercised, the God of miracles leads our lives. We walk by faith, not by sight. That doesn't mean that we live blindly. It means we live in the reality of our God who is physically unseeable at this time but is manifested in every detail around us.

**Joshua 3:9-11** | And Joshua said to the people of Israel, "Come here
and listen to the words of the Lord your God." [10] And Joshua said,
"Here is how you shall know that the living God is among you and
that he will without fail drive out from before you the Canaanites,
the Hittites, the Hivites, the Perizzites, the Girgashites, the Amorites, and the Jebusites. [11] Behold, the ark of the covenant of the
Lord of all the earth is passing over before you into the Jordan.

There are two scriptural allusions here that are pictures of conversion. The first allusion has to do with the twelve spies. They explore the
land of Canaan in Numbers 13-14 and ten of them give up because of
"giants in the land". Joshua begins the do-over, "Choose twelve men"
(3:12). This time no one is afraid. You will recall when 12 spies explored
the promised land and 10 of them ended up refusing to trust God. Here
in Joshua 3, we have a new test of the same kind for this second generation. They must have heard the story of this great failure that led to
forty years in the wilderness. They need to choose twelve men to cross
the Jordan and enter the promised land.

The second allusion is the Red Sea crossing from Exodus 14. Again,
this points to salvation. The Red Sea crossing is the most famous picture of salvation in the Old Testament and is alluded to most throughout the Bible.

## A New Surrender

Watch what happens. Twelve men with the priests surrender to the
supernatural power of God, and God does something incredible. There
is a manifestation when God moves in by faith.

**Joshua 3:12-13** | Now therefore take twelve men from the tribes of Is-
rael, from each tribe a man. [13] And when the soles of the feet of
the priests bearing the ark of the Lord, the Lord of all the earth,
shall rest in the waters of the Jordan, the waters of the Jordan
shall be cut off from flowing, and the waters coming down from
above shall stand in one heap.

This would unmistakably bring in their mind the Red Sea crossing.
This second generation needed to experience the "salvation of the
Lord" as well. Now watch these priests! They have feet of faith! When
they stepped onto the water, the waters parted. But it wasn't until they
took that step of faith. Now we are told that the waters parted from the
Dead Sea to Adam, near Zerethan and Shiloh. That's 20 miles! God has

you where you are at this moment, and he's asking you to take a step of faith. That first step is conversion. You need to be converted.

Another step of every believer is consecration and surrender. We are sometimes so selfish; we don't want to give up our rights. We don't want to give up control. Surrender to Christ today Christian. It's a daily surrender. Walk in the Spirit. Surrender to Christ.

## THE POWER OF MIRACLES (3:14-17)

At the end of the day, nothing happens until God shows up. This is true for all things in life. Once God's presence (symbolized by the ark) is carried into the water, there is a 20 mile gap in the River — from the city of Adam (parallel with Zarethan and Shiloh) all the way to the Dead Sea.

**Joshua 3:14-17** | So when the people set out from their tents to pass over the Jordan with the priests bearing the ark of the covenant before the people, [15] and as soon as those bearing the ark had come as far as the Jordan, and the feet of the priests bearing the ark were dipped in the brink of the water (now the Jordan overflows all its banks throughout the time of harvest), [16] the waters coming down from above stood and rose up in a heap very far away, at Adam, the city that is beside Zarethan, and those flowing down toward the Sea of the Arabah, the Salt Sea, were completely cut off. And the people passed over opposite Jericho. [17] Now the priests bearing the ark of the covenant of the Lord stood firmly on dry ground in the midst of the Jordan, and all Israel was passing over on dry ground until all the nation finished passing over the Jordan.

There was a twenty-mile wide gap in the Jordan River. The water was standing "in one heap" (3:13). That's impossible right? "What is impossible with man is possible with God" (Lk 18:27). Is there anything too hard for the Lord? Twenty miles of dry land! Wow! That's what happens when God shows up!

Consider a warning: miracles won't give you faith. They will build up your faith if you already have some faith. But they don't convert people.

Jesus said, If they do not hear Moses and the Prophets, neither will they be convinced if someone should rise from the dead.—Luke 16:31

But if you are a Christian, your life is a supernatural life. You've crossed the Jordan. You are in the Promised Land. God fights for you. Every step is a miracle. I want to encourage you Christian: live life in the Promised Land of victory, not in the wilderness of defeat! Death and sin are defeated. Don't live in the power of your flesh but walk in the Spirit. Do whatever it takes so that you can see Jesus, our Ark, and follow him. See him, follow him, be transformed by him, from victory unto victory!

## Conclusion

Now let me celebrate Christ here today. The ark of the covenant, representing Christ, went through that Jordan River. Jordan has the meaning of Judgment. Christ your Ark went through that Judgment River for you. He was completely soaked in the justice for your sin. He was punished for sinners.

> He who knew no sin was made sin for us, that we might be made the righteousness of God in him. —2 Corinthians 5:21

We want justice in this world. We're praying for it. But we are not going to get perfect justice here on earth. Perfect justice even on earth only begins to be seen as people get their hearts right with Christ. Jesus is the answer! Christ went to that River of Judgement and he took it all for us. "It is finished," he said.

# 5 | JOSHUA 4
## MEMORIAL STONES

*When your children ask in time to come, 'What do those stones mean to you?' then you shall tell them that the waters of the Jordan were cut off before the ark of the covenant of the Lord. When it passed over the Jordan, the waters of the Jordan were cut off. So these stones shall be to the people of Israel a memorial forever.*

JOSHUA 4:6-7

The children of Israel had come right to the threshold of their Canaan. They were about to cross over the river Jordan. They were about to enter the land and possess the inheritance God had promised to them. They were facing the greatest crisis of their existence. The opportunity to enter the promised land was right in front of them, but the Jordan River was at flood stage with raging rapids, a mile wide at her widest point. Over two million people were waiting to enter.

Have you ever looked straight into the blazing center of a crisis? My hope today is that we will realize that our greatest crisis is what God wants to turn into our opportunity place of growth. God uses all things for good to conform us to Christ (Rom 8:28-30). This is a promise for all of God's people but is perhaps more clearly seen in the life of Job. It was Job who said,

Though he slay me, yet will I trust in him.—Job 13:15

God will take a crisis and grow you. This principle is illustrated by the story of Joshua 3 and 4 when God's people crossed the Jordan River. It was at flood season, and the Jordan was a mile wide during this time at its widest point.[28] God promised once the priests' feet touched the waters of the river Jordan, he would part the waters, turning their crisis into a place of growth. So the priests obeyed. As they entered the Jordan and their feet touch the water, the great river stopped flowing, and it started stacking up like it was held up by a plexiglass shield. The ark of the covenant stopped right there in the middle of the riverbed of the Jordan. God's people went right on through and came up on the other side. For twenty miles across from Adam, near Shiloh in the north, to the south at Gilgal, the Jordan River went dry during this unexpected miracle during flood season. While the water of the Jordan was held back, God commanded his people to set up a monument of twelve stones from the bottom of the river. "This monument was to be a symbol for the people to look on in time of doubt and confusion in order to remember God's awesome power, love, and faithfulness to them and future generations (Josh 4:1–9)."[29] Garrett Higbee summarizes the principle of this story well: "The hard cases are perhaps the greatest opportunities to see the power of God and his Word at work in changing lives."[30] Each of us ought to face a crisis with a deep assurance of God's promises to use this crisis to transform the heart of us (Phil 1:6; 1 Thess 5:23-24).

Here in Joshua 3 and 4, we find one of the climactic events in all of biblical history. The Israelites had waited forty years, but now the time had come. It is a poignant moment as they stride across the riverbed of the Jordan, opened for them by the miraculous power of God. Behind them, they leave the wearying decades of meandering around in a barren wilderness and the tragic memories of countless funerals for an entire generation of people who would not trust God's promises. Slavery in Egypt and the bare survival of nomadic life are bygone experiences now.

Their joy had been magnified by recent events. But when they arrived at the Jordan, they found it is flood stage, menacing in its speed

---

[28] Davis, *Joshua*, 37–38.
[29] Garrett Higbee. "Tony and Bipolar Disorder" in Stuart Scott. *Counseling the Hard Cases*. B&H Publishing. Kindle Edition.
[30] Ibid.

and dangerous in what it could do to the families of Israel. The rapid current left Israel flatfooted. The river was impassible, its crossing impossible. Have you ever had a crisis that seemed to put an impasse in front of what you thought was God's will? It's at those moments we learn the most about our God, as he builds our faith in his power to grow us.

You know the story. God intervened, performing a miracle that paralleled the miracle of the Exodus from Egypt. God rolled back the waters of the Jordan River, just as he had done with the Red Sea. God meant what he had said through Moses years before. Here was his signature again, in the same way, to assure his people that he was good to his word.

While crossing the Jordan, they are told to erect a monument of 12 stones. Later they are told to carry another set of stones out of the Jordan to Gilgal where they were placed, and then Joshua assembled them there (4:21). These stones had great significance to the people of Israel then and to us today. Remember as soon as the priests' feet touched the water, the flow of the water cut off upstream (a total of 20 miles of the Jordan turned to dry land, 3:16), and the river stood up like a wall. Then the ark was brought to the middle of the opening, and all the people were invited to cross on either side of the ark, each side a half a mile away from the ark itself (3:4). This is their conversion and confirmation into the faith of Yahweh. In this passage we see four markers of this new step of faith: the 12 stones, the society, the Shekinah glory, and the city of Gilgal.

## THE MONUMENT'S PURPOSE (4:1-10A)

**Joshua 4:1-6a** | When all the nation had finished passing over the Jordan, the Lord said to Joshua, [2] "Take twelve men from the people, from each tribe a man, [3] and command them, saying, 'Take twelve stones from here out of the midst of the Jordan, from the very place where the priests' feet stood firmly, and bring them over with you and lay them down in the place where you lodge tonight.'" [4] Then Joshua called the twelve men from the people of Israel, whom he had appointed, a man from each tribe. [5] And Joshua said to them, "Pass on before the ark of the Lord your God into the midst of the Jordan, and take up each of you a stone upon his shoulder, according to the number of the tribes of the people of Israel, [6] that this may be a sign among you...

## A Reminder of Salvation

The stones were a personal reminder of the mighty hand of the Lord opening up the Jordan and bringing his promises to pass by bringing them into the promised land. By returning to Gilgal on a regular basis, as they did, since Gilgal was their base of operations, they would see the stones and be reminded of the power and faithfulness of the great God who was with them, leading them in their conquest.[31]

Twelve men hoisted heavy stones to their shoulders from Jordan's floor and then had Joshua arranged them in the promised land, by God's command. They were assembled there as a sign, an unmistakable marker at the very place where God had demonstrated his power to overcome any obstacle to his will.

### A Reminder to Worship!

Before Shiloh or Jerusalem, the Tabernacle was erected here at Gilgal as a place of worship. It was really the first holy city or more like an encampment. It was also a place of training and instruction for the people. Like Shiloh and Jerusalem, the geography of this place has hills surrounding a smaller hill upon which the place of worship is. Gilgal today is a plain surrounded by hills between the Jordan River and Jericho, and the ruins of their "city" are still there today in the shape of a footprint. You can see at the entrance to the footprint are the twelve stones placed in a way so all could see.

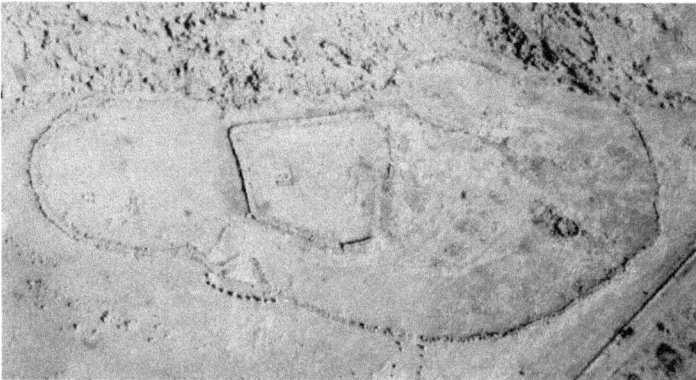

*The ruins of Gilgal outside of Jericho (2018)*

---

[31] Boice. *Joshua*, 40.

*12 Standing Stones*

Here in the above picture, we have an example of a standing stone monument, and then the actual remains of the 12 stones. This is similar to the standing stone monument with 12 stones at Mount Ebal that Joshua erected with the alter in chapter 8 of Joshua. The remains are still there today at Mount Ebal.

What are some memorial stones that you have to look back upon in your life? Several things come to mind that remind me of my conversion: my personal testimony of salvation, God's work of the Spirit to sanctify me, his gifts that I stir up through service, just to name a few. I love seeing my life change. I love seeing your lives change.

My baptism is a memorial stone. The Lord's supper is a memorial stone for us. Most of all the fruit of the Spirit marks God's presence and power in our lives! Indeed, we are all living memorial stones in God's temple. Each of us is alive with the Spirit of God in us.

## A Reminder for Future Generations

The children of this church need to hear about the great victories you have experienced in your life. The stones also were a reminder to the future generations of God's personal interaction and salvation for his people.

**Joshua 4:6b-8** | When your children ask in time to come, 'What do those stones mean to you?' [7] then you shall tell them that the waters of the Jordan were cut off before the ark of the covenant of the Lord. When it passed over the Jordan, the waters of the Jordan were cut off. So these stones shall be to the people of Israel a memorial forever." [8] And the people of Israel did just as Joshua

commanded and took up twelve stones out of the midst of the
Jordan, according to the number of the tribes of the people of
Israel, just as the Lord told Joshua. And they carried them over
with them to the place where they lodged and laid them
down there

**Joshua 4:21-24** | And he said to the people of Israel, "When your chil-
dren ask their fathers in times to come, 'What do these stones
mean?' [22] then you shall let your children know, 'Israel passed
over this Jordan on dry ground.' [23] For the Lord your God dried up
the waters of the Jordan for you until you passed over, as
the Lord your God did to the Red Sea, which he dried up for us
until we passed over, [24] so that all the peoples of the earth may
know that the hand of the Lord is mighty, that you may fear
the Lord your God forever."

Our children need to know that God is alive and well! What kind of
memorial stones do we have today to teach our children? We can mention the church's sacraments of the **Lord's supper** and **baptism**. Sacraments are an outward sign and seal of an inward reality. They are a
dramatization of actual events. They picture the work of Jesus Christ in
his death and resurrection. Each time these sacraments are experienced, there is a memorial, a reminder of the Lord's death and resurrection. This is a wonderful time to teach our children. As the cup and
bread are passed out and our children are not permitted to partake, and
they ask why, we have the privilege to explain the Gospel to them.
"Well, son, Jesus died on the cross for our sins. This cup and bread are
reminders of his shed blood and broken body." Our children may ask
about baptism. "Well, daughter, the waters of baptism are like a tomb
in which the person going into the water is 'buried with Christ' and then
they rise up out of the water 'to walk with him in newness of life." What
a wonderful way to teach our children through these "memorial
stones." Of course, our remembrance of the good news of Christ's death
and resurrection are in no way limited to the sacraments.

How about the memorial stones of the Lord's Day worship? Our kids
don't remember a time when they haven't been in church.

We remember in so many informal ways like keeping journals of
God's work in your life and answers to prayer, prayer meetings and testimony times when we recount God's love and faithfulness, Sunday

worship where we extol the Triune God for his work in our salvation, among hundreds and thousands of other things.

But really, it is those times of crisis that we remember the most. That time when you felt like nothing good could come out of your marriage, but in faith you waited, and you found God was greater than any marriage crisis. The goal is to get your eyes off of your crisis and on to your great God!

## A Warning of Judgment Averted

**Joshua 4:9-10a** | And Joshua set up twelve stones in the midst of the Jordan, in the place where the feet of the priests bearing the ark of the covenant had stood; and they are there to this day. [10] For the priests bearing the ark stood in the midst of the Jordan until everything was finished that the Lord commanded Joshua to tell the people, according to all that Moses had commanded Joshua...

There seems to be two sets of stones: one set is a memorial to God's faithfulness. The other is a memorial to God's judgment. The stones in the river would be forgotten and would in a way "perish." The stones in the Jordan that anyone who doesn't cross into God's promised land will perish and be forgotten.

The name "Jor-dan" is significant. "Jor" (from *yarad*) means to flow down, and "Dan" means to "execute judgment."[32] Hosea confirms the idea with God's proclamation: "...I will pour out my wrath on them like water" (Hos 5:10). Aren't you glad you have been delivered from God's downflowing wrath and judgment? Even our baptism is a sign and seal of God's covenant today, and the picture goes back to the Red Sea and the Jordan River. We pass through the waters of judgment, being united in Christ's death. Our judgment is put on Christ, and we are raised to walk out of that water "in newness of life" (Rom 6:4).

This row of 12 stones at the bottom off the Jordan was never to be seen by future generations. They would never inquire about it, once the Jordan waters flowed again. This 12 stone memorial would perish in the waters of the Jordan, just as the Egyptian army had perished in the waters of the Red Sea so many years before. These 12 stones were a memorial to God's justice. The typological lessons in this account provide an eternal, but disheartening, perspective.

---

[32] James Strong, *Enhanced Strong's Lexicon* (Woodside Bible Fellowship, 1995), Strong's number 1777.

The 12 stones under the waters of the Jordan may be a typological picture of all people who reject the salvation that God offers. They have not been delivered. They have not "crossed over" and received the grace of God. They remain under the waters and are not counted among those who have entered into their inheritance, their promised land.

## A Promise of God's Presence

On the other hand, the stones in the water may simply be another reminder of where they had crossed in the Jordan so that anytime the water went down, they might be able to see the stones in the water where the ark had been, and where the water had been held back by the hand of God. These stones then were a reminder of God's presence.

## THE MONUMENT'S PEOPLE (4:10B-14)

## The People

**Joshua 4:10** | The people passed over in haste.

So many were passing over. Aside from efficiency, why would they pass over "in haste"? We could surmise that they were ready and excited to enter into the promised land. They believed the promises of God. This is a wonderful picture of faith. Isn't it true that when we come to Christ, we rush to him "in haste" because he is so beautiful? We come leaving all behind. I love the words of Jesus who said,

> Come to me, all who labor and are heavy laden, and I will give you rest. [29] Take my yoke upon you, and learn from me, for I am gentle and lowly in heart, and you will find rest for your souls. [30] For my yoke is easy, and my burden is light.—Mathew 11:28-30

The people in Joshua's day were leaving the wilderness behind for the promised land. So every Christian leaves their old life behind to take up Christ's cross. By losing the ambition, reputation, and possibilities of the old life, we actually gain life since we gain eternal life, and so much even in this short, temporal life we live on earth.

## The Priests

**Joshua 4:11** | And when all the people had finished passing over, the ark of the Lord and the priests passed over before the people.

There is a twenty-mile expanse where the Jordan has dried up and the people may cross. In the middle of this great expanse is the ark with the pillar of glory above it. The people can see the ark for miles, but they have to keep that distance. God has already instructed them to keep a half mile distance on both sides of the ark, but they have nine and a half miles of dry expanse to cross on either side.

Notice it is the priests holding the ark that is leading the way. They hadn't chosen this for themselves but were chosen by God through their families, who were from the tribe of Levi. So it is that in the new covenant, we are all priests, chosen by God and set apart for his service. We are all part of a holy priesthood. The duty of a priest is to bring himself and others nearer to God.

We are all called to be priests and to "make disciples of every nation" (Mt 28:19). What about you as a leader? Are you leading the way to God? Your body, the Bible says, is the ark, the habitation of God (1 Cor 6:19)! Are you pointing people to Christ? We all have this responsibility as God's new covenant priests. We believe in the priesthood of every believer. Every member of Christ's body is a minister (Eph 4:11-12).

> But you are a chosen race, a royal priesthood, a holy nation, a people for his own possession, that you may proclaim the excellencies of him who called you out of darkness into his marvelous light. —1 Peter 2:9

Dear saints, you are all priests, with priestly responsibilities. Exercise those duties. Draw yourself and those around you nearer to God.

## The Platoon

**Joshua 4:12-13** | The sons of Reuben and the sons of Gad and the half-tribe of Manasseh passed over armed before the people of Israel, as Moses had told them. [13] About 40,000 ready for war passed over before the Lord for battle, to the plains of Jericho.

Now you have the people from two and a half tribes that had determined to stay on the other side of Jordan but were committed to helping the conquer each tribe's land. Out of all the tribes, there were 40,000 warriors armed and ready for war. The text brings up several questions. Where did they get the armaments and armor? Whatever they had was very limited, as far as human weaponry. They had seen war in the days of Moses. Perhaps they took some weapons from the people they conquered who were very sophisticated in their weaponry having chariots and armaments of iron. In any case, they are trusting in God and ready to lead. Are you experienced in spiritual warfare? There are always those in the church who have had the experience of spiritual warfare and are more mature. We are commanded by the apostle to appoint mature, godly men as elders in the church. Also mature and godly men and women are to disciple those who are more new to the faith (Titus 2).

## The Premier General

**Joshua 4:14** | On that day the Lord exalted Joshua in the sight of all Israel, and they stood in awe of him just as they had stood in awe of Moses, all the days of his life.

Joshua from the very beginning always pointed to the Lord as the main general of Israel, but Joshua is indeed the human general. Like Moses before him, he is meek, and yet they stand "in awe" of Joshua. Why? Because, "On that day the Lord exalted Joshua in the sight of all Israel" (4:14). Like Joseph, we might say "the hand of the Lord" was upon Joshua. "Potiphar noticed this and realized that the LORD was with Joseph, giving him success in everything he did" (Gen 39:3; *cf* 39:23, 40:3). There is a graciousness God grants to leaders who follow the Lord. God always raises up leaders who have his presence and grace upon them.

> Humble yourselves in the sight of the Lord, and he will lift you up. — James 4:10

If you want to be used of God you must face that crisis with humility and grace. The only way to do that is to get your strength from the Lord himself. When you are weak you are strong, because you are empowered by Christ.

## THE MONUMENT'S PICTURE (4:15-24)

## A Picture of Faith

We must be reminded that the ark is the physical and tangible representation of God's presence. Accompanying the ark of the covenant no doubt was the very Shekinah glory of God, his manifest presence in the pillar-like glory cloud. Remember the people had a twenty-mile area to cross the Jordan on dry ground. They could not come near the ark but had to pass a half a mile on each side. They could see the ark but could not touch it. They could see the glory cloud. They were to get a glimpse of that massive display of God's glory and remember it.

**Joshua 4:15-18** | And the Lord said to Joshua, [16] "Command the priests bearing the ark of the testimony to come up out of the Jordan." [17] So Joshua commanded the priests, "Come up out of the Jordan." [18] And when the priests bearing the ark of the covenant of the Lord came up from the midst of the Jordan, and the soles of the priests' feet were lifted up on dry ground, the waters of the Jordan returned to their place and overflowed all its banks, as before.

We must be reminded that the ark is the physical and tangible representation of God's presence. Accompanying the ark of the covenant no doubt was the very Shekinah glory of God, his manifest presence in the pillar-like glory cloud. Remember the people had a twenty-mile area to cross the Jordan on dry ground. They could not come near the ark but had to pass a half a mile on each side. They could see the ark but could not touch it. They could see the glory cloud. They were to get a glimpse of that massive display of God's glory and remember it.

## A Picture of God's Presence

This monument was something only God could provide for. He opened the River so the rocks could be gathered and arranged. Those rocks are still there till this day.

**Joshua 4:18** | And when the priests bearing the ark of the covenant of the Lord came up from the midst of the Jordan, and the soles of the priests' feet were lifted up on dry ground, the waters of the Jordan returned to their place and overflowed all its banks, as before.

This monument was a picture and reminder of the presence of God with his people. Consider the power of God's presence. When the ark moved out of the waters, the waters returned to their place from 20 miles away! So it is that all Christians are like the ark — we carry the presence of God with us.

Do you not know that your body is a temple of the Holy Spirit within you, whom you have from God? You are not your own, for you were bought with a price. So glorify God in your body. —1 Corinthians 6:19-20

Just as the ark could be seen from afar (up to 20 miles away), our testimony for Christ is seen by all those around us. Jesus said,

> You are the light of the world. A city set on a hill cannot be hidden. Nor do people light a lamp and put it under a basket, but on a stand, and it gives light to all in the house. In the same way, let your light shine before others, so that they may see your good works and give glory to your Father who is in heaven. —Matthew 5:14-16

## A Picture of God's Faithfulness

**Joshua 4:19** | The people came up out of the Jordan on the tenth day of the first month, and they encamped at Gilgal on the east border of Jericho.

Until now, the reader knows only that the crossing took place during the flood stage of the Jordan, that is in the spring. Now the text specifies *the tenth day of the first month.* The same date appears in Exodus 12:2–3, where it introduces the preparations for the Passover, which occurs on the fourteenth day [Good Friday].33 It was on the same day forty years before that Israel had begun to prepare for going out of Egypt by setting apart the Passover lamb (Exo 12:2–3).34 So it's four days away till Passover celebration, which will take place in Joshua 5.

## A Picture for our Children

**Joshua 4:20-24** | And those twelve stones, which they took out of the Jordan, Joshua set up at Gilgal. 21 And he said to the people of Israel, "When your children ask their fathers in times to come, 'What do these stones mean?' 22 then you shall let your children know, 'Israel passed over this Jordan on dry ground.' 23 For the Lord your God dried up the waters of the Jordan for you until you passed over, as the Lord your God did to the Red Sea, which he dried up for us until we passed over, 24 so that all the peoples of the earth may know that the hand of the Lord is mighty, that you may fear the Lord your God forever."

Sometimes when we get overwhelmed, we forget how big God is! We need to be telling the stories of our great God to our children! That's

---

33 Richard S. Hess, *Joshua: An Introduction and Commentary,* vol. 6, Tyndale Old Testament Commentaries (Downers Grove, IL: InterVarsity Press, 1996), 126.

34 Carl Friedrich Keil and Franz Delitzsch, *Commentary on the Old Testament,* vol. 2 (Peabody, MA: Hendrickson, 1996), 51.

what the 12 stone monument was for: a testimony to our children and a legacy for generations to come. Let me ask you: are you leaving an eternal legacy of living stones? And you are living stones that God is building into his spiritual temple. What's more, you are his holy priests. Through the mediation of Jesus Christ, you offer spiritual sacrifices that please God (1 Pet 3:5).

## Conclusion

These 12 stones tell a story of deliverance and of remembrance. We need to remember that God wants to turn your greatest crisis into your greatest victory. First, that crisis is one of faith. Are you in Christ? Do you know him? Have you been delivered from your sin? Do you have a testimony of salvation that you can give? How did God bring you across your Jordan of death, hell and sin? Was it through Christ alone? He's the only one that can part our Jordan of judgment!

I love the 12 memorial stones the tell of victory. I can think of another stone. A stone that was moved in front of the tomb of our crucified Savior. That stone was there for three days. I want us to remember that stone. It was rolled away!

Jesus' baptism site is very near where these 12 standing stones were taken out of the water. John the Baptist presented Jesus at this very spot as "the Lamb of God who takes away the sins of the world" (Jn 1:29). Jesus is our Lamb. He takes upon himself the wrath of that River of Judgment. He takes us, like those stones, and makes us living memorials to the grace of God.

# 6 | JOSHUA 5

## THE CAPTAIN OF ANGEL ARMIES

*When Joshua was by Jericho, he lifted up his eyes and looked, and behold, a man was standing before him with his drawn sword in his hand. And Joshua went to him and said to him, "Are you for us, or for our adversaries?" And he said, "No; but I am the commander of the army of the Lord. Now I have come."*

JOSHUA 5:13-14

When we are at our weakest, God is at his strongest. When we feel like giving up in the Christian life, that's often the very dawn of a breakthrough. Though you are weak, if you trust in the Lord, you will find great strength. Isaiah said it best.

> But they that wait upon the Lord shall renew their strength; they shall mount up with wings as eagles; they shall run, and not be weary; and they shall walk, and not faint. — Isaiah 40:31

Today's lesson is about preparing for victory. Three significant events happen here that show us the pathway to victory in the Christian life. God guaranteed victory for his people over the Canaanites if they would trust him. And we are guaranteed the power to live in holiness: the power not to be controlled by anger, despair, fear, or foolishness, but instead be controlled by the Spirit. How do we get there? Three events lead us there:

First, we have the covenant of circumcision. No one was circum-cised in the wilderness. We're going to talk about circumcision, and how it pictures the true circumcision, that of our hearts. If we want victory, we need tender hearts.

Second, we have the celebration of the first Passover in the Promised Land. This points to the Lamb of God, Jesus Christ. If we want victory, we need our eyes focused on Christ.

Third, we are going to be introduced to the Captain of the Lord's angel armies. And we will learn that if we want to have victory, we have to give up our own agenda and will and surrender to the Lord. We need feet that obey.

The children of Israel had just crossed the Jordan River. The nation of Israel arrived safely on the other side of the Jordan River. Their crossing was a great miracle, and it sent a great message to the people of the land (5:1). The Canaanites were already afraid (2:9–11), and now their fears totally demoralized them.[35] God's people were in a place of great strength, but they weren't ready.

**Joshua 5:1** | As soon as all the kings of the Amorites who were beyond the Jordan to the west, and all the kings of the Canaanites who were by the sea, heard that the Lord had dried up the waters of the Jordan for the people of Israel until they had crossed over, their hearts melted and there was no longer any spirit in them because of the people of Israel.

The victory seemed certain. They should strike while they're hot. Nope. God says wait. They can go and take Jericho so easily. It's easy pickins! We have momentum. God says, no. Stop. Wait. Don't get ahead of yourself. Don't get ahead of me. We need to remember God is in sovereign control. He knows what they need. They need to prepare themselves through dedication, specifically, circumcision.

You see, everything in your life can seem in order. It can seem good. But if God's not in it, it will not work.

Unless the Lord builds the house, those who build it labor in vain. —Psalm 127:1

Without me, you can do nothing. —Jesus in John 15:5

God said through the prophet Zechariah:

---

[35] Wiersbe. *Be Strong*, 56.

Not by might, nor by power, but by my Spirit, says the LORD of hosts.
—Zechariah 4:6

If you want to have a true full victory, then you need all of God. Put self and selfish desires aside. It doesn't matter how you feel. Don't be led by the emotions of your deceptive flesh. You need the humility to hear God reveal himself to you. "How do I get there?" you ask. You begin with a tender heart. That's what circumcision represented.

## A TENDER HEART (5:1-9)

After triumphantly crossing the Jordan River, the nation of Israel had to pause at Gilgal while the men submitted to what in essence was painful surgery. Why did God command this ritual at this time?

### The Mark of a Tender Heart

Circumcision was the covenant mark for God's people. It was God's mark of ownership. Israel is a covenant nation—an awesome privilege God has given to no other nation on earth (Rom 9:4–5). God gave circumcision as the sign of the covenant to Abraham and his descendants (17:9-14, 23-27). The men of the nation need to make an outward profession of an inward reality of faith. That's what circumcision is all about. Israel was to be a nation of tender-hearted people, marked by God through this ritual.

**Joshua 5:2-7** | At that time the Lord said to Joshua, "Make flint knives and circumcise the sons of Israel a second time." [3] So Joshua made flint knives and circumcised the sons of Israel at Gibeath-haaraloth [another name for Gilgal] [4] And this is the reason why Joshua circumcised them: all the males of the people who came out of Egypt, all the men of war, had died in the wilderness on the way after they had come out of Egypt. [5] Though all the people who came out had been circumcised, yet all the people who were born on the way in the wilderness after they had come out of Egypt had not been circumcised. [6] For the people of Israel walked forty years in the wilderness, until all the nation, the men of war who came out of Egypt, perished, because they did not obey the voice of the Lord; the Lord swore to them that he would not let them see the land that the Lord had sworn to their fathers to give to us, a land flowing with milk and honey. [7] So it was their

children, whom he raised up in their place, that Joshua circum-
cised. For they were uncircumcised, because they had not been
circumcised on the way.

Through this ritual the Jews became a "marked people" because
they belonged to the true and living God. This meant that they were
under obligation to obey him. The mark of the covenant reminded them
that their bodies belonged to the Lord and were not to be used for sinful
purposes. Israel was surrounded by nations that worshiped idols and
included in their worship rituals that were sensual and degrading. The
mark of the covenant reminded the Jews that they were a special people, a separated people, a holy nation (Exo 19:5–6), and that they were
to maintain purity in their marriages, their society, and their worship
of God.

We, God's people, the church, are marked by God by the Holy
Spirit. We are given the seal, or imprint of God in our hearts. It's a seal
and mark of ownership.

When you believed in him, were sealed with the promised Holy
Spirit, [14] who is the guarantee of our inheritance until we acquire possession of it, to the praise of his glory. —Ephesians 1:13-14

Even the Old Testament speaks of this reality of God transforming
and circumcising the heart. This physical operation on the body was
meant to be a symbol of *a spiritual operation on the heart*. Circumcision pointed to regeneration of the heart — having a tender heart toward God because it has been renewed by the Holy Spirit.

And the LORD your God will circumcise your heart and the heart of
your offspring, so that you will love the LORD your God with all your
heart and with all your soul, that you may live. —Deuteronomy 30:6

Circumcise therefore the foreskin of your heart and be no longer stubborn. —Deuteronomy 10:16

Theologians call this transformation of heart regeneration. No
amount of external surgery can change the inner person. It's when we
repent and turn to God for help that he can change our hearts and make
us love and obey him more. Paul teaches the same thing.

For no one is a Jew who is merely one outwardly, nor is circumcision
outward and physical. [29] But a Jew is one inwardly, and circumcision
is a matter of the heart, by the Spirit, not by the letter. His praise is
not from man but from God. — Romans 2:28-29

Sadly, over the years, the Jews came to trust in the external mark of the covenant and not in the God of the covenant who wanted to make them a holy people. They thought that as long as they were God's covenant people, they could live just as they pleased! Moses warned them about this sin (Deut 30:6), and so did the prophets (Jer 4:4).

> Jeremiah says the same: Break up your fallow ground, and sow not among thorns. [4] Circumcise yourselves to the Lord; remove the foreskin of your hearts. — Jeremiah 4:3-4

When John the Baptist called them to repent, the Jewish spiritual leaders said, "We have Abraham as our father" (Mt 3:9). They were not unlike some people today who feel sure they're saved and are going to heaven because they're baptized, confirmed, and participate regularly in Communion. As good as these religious rites can be, they must never become substitutes for faith in Jesus Christ (cf Rom 2:25-29). Have you experienced regeneration of your heart? Has the Spirit circumcised your heart? That's where tenderness begins.

Over and over in the Scriptures, we are told to have a tender heart. That begins with regeneration, but daily you have to humble yourself. You can't seek your own way. Put away anger. Put away trying to control people around you. Stop punishing people when you don't get your way. That's all idolatry. It's usurping God from your heart. Let God be God. Walk in the Spirit. Surrender to the Holy Spirit.

## A Test for a Tender Heart

This ritual of circumcision was actually a great test. They were essentially to be disabled in enemy territory. They were to trust God implicitly when they felt very vulnerable.

> **Joshua 5:8** | When the circumcising of the whole nation was finished, they remained in their places in the camp until they were healed.

Israel was camped in enemy territory, just a few miles from Jericho. Now they were going to temporarily disable *every male in the nation*, including every soldier in the army! What a golden opportunity for the enemy to attack and wipe them out (cf Gen 34). It took total trust in God for Joshua and the people to obey the Lord, but their obedience to the Scriptures was the secret of their success (Josh 1:7–8). In their weakness they were made strong; and through faith and patience they inherited the promises (Heb 6:12).

After we've experienced an exciting victory of faith, God often permits us to be tested. We get a target on our back. Satan hates the victory of faith. Think about it. Abraham arrived in the land of promise and was confronted with a famine (Gen 12). Elijah triumphed over Baal and was threatened with death (1 Kings 18–19). After Jesus' baptism in the Jordan, the Spirit led Jesus into the wilderness to be tempted by Satan (Mt 3:13–4:11). Since great victories can lead to great pride, God allows us to be tested in order to remind us to depend on him.

## A Mindset of Victory for the Tender-Hearted

Circumcision was ultimately a mark of God's already promised victory. He had cut away their reproach. God's people had been defiled by idolatrous practices that their parents brought from Egypt. That could stop them in their tracks. This circumcision was not just a rolling away of the flesh, but a rolling away of their reproach.

**Joshua 5:9** | And the Lord said to Joshua, "Today I have rolled away the reproach of Egypt from you." And so the name of that place is called Gilgal to this day.

The sins and idolatry of their former lives were rolled away. The walls of the Gilgal camp, if you recall, was in the form of a shoe. They were to trample the enemy and conquer the land. The circumcision of heart gives us a mindset of victory. Do you have that victory mindset?

For sin will have no dominion over you, since you are not under law but under grace. —Romans 6:14

Do you have a tender heart? Are you surrendered to the Spirit, or do you want to legislate your holiness through doing things your own way?

But the fruit of the Spirit is love, joy, peace, patience, kindness, goodness, faithfulness, [23] gentleness, self-control; against such things there is no law. — Galatians 5:22-23

The moment you leave from these things, you are walking in the flesh. Have you lost your first love? Have you lost your joy? Your peace? Humble yourself. Surrender. *Soften your heart!* Give up on your plans and trust God completely.

The men were now marked with circumcision, the sign of a tender heart. But now they would have a celebration of the Passover. This was a sign of their faith in the coming Messiah.

## EYES ON CHRIST (5:10-12)

"Forgetting those things which are behind" (Phil 3:13) is wise counsel for most areas of life, but there are some things we must never forget. That's what the Passover Feast was all about.

### Remember Christ's Goodness in Salvation

In his farewell address to the nation, Moses repeatedly commanded the Jews to remember that they were once slaves in Egypt and that the Lord had delivered them and made them his own people (Deut 6:15; 15:15; 16:12; 24:18, 22). This great truth was embodied in their annual Passover feast. They were never to forget that they were a redeemed people, set free by the blood of the lamb.[36] God commands them through Joshua to celebrate the Passover and remember the goodness of God.

> **Joshua 5:10-11** | While the people of Israel were encamped at Gilgal, they kept the Passover on the fourteenth day of the month in the evening on the plains of Jericho. **11** And the day after the Passover, on that very day, they ate of the produce of the land, unleavened cakes and parched grain.

Exactly forty years before, Israel had celebrated the Passover on the night of their deliverance from Egypt (Exo 11-14). They also celebrated Passover at Mt. Sinai, before leaving for Kadesh Barnea (Num 9:1–14). But they never entered into the Promised Land and all died in the wilderness. The new generation had so much to be thankful for. They were in the Promised Land by the blood of the lamb. Do you remember the moment you were born again and realized that all your sins were forgiven in Jesus?

### Remember Christ's Goodness in Provision

The manna ceased the day after they ate the produce of the land. The produce would have been the first Feast of firstfruits in the land.

---

[36] Wiersbe. *Be Strong*, 63.

**Joshua 5:12** | And the manna ceased the day after they ate of the pro-
duce of the land. And there was no longer manna for the people
of Israel, but they ate of the fruit of the land of Canaan that year.

No more manna! That's a good thing. Now they get to eat the fruit
of the land of Canaan. On the day after Passover, the manna ceased;
and thus ended a forty-year miracle (Exo 16). Isn't God good to provide
for all our needs?

Talk about the verses in the Bible that tell us God will provide for
all our needs.

And my God will supply every need of yours according to his riches
in glory in Christ Jesus. — Philippians 4:19

I have been young, and now am old, yet I have not seen the righteous
forsaken or his children begging for bread. — Psalm 37:25

You keep your eyes on Christ, and you will see his goodness! He's
saved you. He's sanctifying you. You have everything you need in
Christ.

Oh, taste and see that the LORD is good! Blessed is the man who takes
refuge in him! — Psalm 34:8

Pray that the Lord will give you eyes to see the goodness of God in
everything!

We know that for those who love God all things work together for
good, for those who are called according to his purpose. [29] For those
whom he foreknew he also predestined to be conformed to the image
of his Son. — Romans 8:28-29

Good, good, good! Our God is good. If you doubt it, look to Christ.
He's the Lamb of God that takes away the sin of the world! Praise God
for this Passover celebration that reminds us of Christ. By the way they
would celebrate the Passover pretty consistently until the time of the
Judges. They did this between Gilgal and Shiloh among other places.
In fact, the Tabernacle would rest at Shiloh for 369 years, and each year
they would joyfully celebrate the Passover. But then as a judgment on
Eli the priest's disobedient sons, the Lord sent the Philistines to disci-
pline them, and the Philistines burned down the Tabernacle. From that
time until the time of Hezekiah and later Josiah, the Passover was not
celebrated (2 Kgs 23:21-22).

Oh, I want eyes to see Christ! In Christ all the promises of the Old Testament are Yes and Amen! In Christ I have everything I need for life and godliness! In Christ, I have a full and free forgiveness of sins. In Christ I have the promised Holy Spirit so that I can be clothed with power from on high. In Christ I have the victory! In Christ, "No weapon that is formed against you shall prosper" (Isa 54:17). The secret to victory is not to talk about your problems until you are blue in the face. You need to fix your eyes on Christ. You don't need to fix your spouse or fix your job or fix your church. You don't need to fix your problem. Fix your eyes on Jesus! Seek first his kingdom! May Christ, and Christ alone have the pre-eminence in your life. So, we said, for victory, we need tender hearts. We need eyes fixed on Christ. But thirdly, we need feet to obey.

## FEET TO OBEY (5:13-15)

So often, we have heads that are swimming with Bible knowledge, but we have very little application and very little victory. You can have knowledge without having Christ. We need Christ. That's what the end of Joshua 5 is all about. They get a visit from "the commander of the Lord's army" (5:14). And we learn something from him.

### Get Off Your Feet and Worship

The commander of the LORD's army is Jesus. We see him right here in this text. We know this is Jesus because when Joshua sees him a worship service takes place.

**Joshua 5:13-14a** | When Joshua was by Jericho, he lifted up his eyes and looked, and behold, a man was standing before him with his drawn sword in his hand. And Joshua went to him and said to him, "Are you for us, or for our adversaries?" **14** And he said, "No; but I am the commander of the army of the Lord. Now I have come." And Joshua fell on his face to the earth and worshiped...

This paragraph records one of the pre-incarnation appearances of the Lord Jesus Christ recorded in the Old Testament.

- To Abraham the sojourning shepherd, the Lord came as a traveler to share in a friendly meal (Gen 18:1–8).
- To Jacob the schemer, he came as a wrestler to bring him to the place of submission (Gen 32:24–32).

- The three Hebrew young men met him as their companion in the furnace of fire (Dan 3:25).
- And Joshua met him as the Captain of the Lord's armies. Our Lord always comes to us when we need him and in the way we need him.

In John 15:5, Jesus said, "I am the vine; you are the branches. Whoever abides in me and I in him, he it is that bears much fruit, for apart from me you can do nothing."

## Your Feet on Holy Ground

**Joshua 5:14b-15** | … Joshua fell on his face to the earth and worshiped and said to him, "What does my lord say to his servant?" **15** And the commander of the Lord's army said to Joshua, "Take off your sandals from your feet, for the place where you are standing is holy." And Joshua did so.

Joshua was told he was on holy ground. When Joshua discovered the divine Visitor was the Lord, he fell at his feet in worship and waited for his orders. It's so easy to move forward with new and fresh and bold ideas that come from human wisdom. For a while they may seem like they bear fruit.

### Conclusion

I want to be led by Christ, the Captain of the Lord's angel armies. When I see Joshua following after Jesus, the Captain of the Lord's armies, I have to affirm that I have a General. I have a Captain. That's my Jesus. He's King of all kings and Lord of all lords. John and Isaiah both call him "the first and the last, the Almighty". I call him my Lord and my Savior.

If Jesus is your captain, then when you are weak, you will be strong. If he's your captain, he'll take a difficult marriage and turn into a distinctive and divinely touched marriage that expands his kingdom. Do you want him to be your Captain and commander? Stop trying to control your life. Let Christ lead you!

# 7 | JOSHUA 6
## TAKING DOWN STRONGHOLDS

*So the people shouted, and the trumpets were blown. As soon as the people heard the sound of the trumpet, the people shouted a great shout, and the wall fell down flat, so that the people went up into the city, every man straight before him, and they captured the city.*

JOSHUA 6:20

L ife is a battle. You are God's instrument. If you want to win, you have to follow his voice. Jesus said, "My sheep hear my voice and they follow me" (Jn 10:27). In a battle, you have to listen to the general, not to your own ideas. One of the early preachers of the church, known as the "silver tongued preacher" understood the necessity of having a wartime mindset on this earth.

> You are but a poor soldier of Christ if you think you can overcome without fighting and suppose you can have the crown without the conflict. —John Chrysostom (347–407) [37]

Chrysostom was a courageous Syrian preacher and martyr, and he was right. The Christian life involves challenge and conflict whether we like it or not. But just fighting isn't enough. You have to fight the right way.

---

[37] Wiersbe. *Be Strong*, 68.

For the weapons of our warfare are not carnal but mighty in God for
pulling down strongholds. —2 Corinthians 10:4

You will fight, but how? The message of Joshua 6 is about how we
fight life's battles. Will we come with our own plans and methods or
will we hear from the Lord? We need to hear from God. We all need a
leader. The leader of the book of Joshua is not General Joshua, but King
Jesus.

## OUR CHAMPION (5:13-15; 6:1-5)

"Joshua fought the battle of Jericho, and the walls came tumbling
down," so the old spiritual says. True enough, but the real difference
was not Joshua or Israel, but Jesus. The walls certainly collapsed but
not inward, but outward, and "everyone charged straight in, and they
took the city" (6:20). But how? The Lord has to lead. God gave Jericho
into Israel's hands, and the whole account of this dramatic sixth chapter centers on the our glorious General: the Lord himself.[38]

### Worship Him

I can imagine how Joshua might have studied the situation. The
Bible does not tell us what he thought. But it could have been like this.

"I wonder what the best way would be to attack Jericho? The walls
are high. The gates are huge and heavy–and well-guarded. The people
are equipped for war. How can we conquer Jericho?"

Joshua surely remembered that God had promised to defeat the
enemies of the Israelites. Do you think he asked God for help? Suddenly
standing before Joshua was a Man with a sword in his hand.

"Who are you?" Joshua asked. "Are you on our side or the side of
our enemies?"

The man answered, "I am Captain of the Lord's army."

Immediately Joshua realized this was the Lord himself. Listen to
what the Bible says.

**Joshua 5:13-15** | When Joshua was by Jericho, he lifted up his eyes and
looked, and behold, a man was standing before him with his
drawn sword in his hand. And Joshua went to him and said to him,
"Are you for us, or for our adversaries?" **14** And he said, "No; but I
am the commander of the army of the Lord. Now I have come."
And Joshua fell on his face to the earth and worshiped and said to

---

[38] Jackman, *Joshua*, 67.

him, "What does my lord say to his servant?" [15] And the commander of the Lord's army said to Joshua, "Take off your sandals
from your feet, for the place where you are standing is holy." And
Joshua did so.

Joshua had read Moses' plea to God in the Book of the Law:

If your presence does not go with us, do not bring us up from here. —
Exodus 33:15

The Lord had promised to be with Joshua just as he had been with
Moses (Josh 1:5), and now he reaffirmed that promise in a personal
way. Like his predecessor, Joshua refused to move until he was sure the
Lord's presence was with him.

This paragraph records one of the pre-incarnation appearances of
the Lord Jesus Christ recorded in the Old Testament.

* To Abraham the sojourning shepherd, the Lord came as a traveler to share in a friendly meal (Gen 18:1-8).
* To Jacob the schemer, he came as a wrestler to bring him to the
  place of submission (Gen 32:24-32).
* The three Hebrew young men met him as their companion in the
  furnace of fire (Dan 3:25).
* And Joshua met him as the Captain of the Lord's armies. Our
  Lord always comes to us when we need him and in the way we
  need him.

The point is: nothing significant happens in life until Jesus shows
up: that's true in both Old and New Testaments. He's my Captain, and
if you know him, he's yours too. In John 15:5, Jesus said, "I am the vine;
you are the branches. Whoever abides in me and I in him, he it is that
bears much fruit, for apart from me you can do nothing."

It is a striking lesson. But it could easily be misinterpreted. This is
not justification for inactivity. As we shall see, God's people had a large
part to play in the conquest and destruction of the city of Jericho. It was
not delivered to them on a plate, as it were, by overwhelming supernatural intervention that required them to do nothing. But the way in
which the victory came was chosen by the Lord, so that it would be in-
grained in their memory that this first victory was the gift of their gracious, sovereign commander. What happened at the beginning was to

be the pattern for all their future advance into this land of promise and rest.[39] You see Israel feared the Lord, and Jericho feared Israel.

**Joshua 6:1** | Now Jericho was shut up inside and outside because of the people of Israel. None went out, and none came in.

The citizens of Jericho were terrified of what the Lord had done with the Hebrews who had come from Egypt. Remember the waters of the Jordan were split for about twenty miles, from the Dead Sea to the city of Adam (near Shiloh). For twenty miles, the Jordan dried up, with all the water on a heap. Everyone saw this miracle. Even the citizens of Jericho, with their mighty walls, were terrified.

But the news of Israel's exodus from Egypt and their recent victories east of the Jordan had already spread to Canaan and put the people in panic (Josh 2:9–11; cf Deut 2:25; 7:23; 11:25; 32:30). Then after seeing the Jordan River miracle, they were trembling with fear. This was just what God promised. [40]

I will send my terror before you and will throw into confusion all the people against whom you shall come, and I will make all your enemies turn their backs to you [*and run in retreat*]. —Exodus 23:27

As your worship level goes up in your life, you become a more effective witness. People need to see the Lord in you. The people of Jericho feared and trembled as they saw the faith of the people of Israel and God's manifest presence and miracles.

## Trust Him for Victory

Where does victory come from? God had sent his Capitan of the Lord's armies to direct a hidden war. The Lord gave Joshua this encouraging promise: "This is my war, Joshua. I am going to win the battle against Jericho for you. Simply trust me and do exactly as I say." Joshua listened carefully as God explained his plan.

**Joshua 6:2** | And the Lord said to Joshua, "See, I have given Jericho into your hand, with its king and mighty men of valor".

The victory had already been won! All Joshua and his people had to do was claim the promise and obey the Lord. Victorious Christians are people who *know* the promises of God, because they spend time

---

[39] Ibid.
[40] Wiersbe. *Be Strong*, 71.

meditating on God's Word (1:8); they *believe* the promises of God, because the Word of God generates faith in their hearts (Rom. 10:17); and they *reckon* on these promises and obey what God tells them to do. To "reckon" means to count as true in your life what God says about you in his Word.

## Follow His Instructions

"Joshua did not take the city merely by a clever, human military tactic," wrote Francis A. Schaeffer. "The strategy was the Lord's."[41]

**Joshua 6:3-5** | "You shall march around the city, all the men of war going around the city once. Thus shall you do for six days. [4] Seven priests shall bear seven trumpets of rams' horns before the ark. On the seventh day you shall march around the city seven times, and the priests shall blow the trumpets. [5] And when they make a long blast with the ram's horn, when you hear the sound of the trumpet, then all the people shall shout with a great shout, and the wall of the city will fall down flat, and the people shall go up, everyone straight before him" (6:3-5).

Early in the morning Joshua called the people together. "Today we shall begin our attack against Jericho," he announced. "We are going to do it God's way, not ours."

Joshua continued, "Line up in this order: Armed soldiers first. Next, seven priests each with a trumpet. After the trumpeters will be the priests carrying the Ark of God. The rest of the soldiers and other people will follow the Ark."

Everyone obeyed.

Joshua continued his instructions. "Now we shall march around the city of Jericho one time. The priests will blow their trumpets. Everyone else keep quiet. Do not say one word!"

"Ready? Forward march!" Joshua ordered.

Hearing the trumpets, the Jericho guards scurried to the top of the city wall. Wide-eyed, they watched the Israelites march around the entire city only one time. And then they all returned to their camp. How strange!

"What is the matter with that nation?" the people of Jericho must have wondered.

---

[41] Francis A. Schaeffer, *Joshua and the Flow of Biblical History* (Downers Grove, IL: InterVarsity Press, 1975), 102–3.

Early the next day Joshua gave the exact same strange order. Again, the Israelites marched around the city without talking. All that could be heard was the blowing of the trumpets. Then they went back to camp.

Now consider this: the Lord's instructions don't always make sense. But he is all wise and worthy of our trust. For six days, seven priests were to be armed with shofars. They were to lead the people and march around the city once without a word — without a sound, blowing the trumpets continually as they marched once around the city, and then go home. They were to do this for six days.

On the seventh day, they were to march around without a sound seven times, and on the seventh time the priests were to make a long blast of the trumpets. At that time, all the people shall shout with a great shout, and the wall of the city will fall down flat. That's when God's people were to invade the city.

Ok. That makes no sense. But they were to follow God's instructions to the tee. God sometimes seems to delight in using strange methods to achieve great things. He enabled Samson to win a victory over the Philistines by wielding the jawbone of a donkey. He enabled David to slay Goliath with a sling and a stone. Centuries later, God selected an ordinary Jewish girl to bring his Son into this world, and he selected tiny Bethlehem as the place for him to be born. The supreme example, of course, is the cross of Christ. It seems ridiculous to suggest that a Jewish rabbi dying on a Roman cross would provide eternal salvation for sinners. But that cross, so despised and scorned, is the means that God chose for saving sinners. That cross would prove to be a stumbling block to the Jews and a laughingstock to the Greeks, but to those who are saved, it is both the power and the wisdom of God (1 Cor 1:18–25). Why did God choose such a strange means of salvation? It was so all the glory for the salvation of sinners would be given to him (1 Cor 1:26–31).[42]

How do you hear from God? If you are God's child, you definitely will hear from him. But how do we hear from God? Of course, all Christians should say, "The Bible." Just to push back a bit, what about all the Bible loving Jehovah's witnesses or the Mary-worshipping Catholics? What makes us as evangelical or born-again Christians different? I believe the answer is by his Word and through his Spirit. God is interested

---

[42] Ellsworth, *Joshua*, 69.

in being personally involved in your life through his Word. God uses his Word to speak to you, but hear this: God does speak today. He may use a verse or a passage to directly guide you into the circumstances in your life. He promises that if we lack wisdom and ask, that he will give us wisdom without rebuking us (Jas 1:5).

## OUR STRATEGY (6:6-19)

The strategy presented from the Lord through Joshua was to demonstrate the complete powerlessness of God's people and the complete power of the Lord. We have an incredible illustration of walking in the Spirit.

### Faith Defined

The obedience of the people was due to their faith in the Word of God. *Faith is believing that which God tells us even when it seems ludicrous to do so.*

> Faith is the assurance of things hoped for, the evidence of things not seen. —Hebrews 11:1

There is a conviction or assurance of things that are hoped for. Hope in the Bible is not wishful thinking. Hope is a certain and settled expectation. Faith is trusting God based on evidence of unseen things. This is called by philosophers and theologians the *transcendental argument* for God. There are certain things that are settled realities that we cannot see, like the laws of science, laws of logic, and laws of morality and conscience. Faith, in other words, is not blind faith. It is based on settled evidence. God's fingerprints are everywhere. "The heavens declare the glory of God..." (Psa 19:1). DNA is just one example of God's mark of intelligence upon all living creatures.

Christian faith though goes beyond the transcendental evidence for God and looks to actual history when God became a human being. We as Christians believe that the true and living God has been revealed in his Son Jesus Christ of Nazareth who lived and died in Palestine around 2000 years ago.

Joshua had not yet seen the realities of the Gospel that we hold dear, but he was being led by the same Messiah that we are. The Captain of the Lord's armies was leading him, and he and the army of Israel with the priests were following the Lord by faith.

**Joshua 6:6-7** | So Joshua the son of Nun called the priests and said to them, "Take up the ark of the covenant and let seven priests bear seven trumpets of rams' horns before the ark of the Lord." ⁷ And he said to the people, "Go forward. March around the city and let the armed men pass on before the ark of the Lord".

Faith is not believing in spite of evidence, for the people of Israel had been given one demonstration after another proving that God's Word and God's power can be trusted. The Lord had opened the Red Sea, destroyed the Egyptian army, cared for his people in the wilderness, defeated great kings, given Israel their land, opened the Jordan River, and brought his people safely into the Promised Land. How could they do anything other than believe him!

They were given the instructions from the Lord through Joshua, and they obeyed. Although the strategy must have seemed to be utter nonsense to them, there is no record of the people questioning it or complaining about it. This generation had learned from the grumbling, unbelieving generation that had preceded them.

Peter Jeffery writes, "Faith is not an irresponsible step into the unknown, but a reasonable obedience to the will and word of a sovereign, almighty God."⁴³ Indeed, faith is the only pathway to victory.

And this is the victory that has overcome the world—our faith. —1 John 5:4

By faith the walls of Jericho fell down, after they were compassed about seven days. —Hebrews 11:30

Faith always has an object. Faith is not just wishful thinking. You can't just "have faith." That's wishful thinking. Biblical faith always has an object. The object of our faith is the triune God revealed in the Holy Scriptures. We trust in the God revealed in the Bible. Our object is the Lord. "Believe on the Lord Jesus Christ, and you be saved" (Acts 16:31). There's faith's object: the Lord!

Faith is not just believing facts. Faith is a trust in someone or something. It's a surrender of your mind, will, and emotions. Faith is demonstrated by actions. James said, "Faith apart from works is dead" (Jas 2:26). The evidence that a person has true faith is godly obedience

---

⁴³ Peter Jeffery. *Overcoming Life's Difficulties: Learning from the Book of Joshua* (Welwyn Garden City, UK: Evangelical Press, 2007), 71.

from the heart. As Jesus said, "You shall know them by their fruits" (Mt 7:16).

## Faith Supported

**Joshua 6:8** | And just as Joshua had commanded the people, the seven priests bearing the seven trumpets of rams' horns before the Lord went forward, blowing the trumpets, with the ark of the covenant of the Lord following them.

No one has perfect faith. We all look to the Lord, but we also all depend on each other. We see a beautiful pattern of growth. The Captain of the Lord of the Angel Armies (Jesus) is first. Amen! Then Joshua, then the soldiers, then the priests, then the people. Paul said, "Follow me as I follow Christ."

The Lord was at the center of everyone when they crossed. It was important that the ark of the Lord be in its proper place, for it represented the presence of the Lord with his people. When Israel crossed the river, the account mentions the ark sixteen times (Josh 3–4); and here in 6:6-15, the ark is mentioned eight times. Israel could march and the priests blow trumpets until all of them dropped from weariness; but if the Lord wasn't with them, there would be no victory. When we accept God's plan, we invite God's presence; and that guarantees victory (*cf* Exo 33:12-17). People are following you. But where are you leading them? Are you following Christ like Joshua was?

## Faith in Action

You can't say you have faith unless you obey the Lord. Trust and obedience go together. "Faith apart from works is dead" (Jas 2:26). The evidence that a person has true faith is godly obedience from the heart. As Jesus said, "You shall know them by their fruits" (Mt 7:16). What does obedience look like? Obedience is a total surrender. It's a walking in the Spirit, a yielding to God entirely.

### Obedience of Self-Control (6:9-11)

**Joshua 6:9-11** | The armed men were walking before the priests who were blowing the trumpets, and the rear guard was walking after the ark, while the trumpets blew continually. [10] But Joshua commanded the people, "You shall not shout or make your voice heard, neither shall any word go out of your mouth, until the day I tell you to shout. Then you shall shout." [11] So he caused the ark of the Lord to circle the city, going about it once. And they came into the camp and spent the night in the camp.

Marching around the walls, they couldn't make a sound until the seventh day. The only sound was the trumpets the priests were blowing. If the week's schedule was a test of their patience, the divine command of silence was a test of their self-control. People who can't control their tongues can't control their bodies (Jas 3:1-2), and what good are soldiers whose bodies are not disciplined? "Be still, and know that I am God" (Psa 46:10). In the Christian life there's "a time to keep silence, and a time to speak" (Ecc 3:7); and wise is the Spirit-filled child of God who knows the difference. Our Lord is the perfect example of this (Isa 53:7; Mt 26:62–63; 27:14; Lk 23:9).

### Obedience of Self-Discipline (6:12-14)

They walked around the city walls once each day for six days straight and went home. The city of Jericho is about a mile around the entire city, which is around 8 acres in land mass. It isn't a massive city, but a military compound. The scary part was not the size of the city but the soldiers and weapons they had inside the double paned walls. God did not tell them to build chariots, but to be silent and march while the priests blew the trumpets continually (6:13). They didn't necessarily understand, but they obeyed. Proverbs 3:5-6 says that our hearts are not always going to understand God's plans — that's why we can't lean to our own understanding.

**Joshua 6:12-14** | Then Joshua rose early in the morning, and the priests took up the ark of the Lord. [13] And the seven priests bearing the seven trumpets of rams' horns before the ark of the Lord walked on, and they blew the trumpets continually. And the armed men were walking before them, and the rear guard was walking after the ark of the Lord, while the trumpets blew continually. [14] And the second day they marched around the city once, and returned into the camp. So they did for six days.

Day after day, we are to seek the Lord. We are to do what he says. We may see no movement. But we need to surrender to the Lord and realize he knows exactly what he is doing.

### Obedience of Self-Denial (6:15-19)

Their obedience included not taking what they wanted. Some things in the world need to be devoted to destruction.

**Joshua 6:15-19** | On the seventh day they rose early, at the dawn of day, and marched around the city in the same manner seven times. It was only on that day that they marched around the city seven times.[16] And at the seventh time, when the priests had blown the trumpets, Joshua said to the people, "Shout, for the Lord has given you the city. [17] And the city and all that is within it shall be devoted to the Lord for destruction. Only Rahab the prostitute and all who are with her in her house shall live, because she hid the messengers whom we sent. [18] But you, keep yourselves from the things devoted to destruction, lest when you have devoted them you take any of the devoted things and make the camp of Israel a thing for destruction and bring trouble upon it. [19] But all silver and gold, and every vessel of bronze and iron, are holy to the Lord; they shall go into the treasury of the Lord."

This meant that everything was dedicated to the Lord—the people, the houses, the animals, and all the spoils of war—and the Lord could do with it whatever he pleased. In this first victory in Canaan, Jericho was presented to God as "the firstfruits" of the victories to come. Ordinarily the soldiers shared the spoils of war (Deut 20:14), but not at Jericho; for everything there belonged to the Lord and was put into his treasury (Deut 13:16; 1 Kgs 7:51). It was this command that Achan disobeyed, and his disobedience later brought Israel defeat and disgrace and brought Achan and his family death.

Obedience always looks like the fruit of the Spirit. It's not just an outward compliance, but an inward surrender and joy in yielding to God!

Is there a lack of obedience in your life? Is there a stronghold of the flesh? The works of the flesh manifest our unbelief in anger.

Are you angry? Is their cursing in your heart or on your lips? That's the flesh. Are you wanting to control things? The wrath of man works not the righteousness of God (Jas 1:19). God wants us walking in meekness, not anger.

Are you foolish? Do you turn to media, to porn, to worldly music to just check out? Instead of checking out, check in with the wisdom of Jesus.

Are you despairing? Depression isn't a fruit of the Spirit. Nothing should rob you of the joy that comes from knowing Christ by faith. Put it away. Find the root. Put on hope!

Are you worried? Anxiety is also not a fruit of the Spirit. Worry displays unbelief in the heart. We serve a God who is all wise. Trust him. Be filled with the joy of trust.

Obedience puts off the works of the flesh and puts on the fruit of the Spirit!

## OUR VICTORY (6:20-27)

## A Victory for Israel

**Joshua 6:20** | So the people shouted, and the trumpets were blown. As soon as the people heard the sound of the trumpet, the people shouted a great shout, and the wall fell down flat, so that the people went up into the city, every man straight before him, and they captured the city.

The people of Israel had a great victory. They devoted the entire city to destruction. For six days they walked around the city (about a one-mile radius). Each day they would walk once around the city blowing the ram's horns (shofars) continually. After their one-mile, very noisy walk, they went home. They did this for six days. On the seventh day, they did the same thing, but walk around it seven times, blowing their horns continually. At the end of the seventh circuit around the city, after blowing the horns for so long, they were to give a great shout. At that moment, the double wall barrier fell down flat. The people easily went up into the city, and they captured the city.

What a victory this was. This is what we should expect in our Christian walk because of Christ. We may be called upon to do unusual things! I doubt we will be asked to blow any trumpets, but we are called to obey Jesus Christ no matter what. Jesus said, "If you love me keep my commandments" (Jn 14:15). He promises to answer if we obey. We ought to expect God to do great things. That does not mean that we will always see the victory in this life. The hall of faith in Hebrews 11 closes with these sobering words: "All these, though commended through their faith, did not receive what was promised" (Heb 11:39). We may not receive it now, but we will have the victory when our faith is made sight at Jesus' coming.

## A Victory for Rahab and Her Family

**Joshua 6:22-23** | But to the two men who had spied out the land, Joshua said, "Go into the prostitute's house and bring out from there the woman and all who belong to her, as you swore to her." ²³ So the young men who had been spies went in and brought out Rahab and her father and mother and brothers and all who belonged to her. And they brought all her relatives and put them outside the camp of Israel.

Remember the words of Hebrews 11 about Rahab,

By faith Rahab the prostitute did not perish with those who were disobedient, because she had given a friendly welcome to the spies. — Hebrews 11:31

How amazing that Rahab is found in Matthew 1, in the very genealogy of Jesus, where there are two are Gentile women: Rahab the Cananite from Jericho (who, according to Jewish tradition, apparently married one of the spies, Salmon); the other is Ruth the Moabitess.

Rahab and her family had a great victory as well. When the walls of the city Jericho fell down, it appears that the section of the wall that held Rahab's house (2:17) *didn't fall down!* It wasn't necessary for the spies to look for a window with a red cord hanging from it (2:18-19), because the only house that was preserved was the house in which Rahab and her family waited. When the spies made their covenant with Rahab, they didn't know exactly how God would give them the city. The cord was there to preserve her and her family from destruction.

God saved and protected Rahab because of her faith (Heb 11:31); and because she led her family to trust in Yahweh, they were also saved. These Gentile believers were rescued from a fiery judgment because they trusted the God of Israel, for "salvation is of the Jews" (Jn 4:22). They were "afar off" as far as the covenants were concerned (Eph 2:11–12), but their faith brought them into the nation of Israel; for Rahab married Salmon and became an ancestor of King David *and of the Messiah!* (Mt 1:5).⁴⁴

## A Victory Costly to Jericho

Jericho could never be rebuilt. This is the Lord's victory. They were to destroy the people (6:21).

---

⁴⁴ Wiersbe. *Be Strong*, 78–79.

**Joshua 6:21, 24-25** | Then they devoted all in the city to destruction, both men and women, young and old, oxen, sheep, and donkeys, with the edge of the sword.

[24] And they burned the city with fire, and everything in it. Only the silver and gold, and the vessels of bronze and of iron, they put into the treasury of the house of the Lord. [25] But Rahab the prostitute and her father's household and all who belonged to her, Joshua saved alive. And she has lived in Israel to this day, because she hid the messengers whom Joshua sent to spy out Jericho.

### Destroy the inhabitants (6:21)

Although God's command meant total destruction for Jericho, this does not mean that there could not have been mercy. The command is only one aspect of God's plans for nations. This in particular is a fulfillment of prophecy in Leviticus. That wickedness or uncleanness is graphically described in Leviticus 18, with its focus on sexual perversions, child sacrifice, and other "abominations" to the Creator.[45]

> For by all these [things] the nations I am driving out before you have become unclean, and the land became unclean, so that I punished its iniquity, and the land vomited out its inhabitants. —Leviticus 18:24, 25

Elsewhere it is clear that nations do have a choice. Even a people whose wickedness is reaching the point of no return (like Israel and Nineveh, even Sodom and Gomorrah) can repent and find forgiveness and mercy from God (2 Chr 7:14; Jer 18:5–10; Jonah 4:11).[46] Why did all the inhabitants of the city have to die? Is it right that God could command Israel to kill everyone in Jericho, including women and children? Essentially, God prophesied the nations would be vomited out of the land because of their wickedness.

God, in another prophesy says, "Let the sins of the Amorites accumulate for 400 years so that they would be full" (Gen 15:16), and then sends his own people in as instruments of judgment. God is sovereign and has the right to choose when and how people die. 50,000 people die every day. Because this was a theocracy, God chose to use Israel. So God has his times and seasons for when he shares his authority to take

---

[45] Jackman, *Joshua*, 72.
[46] Richard S. Hess, *Joshua: An Introduction and Commentary*, vol. 6, Tyndale Old Testament Commentaries (Downers Grove, IL: InterVarsity Press, 1996), 146.

and give life. And the church today is not Israel, and we are not a political entity. Therefore, the word we have from the Lord today is, "Love your enemy. Pray for those who abuse you. Lay your life down for the world. Don't kill in order to spread the gospel but die to spread it."[47]

## Burn the City (6:24)

"God is a consuming fire" was spoken by Moses in Deuteronomy 4:24 long before it was quoted by the Holy Spirit in Hebrews 12:29. Moses was warning the Jewish people against idolatry and the danger of following the religious practices of the people in Canaan. Moses added a phrase that isn't quoted in Hebrews but is still important for us to know: "even a jealous God." God is jealous over his people and will not permit them to divide their love and service between him and the false gods of the world (Exo 20:5; 34:14). We cannot serve two masters.

Jericho was a wicked city, *and sin is only fuel for the holy wrath of God.* Jesus compared hell to a furnace of fire (Mt 13:42), fire that is eternal (25:41, 46); and John compared it to a lake of fire (Rev 19:20; 20:10, 14). John the Baptist described God's judgment as "unquenchable fire" (Mt 3:12). The burning of Jericho, like the destruction of Sodom and Gomorrah (Jude 7), is a picture of the judgment of God that will fall on all who reject the truth.[48]

**Joshua 6:26** | Joshua laid an oath on them at that time, saying, "Cursed before the Lord be the man who rises up and rebuilds this city, Jericho. "At the cost of his firstborn shall he lay its foundation, and at the cost of his youngest son shall he set up its gates."

Even after he had burned the city, Joshua put a curse on Jericho. This would warn any of the Jews or Rahab's descendants who might be tempted to rebuild what God had destroyed.[49] Many years later, this curse found a fulfillment when Hiel, a man from Bethel, "rebuilt Jericho. He laid its foundations at the cost of his firstborn son Abiram, and

---

[47] John Piper, "What Made it Ok for God to Kill Women and Children in the Old Testament?" Accessed July 11, 2018. https://www.desiringgod.org/interviews/what-made-it-okay-for-god-to-kill-women-and-children-in-the-old-testament
[48] Ibid., 81–82.
[49] Wiersbe. *Be Strong*, 82.

he set up its gates at the cost of his youngest son Segub, in accordance with the word of the Lord spoken by Joshua son of Nun" (1 Kgs 16:34).[50]

## A Famous Victory

All Israel rejoiced in what God had done through Joshua. Joshua did nothing except trust in the Lord. We can do that, can't we?

**Joshua 6:27** | So the Lord was with Joshua, and his fame was in all the land.

The statement here about the Lord's being with Joshua and his fame spreading throughout the land echoes two earlier statements, where God promised Joshua his presence, just as he had been with Moses (3:7) and where God began to exalt Joshua in the eyes of the people (4:14). This statement builds naturally upon those, reiterating that God was with Joshua, but adding that his fame now spread throughout all the land.[51] Joshua's name was known for the right reasons. He loved the Lord. What are you known for?

### Conclusion

The fight is upon us. Are you seeing real victory in your life? Is there a stronghold in your life? Are you following Christ, your Captain? Are you walking by faith? Are you experiencing the victory in your life?

When I think of tearing down strongholds, I think of my old heart of stone. Jesus went into my heart and tore down my heart of stone. He replaced it with a heart of flesh. My Jesus tells me that no enemy can defeat me. No weapon formed against me shall prosper. If I walk in him, I have total victory. In all our trials, Pauls says:

In all these things we are more than conquerors through him who loved us. [38] For I am sure that neither death nor life, nor angels nor rulers, nor things present nor things to come, nor powers, [39] nor height nor depth, nor anything else in all creation, will be able to separate us from the love of God in Christ Jesus our Lord. —Romans 8:37-39

---

[50] Howard. *Joshua,* 176.
[51] Ibid.

# 8 | JOSHUA 7
## SIN IN THE CAMP

*Israel has sinned; they have transgressed my covenant that
I commanded them; they have taken some of the devoted
things; they have stolen and lied and put them among their
own belongings. Therefore the people of Israel cannot stand
before their enemies.*
JOSHUA 7:11-12

The only thing keeping you from a life of total victory is you. You are
your own worst enemy. If you will get out of the way, Jesus will
transform you. Spiritual disaster is avoidable. Let me say that
again: spiritual disaster is avoidable.

The date was June 1, 2009. Air France Flight 447 which took off
from Rio de Janeiro and was headed to Paris, France, but it never made
it. It crashed into the Atlantic Ocean, killing all 228 people on board. It
would take two years for the black box to be found. When it was opened
up, investigators found out something shocking: The crash was avoidable. It didn't have to happen. Apparently, the pilots ignored the "en-
gine stall" warnings. And don't miss this: they didn't follow the manual.
The crash happened because they ignored the signs and didn't do what
they were trained to do.

I mention this because in Joshua 7, we are going to see a crash. It
was avoidable. It happened because they didn't do what they were told.

This theme is a major contrast from the previous chapter. The battle of Jericho is a great victory. The battle of Ai is Israel's greatest defeat. It's the only battle where Israel's army loses any soldiers: 36 to be exact. So Israel goes from the highest spiritual high of crossing the Jordan, defeating Jericho, and then total defeat by a city that was quite a bit smaller and less formidable than Jericho.

Jericho was a formidable victory. Jericho is in the middle of Israel, not terribly far from Jerusalem. This meant so much to the invasion: it meant that they could in essence split Canaan in two so that their enemies could not rally together. The mood is high in Joshua 6. God promised a victory, and God kept his promise.

Little did they know that as they were on this high at the battle of Jericho that they were more vulnerable to defeat than they had ever been. Only the threat was not outside, but inside the camp. Why is that?

The greatest single challenge any person will face is his own success. Why? Because success can become a fertile breeding ground for pride and self-reliance. We become complacent in victory, and we begin depending on the flesh. Before we know it a Christian can go from being on fire to stagnant and stuck.

God's people were on a spiritual high. The Bible says the hearts of the Canaanites melted. The nations in Canaan all knew that God had parted the Jordan River. They knew he crumbled the walls of Jericho. But the spiritual high would not last. Spiritual failure would come to Israel. But it was totally avoidable.

## THE LESSON OF SIN'S HOOK (7:1-15)

In the first 15 verses, we are going to look at the hook of defeat. You fisherman know how a fish loses. It goes for the bait. The hook of defeat is hidden by the bait. I want to teach you a powerful principle of the works of the flesh. The promise everything, and they even feel good for a short time, but defeat is inevitable. Because behind the bait, there is a hook. And here's my advice: "Don't take the bait." Before we look at the bait, I want you to see the hook behind the bait.

### The Hook Behind the Bait

The Bible says in Romans 6:23, "The wages of sin is death, but the gift of God is eternal life through Jesus Christ our Lord." There's the hook. The bait of sin might be pleasurable for a short time, but there is always misery and destruction that follow the bait. Bitterness feels good and justified until it starts eating you away, consuming you like a cancer. Foolishness feels like a great escape until it robs you of your family, your finances, your conscience, and your soul. Despair and self-pity feels right until it paralyzes you and robs you of your vitality. Worry and fear feel productive until you realize your ability to handle life in your own power has a shelf life. The bait of sin is so tempting. But stay far away because a hook of death is sure to closely follow. We see this in the first 15 verses.

**Joshua 7:1-5** | But the people of Israel broke faith in regard to the devoted things, for Achan the son of Carmi, son of Zabdi, son of Zerah, of the tribe of Judah, took some of the devoted things. And the anger of the Lord burned against the people of Israel. [2] Joshua sent men from Jericho to Ai, which is near Beth-aven, east of Bethel, and said to them, "Go up and spy out the land." And the men went up and spied out Ai. [3] And they returned to Joshua and said to him, "Do not have all the people go up, but let about two or three thousand men go up and attack Ai. Do not make the whole people toil up there, for they are few." [4] So about three thousand men went up there from the people. And they fled before the men of Ai, [5] and the men of Ai killed about thirty-six of their men and chased them before the gate as far as Shebarim and struck them at the descent. And the hearts of the people melted and became as water.

Thirty-six men died. That's the hook. The little city of Ai was much less respectable or renowned than Jericho. Ai was a humble city they should have easily defeated. So what was the problem? We see it in verse 1.

**Joshua 7:1** | But the people of Israel broke faith in regard to the devoted things, for Achan the son of Carmi, son of Zabdi, son of Zerah, of the tribe of Judah, took some of the devoted things. And the anger of the Lord burned against the people of Israel.

Achan had to take the bait. Easy escape. Easy pleasure. Sin is so easy, but the price is steep. Thirty-six men suffer death because of one man's sin. I want to focus on how a New Testament Christian can suffer defeat.

Obviously, we have the victory in our Lord Jesus Christ, but we also must stay away from those things that are devoted to destruction. I want to emphasize that all that the flesh offers is empty: it can only lead to misery and destruction. Anything you put in the place of the Lord is an idol, and it cannot fulfill you. This could be a marriage, a job, the desire for obedient children. All these things are good, but they are not to be made a demand. If you highest desire is anything but Jesus, it's an idol, and it will leave you and your family in shambles.

In the 1970s, Dan Wakefield wrong the best-selling book, "Going All the Way". He quickly sold 800,000 copies. This is what he had always dreamed. But when he got to the top and achieved all his dreams, what he found surprised him. He said:

> The dream of a lifetime had been realized, and I was delighted. I was also nervous and anxious... I learned what people have testified since the beginning of time, but that no one really believes until he has the experience—success and achievement and rewards are all fin, but they do not transform you, they do not bring about a state of built-in contentment or inner peace or security, much less salvation... The novel was not The Answer to all life's problems. So I went out and had another drink.[52] —Dan Wakefield

The bait of the flesh never satisfies. It can never calm your conscience. Sin can only kill your conscience. You have to have a clean conscience to be happy. The Christian cannot stay stuck in this emptiness for very long. We have the Spirit of God in us. We know that the world will offer you everything and leave you hungry. We know that true rest and satisfaction comes from Jesus alone. Remember his most famous invitation.

> Come to me all you who labor and are burdened, and I will give you rest. —Matthew 11:28

We learn about one man named Achan who thought he could gain some riches, but he ended up in complete defeat. That's how the sinful world works. It offers you everything, but leaves you empty every time. Are you stuck? Have you chased after the world, but you feel empty? We are going to learn that the soul can only be satisfied by gazing on the perfection of deity. You have to not only have a good theology to be happy—you have to engage with what you believe. You have live a life of faith, trusting God implicitly without the prejudice of your own bent heart or the world's noise, discouragement, and distractions.

---

[52] Dan Wakefield. *Returning: A Spiritual Journey* (Boston: Beacon Press, 1997), 198-199.

## The Catch

Like a fish caught by the hook, sin paralyzes us. Now for Joshua and the elders, they know they have lost their power. There is sin in the camp. There is compromise. The power and the confidence are gone. That's what sin does. It robs the child of God of assurance and power. It doesn't have to be that way. Joshua is dismayed.

**Joshua 7:6-9** | Then Joshua tore his clothes and fell to the earth on his face before the ark of the Lord until the evening, he and the elders of Israel. And they put dust on their heads. [7] And Joshua said, "Alas, O Lord God, why have you brought this people over the Jordan at all, to give us into the hands of the Amorites, to destroy us? Would that we had been content to dwell beyond the Jordan! [8] O Lord, what can I say, when Israel has turned their backs before their enemies! [9] For the Canaanites and all the inhabitants of the land will hear of it and will surround us and cut off our name from the earth. And what will you do for your great name?

The small army of two to three thousand men were faithful to God. They followed God's instructions as we see from the account. Yet God's anger is set against the nation for one man's sin. The anger of the Lord burned against the people of Israel (7:2). This is a great shock to Joshua. He had waited his whole life for this.

Remember, Joshua is eighty years old. He had gone through this before in the wilderness (Num 13). He was one of the twelve spies. Ten of the spies were fearful of entering the land, but Joshua stood with Caleb. They were the only two of that generation that got to enter the Promised Land. Now Joshua is completely confused. He is faithful. He's done nothing wrong. Yet God holds him and the nation accountable. After this surprising defeat and understandable dismay, Joshua prostrates himself before the Lord.

Joshua was shattered by the catastrophe at Ai. He and the elders of Israel put dust on their heads and fell before the ark of the Lord. Give them credit for taking the defeat very seriously and for going to the Lord![53] Joshua was so strong when they fought Jericho, but now he and the whole army have no strength and no confidence. Why? Because they have no power.

---

[53] Ellsworth, *Joshua*, 72.

You see when we're not doing the thing God wants us to do, we will lack the confidence that God wants us to have. Everything falls apart. Everything turns against us when we are not walking right with God. Nothing can be right when you dear child of God, are walking in the flesh.

### Deal with Sin Together

Sin will occur in the believer's life. That wasn't the problem. Achan's problem was not that he sinned, but how he hid his sin. As a result, God puts Joshua and the entire nation to the test. The only way to get victory for Israel is to deal with the sin in the camp. If the believer won't deal with sin, his community will have to.

**Joshua 7:10-15** | The Lord said to Joshua, "Get up! Why have you fallen on your face? [11] Israel has sinned; they have transgressed my covenant that I commanded them; they have taken some of the devoted things; they have stolen and lied and put them among their own belongings. [12] Therefore the people of Israel cannot stand before their enemies. They turn their backs [*and run*] before their enemies, because they have become devoted for destruction. I will be with you no more, unless you destroy the devoted things from among you. [13] Get up! Consecrate the people and say, 'Consecrate yourselves for tomorrow; for thus says the Lord, God of Israel, "There are devoted things in your midst, O Israel. You cannot stand before your enemies until you take away the devoted things from among you." [14] In the morning therefore you shall be brought near by your tribes. And the tribe that the Lord takes by lot shall come near by clans. And the clan that the Lord takes shall come near by households. And the household that the Lord takes shall come near man by man. [15] And he who is taken with the devoted things shall be burned with fire, he and all that he has, because he has transgressed the covenant of the Lord, and because he has done an outrageous thing in Israel.

When one member of the Body of Christ sins, all are affected. We must begin with an understanding that God's people are one. The church always has to be a body who deals radically with sin, or it dies.

Who stole? Who lied? All Israel? No, just Achan. Why does God accuse the nation as transgressing his covenant? Because God treats them as one. God insists that they act as one, or he is leaving them. The New Testament also has this kind of talk.

Paul says, "Do you not know that a little leaven leavens the whole lump? [7] Cleanse out the old leaven that you may be a new lump, as you really are unleavened" (1 Cor 5:6b-7).

God is dealing with one immoral man, but he calls them to act as one in purging out sin. Why? Because the yeast of sin spreads rapidly through the whole church. God's people must take sin seriously in their camp. We must learn from this that God takes sin seriously, even if we do not, and that sin is the real cause of defeat for God's people.[54] They were to all come to account together before God. God takes sin very seriously. We are all going to be brought to account, not just for our own sin, but also how we maintained holiness in the camp. The camp in our context is the local church. Are you taking not only your sins but others' sins seriously?

## THE LESSON OF SIN'S BIRTH (7:16-21)

In the next verses we see what happens. How is sin birthed into existence in the heart? James gives us the conception and birth of a sin.

Let no one say when he is tempted, "I am being tempted by God," for God cannot be tempted with evil, and he himself tempts no one. [14] But each person is tempted when he is lured and enticed by his own desire. [15] Then desire when it has conceived gives birth to sin, and sin when it is fully grown brings forth death. —James 1:13-15

Sin begins with enticement in the heart. That's where it has to be cut off. Every Christian has the responsibility to put away sin at the root. That's what James is saying. Once sin is conceived and birthed, it brings forth a misery that ends in death and eternal damnation. Not so for the Christian. The Christian quickly becomes skilled in cutting off sin in the heart. Let's look at what Achan did to see how we can cut sin off before it starts. Look how it started for Achan.

**Joshua 7:16-21** | So Joshua rose early in the morning and brought Israel near tribe by tribe, and the tribe of Judah was taken. [17] And he brought near the clans of Judah, and the clan of the Zerahites was taken. And he brought near the clan of the Zerahites man by man, and Zabdi was taken. [18] And he brought near his household man by man, and Achan the son of Carmi, son of Zabdi, son of Zerah, of the tribe of Judah, was taken. [19] Then Joshua said to Achan, "My

---

[54] Boyce. *Joshua*, 58.

son, give glory to the Lord God of Israel and give praise to him. And tell me now what you have done; do not hide it from me." **20** And Achan answered Joshua, "Truly I have sinned against the Lord God of Israel, and this is what I did: **21** when I saw among the spoil a beautiful cloak from Shinar [*Babylon*], and 200 shekels of silver, and a bar of gold weighing 50 shekels, then I coveted them and took them. And see, they are hidden in the earth inside my tent, with the silver underneath."

What was it that led Achan to this sad act of disobedience? I suggest the following root elements.

## Sin's Conception

Why was Israel defeated? What is the key to constant and perpetual victory? How did they miss it? What happened? Sin conceived in the heart of a man named Achan.

Sin is conceived when we want what we want, and we are willing to sin to get it. Achan was a rich man. He didn't need anything. The Scripture says he had lots of herds of animals. But he wanted what he wanted, and he was willing to sin to get it.

*Use your imagination.* I can imagine a scene like this. It's midnight now. Over the ruins of Jericho, the city lies in rubble, there are broken columns and crumbled walls, disarray. Outside Jericho the camp of Israel is pitched and here is each tribe in its place and the tents are there. The moon is looking down on that scene, of desolation, as the walls came tumbling down. Everybody is asleep, it's quiet. Did I say everybody was asleep? There's one man who's not asleep. You already know Achan. He got sinned against the Lord, and got his family involved in the cover up. He's a rich man who really needed nothing. Yet he let sin conceive. He could have avoided this defeat personally and for his family and for his nation. That's how sin is. It knows no boundaries.

I see him as he comes to the door of his tent and opens it, quietly, stealthily makes his way from that tent and out of the place where his tribe is encamped. He makes his way over those fallen brick and rock, over that fallen wall. He makes his way into the city there, into the marketplace, and he begins to look around and the moonlight shines down on something that is silvery. And he notices that there's a bag there and the mouth of that bag is open. He picks up the bag and looks and there are two hundred, two hundred shekels of silver. He's a soldier, he's never held that much money in his hand in one time. He picks it up and it runs through his fingers like, like water. He puts it back in the bag and holds it in his trembling hand and there he sees something flashing like fire. Is it a piece of cheese? No! It's a wedge of gold, pure gold! He picks it up, shines it, holds it. He's never seen that much gold at one time. He's got the silver, he's got the gold. And then there's something else, flashing, sparkling. It's an ornament, a beautiful ornament. It, it's on a garment, he picks it up, shakes the dust off it, why, that came from Babylon, why that's, that's beautiful. He holds it up. His heart is beating wildly. He says, This I want, this I will have, and he, he takes the silver and the gold, wraps it up in the Babylonian garment, makes his way back over the rubble, back to his tent, looks around, nobody has seen him yet he thinks. He goes into his tent and rolls back his sleeping mat and scoops out the dirt and he puts the Babylonian garment in there and he puts the 200 shekels of silver and he puts the wedge of gold and he covers it, then rolls out his sleeping mat and lies down and goes to sleep, at least he tries to sleep. There's a smile on his face, he says, I have done it, and nobody has seen me.

And he was right almost. There was one who had seen the whole thing—Almighty God, watching from heaven. What had he done? He had committed a trespass and a terrible trespass.

Israel lost the battle as well because of self-reliance. Instead of bringing their full team, they instead gave an encore performance. They didn't bring their A-game to Ai. They didn't come prepared. Ai was a small city of 12000 people, 3000 soldiers. 15 miles away. It looks like after their victory, they didn't seek the Lord. They didn't worship before war. They went out in the power of the flesh. The Ark of the covenant isn't mentioned until after their defeat. Saints, we have to constantly worship in complete dependence and self-surrender to God. We cannot go in our own power.

## Sin's Deception

Achan was one of Israel's soldiers in the battle of Jericho. We find out later that he's a rich man already, with great herds. He didn't need the money. But that's how the flesh is. It's deceitful.

...put off your old self, which belongs to your former manner of life and is corrupt through deceitful desires, [23] and to be renewed in the spirit of your minds, [24] and to put on the new self, created after the likeness of God in true righteousness and holiness. —Ephesians 4:22-24

Why would a rich man think he needed more? And where was he going to spend that massive amount of gold and silver. And what about the Babylonian garment? Would his wife wear it to dinner? That's be suspicious. Sin was so deceitful that Achan was willing to get his family involved. He buried it *inside* his tent, not *outside* the camp.

One of God's commands was that the entire city of Jericho be destroyed. All metal articles (gold, silver, bronze, iron) were to be taken to the treasury of the Lord as the spoils of the conquest, but everything else was to be consumed by fire. The people were to be killed. Achan heard those commands along with everyone else. But when he entered the city and actually saw some of the forbidden spoil before him, he coveted what he saw and took it.[55]

## Sin's Dissatisfaction

Another obvious fact is that Achan dissatisfied. There's a hunger for more and more and more, but you can never be filled. The sad thing is that God was in the process of leading Achan, along with the other members of the nation, into a new land of great wealth and opportunity. The godly, in normal circumstances, will prosper financially because of good decision making. He could have had it all, but with sin, nothing is ever enough.

Achan was inheriting a country in which each family was to possess its own land, own its own house, and sit beneath its own vines and fig tree. But Achan's mind was not on the blessings that lay ahead, but on what he could get now.[56] Like Adam and Eve in the garden, he doubted God's goodness in fulfilling his promise. Achan's dissatisfaction, which was itself a sin, gave birth to disobedience. This was a rich man that just wanted more. Sin will never be satisfied. The flesh can never have enough.

The foolishness of wanting more can ensnare any of us. It will halt your victory. Don't steal from God. You always get more out of less. You put God first and all the rest will follow (Mt 6:33). Seek first the kingdom of God and his righteousness!

---

[55] Boyce. *Joshua*, 58–59.
[56] Ibid., 59.

God cares about what we give. God owns it all, but in the Old Testament they gave 10% at minimum. If they did that in the Old Testament, that's a good place to start, not out of compulsion but out of love. But listen to what God told them in the Old Testament.

> Malachi 3:8, Will man rob God? Yet you are robbing me. But you say, 'How have we robbed you?' In your tithes and offerings.

If we hold anything back of our time or our treasure, we rob God. We to be completely satisfied and invested in him. God cares about how we give. Remember Ananias and Saphira (Acts 5). They gave for show. We don't give for show. We don't let our left hand know what our right hand is doing. We give privately, but generously. Giving means you are invested. According to Jesus, where you spend your money reveals the values of your heart.

> Where your treasure is that's where your heart is and will be. —Matthew 6:21

You invest in a stock you will pay attention to the stock. It's wonderful to be satisfied in God alone, because it frees us up to give generously! We don't have to steal from God.

## Sin's Betrayal

Under the rules of war, a conqueror can seize the possessions of the one he defeats, and perhaps Achan was thinking along these lines. But this was his error. Achan may have been part of the invading army and may have wielded his sword effectively, but he was not the conqueror of Jericho. Nor were the other Jewish soldiers' conquerors. God was the conqueror. God was giving the city of Jericho to Israel's armies, and it was he (not Joshua or any of the other generals) who had demanded that spoil from the battle go into the temple treasury and that everything else be destroyed.[57] That is why God explained the defeat to Joshua by saying, "Israel has sinned; they have transgressed my covenant that I commanded them; they have taken some of the devoted things; they have stolen and lied and put them among their own belongings" (7:11). We don't belong to ourselves. Our heart and our lives and our fellowship are God's.

---

[57] Ibid., 60.

You were ransomed... not with perishable things such as silver or gold, [19] but with the precious blood of Christ, like that of a lamb without blemish or spot. —1 Peter 1:18-19

Christian, everything you are and ever will be is God's. Walk in the Spirit. Sin steals that worship and that walk from you because ultimately, it's a betrayal of our loving heavenly Father and it is a betrayal of the cross. Now if you are sinning, come back to the Lord. Come clean. Don't stay silent. Don't let sin remain in your heart. It's a betrayal of the highest love possible.

## THE LESSON OF THE STONES (7:22-26)

Here we see an awful price for sin, and we see a lesson from the stones.

**Joshua 7:22-26** | So Joshua sent messengers, and they ran to the tent; and behold, it was hidden in his tent with the silver underneath. [23] And they took them out of the tent and brought them to Joshua and to all the people of Israel. And they laid them down before the Lord. [24] And Joshua and all Israel with him took Achan the son of Zerah, and the silver and the cloak and the bar of gold, and his sons and daughters and his oxen and donkeys and sheep and his tent and all that he had. And they brought them up to the Valley of Achor. [25] And Joshua said, "Why did you bring trouble on us? The Lord brings trouble on you today." And all Israel stoned him with stones. They burned them with fire and stoned them with stones.[26] And they raised over him a great heap of stones that remains to this day. Then the Lord turned from his burning anger. Therefore, to this day the name of that place is called the Valley of Achor [*Trouble*].

### The Misery Monument

Here is a lesson from the pile of stones that were a monument to misery. Not just the man, but his sons, his daughters, his wife, they're all stoned and burned with fire. You say that's not fair, that's not right! Well you see, what happened is, he corrupted his family. Where did he hide this? Not outside the tent, in the tent. They had become partakers of this crime and now his children are destroyed because of his lie. And, mister, if you go to hell, that's one thing, but God have mercy upon you if you drag your sons and daughters into hell, too, because of your sin. Hidden sin, wicked sin, vile sin destroys loved ones.

To whom much is given, much will be required. —Luke 12:48

Judgment is always the harshest where revelation is the fullest. Achan had been given much. He saw the Jordan River parted. He saw God take down the walls of Jericho. How could Achan think that he would get away with his sin?

Judgment begins at the house of God. —1 Peter 4:17

We as a people have had more access to the truth and the Gospel than anyone in the history of the world. We have reaped the blessings are a result. There in the Valley of Achor, Trouble Valley, learn this lesson: sin always brings suffering and misery. It can lead to eternal damnation if a person won't repent and put their faith in Christ.

## The Miracle Monument

We need to learn from these stones. Now the nation of Israel has two piles of stones. They piled up rocks as a monument of God parting the river. That's the Miracle Memorial of 12 stones at Gilgal. This is what happens when we follow God in faith.

Valley of Achor piles of stones is what happens when we live in unbelief. With unbelief you can only reap destruction. If you live in the flesh, you can only get misery. Foolishness will harden your heart and lead your life to tear apart. Bitterness and anger, of which we have all experienced, never got us one step closer to God or righteousness. Worry never helped any situation get better. Your despair and depression cannot get you out of the pit. But Jesus can. Stop living in the flesh. Stop living in unbelief. Walk in the Spirit. Walk in his joy, his love, his peace. Learn from the stones. You need to be putting up miracle monuments, not misery monuments.

### Conclusion

I want you to imagine a scene that did not happen. I want you to see Achan as he plants all of that in his tent there and covers it up, rolls out his bed mat over it and tries to sleep and then he says, "Oh Lord, what have I done? How could I have been so foolish? Wife, wake up, children, get up. Pray, look what we've done, how could we do such a thing? Dig it up, put it, give it to me. Where's Joshua's tent? Joshua, get up, get up, Joshua. Joshua, let me tell you what I've done. Oh, Joshua, I was a fool! God said not to do this but I've done it. Joshua, here's the silver. Joshua, here's the gold, here's the garment. Pray for me, Joshua, I've sinned against God. Pray for me, Joshua, I've sinned against God. Joshua, let's get an animal, let's make a blood sacrifice. I need to be forgiven." Would God have forgiven him? Absolutely.

> He that covers his sin shall not prosper, but whoever confesses and forsakes it shall have mercy. —Proverbs 28:13

Justice is God giving us what we deserve. Mercy is God not giving us what we deserve. We don't need justice, we need mercy. Look to the cross, and with the blood of Christ comes rivers and oceans of mercy! Our sin is great, but his mercy is more!

# 9 | JOSHUA 8
## LEAVING FAILURE BEHIND

*And the Lord said to Joshua, "Do not fear and do not be dismayed. Take all the fighting men with you, and arise, go up to Ai. See, I have given into your hand the king of Ai, and his people, his city, and his land.*
JOSHUA 8:1

Your worst failure can be the beginning of great humility and amazing usefulness for the Lord. For Joshua and the people of Israel, they had gotten a great victory, and as is the case among all of us at times, pride entered in. And they went to a much smaller city, Ai, and lost. They give God the leftovers. They sent a tiny contingent of men (3000) and ended up turning tail in defeat. What do you do after a defeat? God wants you to get up and keep going!

Whether it's a director on a movie set, a coach on a athletic field, or a conductor in an orchestra pit, the best leaders have an ability to know how to get the best out of those they lead. They can tell the difference between someone who is just going through the motions and someone who is giving all their heart. A good leader doesn't just want the mere technicalities and mechanics, but true heart and commitment.

God wants us to not settle for mere mechanics in the Christian life. He wants your whole heart's worship. You can't do that if you give up in your failures and sins. Don't settle for Christian mediocrity! Leave your sins and failures behind. God wants to use you. Don't be afraid when you fail. Get up!

> Though a righteous person falls seven times, he will get up, but the wicked will stumble into ruin. —Proverbs 24:16, CSB

Repentance means you get up and fix your eyes on Jesus. Repentance can bring revival where some amazing things happen. The first thing that happens when we repent is:

## MOMENTUM IS REGAINED (8:1-9)

### Momentum Begins with Worship

There's all this failure in Ai. They hadn't sought the Lord. They gave the Lord the leftovers instead of giving the Lord their best. They send 3000 to fight. They put confidence in the flesh.

> We are the circumcision, who worship by the Spirit of God and glory in Christ Jesus and put no confidence in the flesh. —Philippians 3:3

What happens when you put confidence in the flesh? God starts talking to them. They start worshipping and momentum is regained. They stop going according to their own plan and God gives them his perfect plan.

**Joshua 8:1-2a** | And the Lord said to Joshua, "Do not fear and do not be dismayed. Take all the fighting men with you, and arise, go up to Ai. See, I have given into your hand the king of Ai, and his people, his city, and his land. ²And you shall do to Ai and its king as you did to Jericho and its king...

Momentum begins with worship. Whatever failure you've endured, look for the Lord to be gracious and kind. He's no longer your judge. He's your heavenly Father. Achan was judged because he was caught. As God's children we need to learn to worship the Lord even in our failures. Look for the Lord to be close behind any sin and failure in your life. And, God now says, "Since you've dealt with your sin..." "I have given into your hand the king of Ai." And, notice what God says: "You shall do to Ai and its king as you did to Jericho and its king." Just as I gave you Jericho, I'll give you Ai. In other words, the same God who defeated Jericho is going to defeat Ai.

## Momentum Starts with Willingness

But God gives Joshua a different strategy. They marched around the walls of Jericho, gave a shout and the walls came down. But, this time God says, "You're going to Ai by a strategy, you're going to take them by an ambush."

**Joshua 8:3-9** | So Joshua and all the fighting men arose to go up to Ai. And Joshua chose 30,000 mighty men of valor and sent them out by night. [4] And he commanded them, "Behold, you shall lie in ambush against the city, behind it. Do not go very far from the city, but all of you remain ready. [5] And I and all the people who are with me will approach the city. And when they come out against us just as before, we shall flee before them. [6] And they will come out after us, until we have drawn them away from the city. For they will say, 'They are fleeing from us, just as before.' So we will flee before them. [7] Then you shall rise up from the ambush and seize the city, for the Lord your God will give it into your hand. [8] And as soon as you have taken the city, you shall set the city on fire. You shall do according to the word of the Lord. See, I have commanded you." [9] So Joshua sent them out. And they went to the place of ambush and lay between Bethel and Ai, to the west of Ai, but Joshua spent that night among the people.

Joshua was to take a group of men about thirty thousand, put them up in the mountains behind Ai, and then Joshua came up with the rest of the army in front of Ai. And, when the men of the city of Ai came out against Joshua, Joshua fled out into the wilderness, drew the men out. The men up in the mountain by an ambush came down into the city and burned the city. The men of Ai turned around, saw their city burning, went around and tried to flee back, but the men came out of the city. And, those men who'd been fleeing from Ai turned around, and they caught them and crushed them, and they were destroyed. It was a marvelous strategy.

As a matter of fact, did you know that they study the campaigns of Joshua in the military archives and schools of Israel today? They study what Joshua did because it was a great strategy. God gave Jericho to the Israelites and God gave Ai to the Israelites. But, God did it in two separate ways.

Now, you see so many times we need to learn a lesson and it is this lesson. It's a lesson of radical obedience. God works at different times and in different ways. The methods of God often change. The *who* is a whole lot more important than the *how* and sometimes we get hung up on the *how*. Sometimes we think God has to do the same thing in the same way, and we get uncomfortable if God doesn't do it exactly tomorrow like he did it yesterday. One day God says "March around Jericho." The next day he gives a military strategy to defeat Ai.

God uses methods and programs and all the mechanical stuff, but that's not the main thing. The main thing is that God is in it. One of the worst things that can happen a Christian or a church is to fall into a rut? We must not trust in programs or methods but in the Living God. Someone said, "Do you know what the seven last words of the church are?" "We never did it that way before." Just because God does something a certain way before, he is not bound to do it that way always. Our God is a dynamic God and meets each culture in fresh new ways.

Now some things must not change: who God is, who Jesus is, the work of Christ, the Gospel. But God does things in different ways. we get into an argument with people over methods. You see, the important thing is not how God does it. The important thing is that God does it, right? God's methods change. God's methods change, but God's personality, and God's character, and God's principles never change. And, I want you to notice three things in this passage of Scripture, not about the method of God, but about the character of God. The methods change, but the character of God never changes.

## WAITING IS REWARDED (8:10-23)

God's people in Joshua 7 were a wayward people. They disobeyed the Lord and yet God pardoned them. God forgave them and God gave them a brand-new fresh start. And, I want to tell you it is the nature of God to forgive sin. Isn't that wonderful? And look what victory God gave. There's a little detail in verse 2 that is important to catch.

### Rewarded with Provision

**Joshua 8:2** | "…And you shall do to Ai and its king as you did to Jericho and its king. Only its spoil and its livestock you shall take as plunder for yourselves. Lay an ambush against the city, behind it."

They get the spoil. Had Achan have waited, he could have had the gold and the silver and the Babylonian coat. God's not stingy. But you have to learn a major principle of faith. You have to wait on the Lord.

All those who wait on the Lord will be rewarded. We know this principle. We have to put God first. Israel put God first at Jericho, and all but
Achan gave the spoil to the Lord. And in Ai, God says, now that you are
worshipping me and you've put me first, all the spoil is now yours. God
rewards those who put him first and wait on him.

> Seek first the kingdom of God and his righteousness, and all these
> things will be added to you. —Matthew 6:33

## Rewarded with Power

So they get all the spoils. And look at this: they get the king and the
victory. They have their spiritual power restored. No one from Ai es-
capes this time. No one from Israel dies! Look at Joshua 8:10-23.

**Joshua 8:10-23** | Joshua arose early in the morning and mustered the
people and went up, he and the elders of Israel, before the people
to Ai. [11] And all the fighting men who were with him went up and
drew near before the city and encamped on the north side of Ai,
with a ravine between them and Ai. [12] He took about 5,000 men
and set them in ambush between Bethel and Ai, to the west of
the city. [13] So they stationed the forces, the main encampment
that was north of the city and its rear guard west of the city. But
Joshua spent that night in the valley. [14] And as soon as the king of
Ai saw this, he and all his people, the men of the city, hurried and
went out early to the appointed place toward the Arabah to meet
Israel in battle. But he did not know that there was an ambush
against him behind the city. [15] And Joshua and all Israel pretended
to be beaten before them and fled in the direction of the wilderness. [16] So all the people who were in the city were called together
to pursue them, and as they pursued Joshua they were drawn
away from the city. [17] Not a man was left in Ai or Bethel who did
not go out after Israel. They left the city open and pursued Israel.
[18] Then the Lord said to Joshua, "Stretch out the javelin that is in
your hand toward Ai, for I will give it into your hand." And Joshua
stretched out the javelin that was in his hand toward the
city. [19] And the men in the ambush rose quickly out of their place,
and as soon as he had stretched out his hand, they ran and entered the city and captured it. And they hurried to set the city on
fire. [20] So when the men of Ai looked back, behold, the smoke of
the city went up to heaven, and they had no power to flee this
way or that, for the people who fled to the wilderness turned back
against the pursuers. [21] And when Joshua and all Israel saw that

the ambush had captured the city, and that the smoke of the city went up, then they turned back and struck down the men of Ai. [22] And the others came out from the city against them, so they were in the midst of Israel, some on this side, and some on that side. And Israel struck them down, until there was left none that survived or escaped. [23] But the king of Ai they took alive, and brought him near to Joshua.

Those who wait on God are rewarded! You know, so many times we think of God as being so stern, so unyielding, and sometimes we may think holds a grudge. But as we see God's forgiveness and victory at Ai, we must understand that there is no one like God! We ask with the Prophet Micah:

> Who is a God like you, pardoning iniquity and passing over transgression for the remnant of his inheritance? He does not retain his anger forever, because he delights in steadfast love. —Micah 7:18

God is the God of a second chance. God is the God of grace. God is a God of forgiveness. God is a God of beginning again. Look at the great victory at Ai. I want to tell you that failures are not fatal and failures are not final as long as there's a God in Heaven. He's a God who wants to give you another chance. And, here in Joshua 8:1 we read where God said to Joshua: *Joshua, I'm giving you another chance. I'm giving you another day. You failed at Ai. Don't give up. You disobeyed before. I forgive you. Let's do this again.*

Do you know there are some people who have failed and because they failed they just simply quit? They just quit and they're always going around moaning, groaning, talking about, "What a fool I was." The Bible says we are to forget *"... those things which are behind..."* past guilt and past glory (Phil 3:13). Forget your success at Jericho and your failure at Ai. Forget those things. There's a land out here to be conquered and the same God who wants to give you a second chance will give you a second chance.

He gave Samson another chance didn't he? Do you remember how Samson got his hair cut in the devil's barbershop? Lost his power and yet Samson said, "Oh God, hear me one more time." And, he was more victorious in his death than he was in his life.

He gave Jacob a second chance. Do you remember Jacob went to Bethel? There he met the Lord, he saw a ladder descending out of Heaven (Gen 28). He made vows with God, and then later on he got away from God, and fled from Esau in fear. But, the Bible says, "He went back to Bethel" (Gen 35). He got a new name. God changed his name from Jacob to Israel: Prevailer with God. God gave him a second chance.

He gave John Mark a second chance. Paul said, "Mark, he's been a failure, he's been a deserter." And, yet God gave him a second chance. And, he wrote the Gospel of Mark.

He gave Peter a second chance. Simon Peter cursed, and swore, and denied Christ. And, yet Simon Peter was a great preacher on the day of Pentecost. Aren't you glad that God is the God of a second chance?

And, I want to tell you right now that you bring your sin to him, if you confess your sin, he will forgive your sin. He will give you a brand new start and after you get this new start you may serve him better than ever because you've learned a lesson. You've known the thrill of victory, and the agony of defeat, and now you're ready to serve the Lord with all power that you never had before.

Remember the words of Jeremiah when Israel was quite obliterated by Babylon. But he knew this wasn't the end for Israel. There is are always new morning mercies when God is involved.

> It is of the Lord's mercies that we are not consumed, because his compassions fail not. They are new every morning: great is thy faithfulness. —Lamentations 3:22-23

Aren't you glad that regardless of what happened yesterday that today "is the day which the Lord has made, let us rejoice and be glad in it" (Psa 118:24)? Aren't you glad that he's the God of a second chance? Aren't you glad that he's the God of a fresh start? I'll tell you there's something about the nature and character of God we see in Joshua 8:1. And, it is that the God who judges failure is also the God who is willing to forgive sin when it's confessed, repented of, forsaken and put away. God will give us a second chance.

## FAILURE IS REPURPOSED (8:24-35)

As in the lives of all who repent, we see the failure of Israel is repurposed. Instead of being stained with failure they are washed in victory. They are now known as overcomers. And their failure is completely repurposed.

## Repurposed for Humility

One of the things that happens in victory is we get proud. We forget to give God the glory. If you haven't learned that lesson, you have a lot of crushing failure coming your way.

God resists the proud but gives grace to the humble. —James 5:5

Here we see this failure of Israel keeping them humble and sober in their victory.

**Joshua 8:24-29|** When Israel had finished killing all the inhabitants of Ai in the open wilderness where they pursued them, and all of them to the very last had fallen by the edge of the sword, all Israel returned to Ai and struck it down with the edge of the sword.[25] And all who fell that day, both men and women, were 12,000, all the people of Ai. [26] But Joshua did not draw back his hand with which he stretched out the javelin until he had devoted all the inhabitants of Ai to destruction. [27] Only the livestock and the spoil of that city Israel took as their plunder, according to the word of the Lord that he commanded Joshua. [28] So Joshua burned Ai and made it forever a heap of ruins, as it is to this day. [29] And he hanged the king of Ai on a tree until evening. And at sunset Joshua commanded, and they took his body down from the tree and threw it at the entrance of the gate of the city and raised over it a great heap of stones, which stands there to this day.

Joshua utterly destroyed all the inhabitants. What a stark contrast we have here. Not only is it God's nature to pardon sin, it is also God's nature to punish sin. There's no contradiction. "If we confess our sin he's faithful and just to forgive us our sin" (1 Jn 1:9). But, if we don't he is faithful and just to judge our sin. We need to learn this about the nature of God. Oh, both the goodness and the severity of God (Rom 11:22). Sometimes pastors who will preach the wrath of God. Leaving out the love of God, he'll preach in terms about sin, and judgment, and damnation, and Hell, and terror. What they preach is true, but it's not good news unless it has the Gospel and redemption. Without the Gospel, people get a hopeless idea about God. Then some other pastors will come with all sweetness, and sugar, and honey, and syrup, and just sort of spray that sweetness all over the congregation. And he'll talk about the goodness of God, and the gentleness of God. But people can't appreciate the good news unless they hear the bad news first. We need to understand that on the one hand it is God's nature to pardon, but on the other hand it is God's nature to punish if we refuse to be pardoned. Both the goodness and the severity of God we see here.

Now, I know that some people think that what Joshua did to Ai was very severe, but I want you to remember that Joshua did not instigate this. These people had their chance. They had an opportunity to repent, but they passed it up. The Amalekites were part of these Canaanite people. [58] They refused mercy, so they get wrath. That's the only two options. Pardon or wrath. The Amalekites chose to reject God's pardon, so the Bible says, "The Lord will war against Amalek from generation to generation" (Exo 17:16); He says, "I will blot out the memory of Amalek" (Exo 17:14).

The Amalekites were the first to attack Israel after the exodus (Num 24:20). Israel won the initial battle (Exo 17:8–16), but later were driven back into the Sinai wilderness by a coalition of Amalekites and Canaanites (Num 14:39–45). Thereafter the Amalekites and Canaanites, and surely some from Ai and the surrounding cities, waged a barbaric guerrilla war against Israel (Deut 25:17–19). Fighting continued after Israel settled in Canaan.[59] John Milton describes the Amalekites:

> The Amalekites delighted in oppressing weaker people. Their wars were wars of ambush against the weak, the aged, the helpless. They would wait until a neighbor's crops were ready for harvest then they would invade his land, driving the herds before them. In war the Amalekites were especially cruel. They tortured captives by hacking off limbs, knocking out teeth, and gouging out eyes. The women and the children they drove ahead of them as slaves. They burned cities and destroyed objects of art and things sacred to the people of the land. For hundreds of years they harassed and plagued the people of God. And, in their fights with Israel they would mutilate the bodies of the captives. They would cut off parts of men while these men were still alive and hurl those pieces of flesh into the sky as they jeered at Israel's God.[60]

---

[58] A. Colin Day, *Collins Thesaurus of the Bible* (Bellingham, WA: Logos Bible Software, 2009).

[59] LeBron Matthews, "Amalekite," ed. Chad Brand et al., *Holman Illustrated Bible Dictionary* (Nashville, TN: Holman Bible Publishers, 2003), 54.

[60] See John Milton. *Complete Works* (Hastings, East Sussex, UK: Delphi Classics, 2015) — reprint.

How awful. Yet God gave people like this space to repent. Judgment comes for the Amalekites and all the Canaanites, including those at Ai. Why? They would not repent. But God is gracious to Israel. They repented, and their failure is completely repurposed. They are humble as they see the mighty hand of God working great things for them.

What a contrast: mercy for Israel. Judgment for Canaan. What's the difference? Simply the humility of repentance. When we come to God humbly in our sin, he exalts us, and uses us. I want you to learn this about the nature of God. We know that he pardons iniquity, but he also punishes it. When you fail as a Christian, it is not God condemning you. It is God crushing you. You want that sin: you are going to get failure and misery until you come to him anew and afresh. He's crushing you. He's humbling you.

> Humble yourselves before the Lord, and he will exalt you. —James 4:10

## Repurposed for Worship

When you fail, and you get up and look to the Lord for mercy, you can expect an increased life of worship. Deep rich worship comes to those who have been forgiven much. Do you know how much you've been forgiven? What did Jesus say to the sinful streetwalking woman, whom he had forgiven so much?

> I tell you, her sins—and they are many—have been forgiven, so she has shown me much love. But a person who is forgiven little shows only little love. —Luke 7:47

So it is with Israel. They had been forgiven so much. They got up in humility and got a great victory. In response to this great victory, Joshua teaches the people how to worship.

**Joshua 8:30-35** | At that time Joshua built an altar to the Lord, the God of Israel, on Mount Ebal,[31] just as Moses the servant of the Lord had commanded the people of Israel, as it is written in the Book of the Law of Moses, "an altar of uncut stones, upon which no man has wielded an iron tool." And they offered on it burnt offerings to the Lord and sacrificed peace offerings. [32] And there, in the presence of the people of Israel, he wrote on the stones a copy of the law of Moses, which he had written.[33] And all Israel, sojourner as well as native born, with their elders and officers and their judges, stood on opposite sides of the ark before the Levitical priests who carried the ark of the covenant of the Lord, half of them in front of Mount Gerizim and half of them in front of Mount Ebal, just as Moses the servant of the Lord had commanded at the first, to bless the people of Israel. [34] And afterward he read all the words of the law, the blessing and the curse, according to all that is written in the Book of the Law. [35] There was not a word of all that Moses commanded that Joshua did not read before all the assembly of Israel, and the women, and the little ones, and the sojourners who lived among them.

Suddenly, the war movie is cut and we are left looking at a slide of a worship service. We are wrenched from conquest to covenant.[61] Let's look at the historical background and the geographical background. After conquering Jericho and then Ai, God's people came to a beautiful valley town called Shechem. In Shechem, there are two mountains: Mount Gerizim and Mount Ebal. Mount Ebal is a big mountain in a sense, but rocky and barren nothing much wants to grow on Mount Ebal looks foreboding.

Then there's a valley of about five hundred yards of beautiful green verdant with a stream running through it. It's actually a natural amphitheater. God is going to have Joshua teach the people how to worship in that valley. On one side, you have rocky Mount Ebal. And on the other side green Mount Gerizim. Now, Mount Gerizim is very fruitful, beautiful, green lush mountain, and a lot of vegetation grows on Mount Gerizim, even to this day. There's a valley in between. Joel 3:14 says, "Multitudes, multitudes, in the valley of decision! For the day of the LORD is near in the valley of decision." That's what the city of Shechem was. It lay between Mount Ebal and Mount Gerazim. It was a valley of decision. What we do with God determines everything.

Mount Ebal is considered the mountain of cursing and Mount Gerizim is called the mountain of blessing. God gave these two mountains as visual illustrations knowing that the mountains would be there as long as the children of Israel were there. And, every time they looked at these two mountains it reminds them that God is the God who gives them a choice. God says, "I've set before you this day "the blessing and the curse" (8:34). I've set before you this day death and life. The Lord wanted to reinforce this so much that he just divided the people in half.

---

[61] Davis, *Joshua*, 71.

Now Joshua, in putting together that altar, and in writing out the law, was fulfilling a command in the law of Deuteronomy 27. It's fascinating.

On the day you cross over the Jordan to the land that the Lord your God is giving you, you shall set up large stones and plaster them with plaster. [3] And you shall write on them all the words of this law, when you cross over to enter the land that the Lord your God is giving you, a land flowing with milk and honey, as the Lord, the God of your fathers, has promised you. [4] And when you have crossed over the Jordan, you shall set up these stones, concerning which I command you today, on Mount Ebal, and you shall plaster them with plaster. [5] And there you shall build an altar to the Lord your God, an altar of stones. You shall wield no iron tool on them; [6] you shall build an altar to the Lord your God of uncut stones. And you shall offer burnt offerings on it to the Lord your God, [7] and you shall sacrifice peace offerings and shall eat there, and you shall rejoice before the Lord your God. [8] And you shall write on the stones all the words of this law very plainly. —Deuteronomy 27:2-8

In 1980, the famous archeologist Adam Zertal, discovered this very altar. It was made of unhewn stones, just as the Joshua and Deuteronomy accounts say. Charred animal bones and ash were found inside this altar. There was also a lot of pottery that matched to the date of the time of Joshua. It was so fascinating to him that he went from being an atheist to a monotheistic Jew. He stayed and studied that altar for almost ten years (1982-1989).

The altar they found on Mount Ebal is a prototype, almost an exact replica of the altars for Solomon's temple as well as the second temple of Jesus' day.[62] How did this altar survive? Likely in Joshua's own lifetime, the altar was covered with stones to decommission it. It stayed in that state until 1980 when archeologist Adam Zertal discovered it.[63] The photo that follows is what they found in 1980.

---

[62] Adam Zertal. "Shechem and Mount 'Ebal in the Bible: Is this indeed Joshua's altar?". University of Haifa.

[63] Zvi Koenigsberg. (2020, September 3). Joshua's Altar on Mount Ebal: Israel's Holy Site Before Shiloh. Retrieved September 06, 2020, from https://www.thetorah.com/article/joshuas-altar-on-mount-ebal-israels-holy-site-before-shiloh

Rock by rock they carefully uncovered this altar over a period of years. By 1989, this is what they found underneath the pile of rocks.

Rock by rock they carefully uncovered this altar over a period of years. By 1989, this is what they found underneath the pile of rocks. Absolutely incredible. This altar is identical to the descriptions and measurements of the altars in Solomon's temple and the Temple of Jesus' day, as well as the altar to the golden calf that is still standing (in Tel Dan). One of the archeologists that worked with Zertal on site said this:

There were more than three thousand animal bones. These bones had been burnt on an open flame, and many had butcher marks, implying that at least parts of them had been eaten. — Zvi Koenigsberg [64]

In fact, all the animal bones were kosher. That is, they all those specific animals prescribed by the Levitical law, all those typical of what a Jew would bring to offer.

Not only did they find animal bones, but Egyptian royal medals with the royal marking of Pharoah Thutmoses III. These were valuables (with Thutmoses' royal imprint of the scarab—beetle) that are from the very time of the Exodus.[65] These little limestone beetles were given out at Pharoah Thutmoses III's wedding. He was either the Pharoah of the Exodus, or just before the Exodus. So this commemoration was found around the Mt. Ebal altar. Again, the Bible is not mythology, but history.

Another amazing fact is that Joshua made this altar as part of a new Gilgal camp, like the one they made by the Jordan River. So if you look at this from the sky, the wall around it is in the shape of a shoe. This is another testimony to their faith. God's keeps his promises.

[64] Zvi Koenigsberg. (2018). *Joshua's Altar on Mount Ebal: Israel's Holy Site Before Shiloh*. Retrieved December 24, 2020, from https://www.thetorah.com/article/joshuas-altar-on-mount-ebal-israels-holy-site-before-shiloh

[65] Stephen Gabriel Rosenberg. (2015, April 01). *Who was the Pharaoh of the Exodus?* Retrieved September 6, 2020, from https://www.jpost.com/opinion/who-was-the-pharaoh-of-the-exodus-395885

You can see the clear footprint in the photo. Why make another Gilgal camp? There are five mentioned in the Bible and five that Zertal discovered. The reason Joshua made another camp in the shape of a foot was because of the promise of God in Joshua 1:3.

Every place that the sole of your foot will tread upon I have given to you, just as I promised to Moses. —Joshua 1:3

Now after this victory at Ai, Joshua reads the Law of Moses, the first five books of the Bible, just as he was commanded to do when he enters the land. So Joshua writes the Law down on stone, and then he reads it—in it's entirety.

The people are to go to these two mountains: half on Mount Ebal, and half on Mount Gerazim. Ebal is rocky, representing the curse of sin. Mount Gerazim is green, representing the blessing of life in God.

God said, "I want half of you to go up here on Mount Ebal, the mountain of misery. And, then I want half of you to go up here on Mount Gerizim, the mountain of mercy." And, then Joshua said, "I'm going to be down here in the valley in between them." And, he said, "I'm going to begin to read the law of the Lord as Moses gave it. I'm going to read both the blessings and the cursing, and as I read the blessings and the cursing." I want you to say, "Amen."

Now, those mountains come down in terraces, they're almost like benches. It's one of the world's greatest natural amphitheaters and these voices could be heard resounding all around that valley. It must have been something to see.

What did they read? They read the entire Law, and Joshua put specific emphasis on the blessings and the cursings. For example, they most certainly read from Deuteronomy 27.

> And these shall stand on Mount Ebal for the curse: Reuben, Gad, Asher, Zebulun, Dan, and Naphtali. [14] And the Levites shall declare to all the men of Israel in a loud voice: [15] "'Cursed be the man who makes a carved or cast metal image, an abomination to the Lord, a thing made by the hands of a craftsman, and sets it up in secret.' And all the people shall answer and say, 'Amen.' [16] "'Cursed be anyone who dishonors his father or his mother.' And all the people shall say, 'Amen.' [17] "'Cursed be anyone who moves his neighbor's landmark.' And all the people shall say, 'Amen.' [18] "'Cursed be anyone who misleads a blind man on the road.' And all the people shall say, 'Amen.' [19] "'Cursed be anyone who perverts the justice due to the sojourner, the fatherless, and the widow.' And all the people shall say, 'Amen.' —Deuteronomy 27:13-19

And that went on right on, there are a lot of cursings. Let's go on and get some of the blessing because I want to hear from Mount Gerizim. I'd a lot rather hear from Mount Gerizim than Mount Ebal. So listen to these blessings in Deuteronomy 28.

> "And if you faithfully obey the voice of the Lord your God, being careful to do all his commandments that I command you today, the Lord your God will set you high above all the nations of the earth. [2] And all these blessings shall come upon you and overtake you, if you obey the voice of the Lord your God. [3] Blessed shall you be in the city, and blessed shall you be in the field. [4] Blessed shall be the fruit of your womb and the fruit of your ground and the fruit of your cattle, the increase of your herds and the young of your flock... [10] And all the peoples of the earth shall see that you are called by the name of the Lord, and they shall be afraid of you. —Deuteronomy 28:1-15, 10

There is Joshua with an altar on Mount Ebal representing the cross of the Lord Jesus Christ, and there he is reading the Word of God, and there he is saying, "It is God's mercy to pardon and it is God's justice to punish." Which will you have? It is God's nature to pardon, and God's nature to punish. It is God's nature to bless the forgiven and it is God's nature to curse in unrepentant. And, it all depends what you do with God. Will you surrender in childlike faith? That's not just a one-time thing, it's a way of life. Now what's the point of all this? It's not the animals sacrificed at Mount Ebal. Those pointed forward to Jesus. John the Baptist said,

Behold the Lamb of God who takes away the sin of the world. —John 1:29

You've got to embrace the Christ of Mount Ebal: that rocky foreboding mountain. It is there that the sacrifices are made. It is there that the curses are read. It is representative of curse that Jesus took on another Mountain: Mount Calvary, Golgotha, the place of the skull. There it was that our Lord became a curse for us! God wants us to go on in victory after we have failed. Jesus became the curse for us on that Mount Ebal, so that we could live on Mount Gerazim. This is our covenant. It's a covenant of grace from beginning to end. If you've failed, remember your covenant with Jesus.

## Conclusion

The Bible says, "Today, if you'll hear His voice, harden not your heart" (Heb 3:8). God loves you. The Lord wants to save you. But, I want to tell you one day your heart can get so hard that you will so insult the Holy Spirit that he won't speak to you any longer. Alexander MacLaren said, "Christ has last knocks."[66] You may be here without Christ. Turn to him today.

God has put you in a valley, a mountain of mercy, and a mountain of misery, and you can go to the north or to the south. You can choose life or you can choose death. Choose life. I beg you in the name of Jesus, with all of the unction and function of my soul, come to Jesus Christ and do it today.

---

[66] Andrew Bonar. *Robert Murry McCheyne* (Carlisle, PA: Banner of Truth, 1960), 143.

# 10 | JOSHUA 9
## DOUBLE CROSSED

*But when the inhabitants of Gibeon heard what Joshua had done to Jericho and to Ai, they on their part acted with cunning and went and made ready provisions and took worn-out sacks for their donkeys, and wineskins, worn-out and torn and mended, with worn-out, patched sandals on their feet, and worn-out clothes. And all their provisions were dry and crumbly. And they went to Joshua in the camp at Gilgal and said to him and to the men of Israel, "We have come from a distant country, so now make a covenant with us."*
### JOSHUA 9:3-6

Common sense is not enough for wise living. The flesh will always deceive you and lead you astray. Seek the Lord in his Word and by his Spirit if you want to live the abundant life. Mere Bible knowledge is not enough. We need to know God personally. We cannot just function on principles. Don't get me wrong. We need Biblical principles. Without solid theology you will certainly fail. But mere knowledge puffs up. Love edifies. Saul of Tarsus had an incredible knowledge of the Bible, but without the living God active in his life, that superficial knowledge was twisted and led him to kill Christians.

In other words, we need a heart that is constantly seeking God himself, through the Word if we are going to make godly choices in life. Knowing God makes you humble, content, at rest, and filled with love and hope. I want that. Paul calls this mindset for the New Testament Christian: "walking in the Spirit". John calls it "walking in the light". That's what we want. Are you making godly choices in your life? Media, friendships, family, marriage? Are you still falling into the same wrong choices? How can you and I change today? We are going to learn how to walk with wisdom.

Our lesson comes from the story of how Israel was deceived by a group of Canaanites form Gibeon. Israel failed to seek the Lord for wisdom. We don't have to make the same mistake.

## Introducing the Gibeonites

These two verses describe how the natives of Canaan, alarmed by the news of Israel's victories, banded together to fight the Israelites.

**Joshua 9:1-2** | As soon as all the kings who were beyond the Jordan in the hill country and in the lowland all along the coast of the Great Sea toward Lebanon, the Hittites, the Amorites, the Canaanites, the Perizzites, the Hivites, and the Jebusites, heard of this, [2] they gathered together as one to fight against Joshua and Israel.

One group of Canaanites did not join this confederacy—the Gibeonites. Convinced that Israel could not be defeated, these people decided to try a strategy which proved to be effective in deceiving Israel and in securing survival for themselves. Israel was forbidden from making covenants with close neighbors. The law of God was that Israel had to destroy their close neighbors, and the Gibeonites were a mere 25 miles away. Now Israel was allowed to make treaties outside the borders of the Promised Land. So the Gibeonites had an ingenious plan. We can't blame them. We all might have done the same thing.

## Spiritual Warfare

God's people should have known better. Remember from the beginning, the serpent was "crafty" more than any of the other creatures in Eden. That serpent beguiled Eve and is ready to beguile every one of us. After an experience of great blessing, God's people should have been especially prepared to confront the enemy. But Israel's greatest enemy wasn't the confederation of the armies of Canaan. It was a group of men from Gibeon who were about to enter the camp and deceive Joshua and the princes of Israel.

Satan sometimes comes as a devouring lion (1 Pet 5:8), sometimes as a deceiving serpent (2 Cor 11:3), and sometimes as an angel of light. We must be alert and protected by the spiritual armor God has provided for us (Eph 6:10–18).[67] How well do you know the enemy of your soul? The Bible says we are not to be ignorant of Satan's devices (2 Cor 2:11). He has a bag of tricks that he has found to be extremely effective in tripping God's people up. If we are aware of how he operates we can avoid being caught off guard when he comes against us with these tricks.

I think the attack we are usually waiting for is the direct attack. Where Satan comes charging at us like a roaring lion, teeth bared, blood on his mind. It happens. But we need to remember that he also loves to show up as a slithering serpent. I think this is a far more effective tactic. Because while a direct attack causes us to brace ourselves for impact, when he comes incognito as "an angel of light" we are lulled into complacency and then set up for a sucker-punch.

We see this in action in the Old Testament book of Joshua. Moses had died. Joshua was leading God's people into the Promised Land. Army after army came against them in battle and each time in the end God's people came out victorious. But then they were bested by the men from Gibeon. This defeat didn't take place on the battlefield. There was no actual battle. The Gibeonites won by taking off their weapons, putting on raggedy clothes and carrying dry and moldy bread. We see three very powerful things in this passage. We're going to talk about the power of the enemy, the power of prayer, and the power of redemption.

## THE POWER OF THE ENEMY (9:3-13)

You must never try to outsmart the enemy. You are not smarter than Satan and his demons. If you are to live in victory over sin, you must live in close fellowship with the Lord. Without fellowship, you will be deceived every time. We see this in Joshua 9.

Gibeon was located only twenty-five miles from the camp of Israel at Gilgal and was on Joshua's list to be destroyed. Gibeon was part of a seven-nation coalition, but they pulled out of it because they believed it was a losing cause. They knew they could never beat the God of Israel.

---

[67] Wiersbe. *Be Strong*, 107.

Double Crossed

So, if you can't beat 'em, join 'em! So the Gibeonites deceived Joshua. Despite the fact that God had instructed them to take out all the inhabitants of the land of Canaan, Joshua signed the peace treaty promising not to fight with the Gibeonites.

The problem is, Israel could not make covenants with the people inside the boundaries of the Promised Land. In Deuteronomy 20:10–20, God's law stated that Israel must destroy all the cities in Canaan. If after the Conquest Israel was involved in other wars, they could offer peace to cities that were outside the land. Somehow the Gibeonites knew about this law and decided to use trickery for their own protection. God's enemies in Gibeon knew they couldn't win, so they deceived Israel into making a covenant and coalition with the Gibeonites.

**Joshua 9:3-13** | But when the inhabitants of Gibeon heard what Joshua had done to Jericho and to Ai, [4] they on their part acted with cunning and went and made ready provisions and took worn-out sacks for their donkeys, and wineskins, worn-out and torn and mended, [5] with worn-out, patched sandals on their feet, and worn-out clothes. And all their provisions were dry and crumbly. [6] And they went to Joshua in the camp at Gilgal and said to him and to the men of Israel, "We have come from a distant country, so now make a covenant with us." [7] But the men of Israel said to the Hivites, "Perhaps you live among us; then how can we make a covenant with you?" [8] They said to Joshua, "We are your servants." And Joshua said to them, "Who are you? And where do you come from?" [9] They said to him, "From a very distant country your servants have come, because of the name of the Lord your God. For we have heard a report of him, and all that he did in Egypt, [10] and all that he did to the two kings of the Amorites who were beyond the Jordan, to Sihon the king of Heshbon, and to Og king of Bashan, who lived in Ashtaroth. [11] So our elders and all the inhabitants of our country said to us, 'Take provisions in your hand for the journey and go to meet them and say to them, "We are your servants. Come now, make a covenant with us."' [12] Here is our bread. It was still warm when we took it from our houses as our food for the journey on the day we set out to come to you, but now, behold, it is dry and crumbly. [13] These wineskins were new when we filled them, and behold, they have burst. And these garments and sandals of ours are worn out from the very long journey.

Joshua made a terrible mistake. He trusted the enemy instead of consulting the Lord. Since the enemy knows how to use the Word of God for his own purposes, God's people must keep alert (Mt 4:5-7). How does the enemy deceive us?

## The Gibeonites' Attack

Even though the Gibeonites actually lived 25 miles away they made themselves look like they had traveled hundreds of miles. They made a great show of telling Joshua that they had set out with piping hot bread and brand-new clothes, but now their provisions were rotten, and their clothes were all old and used. They knew that God's people were not allowed to make a treaty with a nearby enemy, but they were allowed to do so with a people that lived far away. It worked.

The Gibeonites assembled a group of men and equipped them to look like an official delegation from a foreign city. Their clothing, food, and equipment were all designed to give the impression that they had been on a long and difficult journey from a distant city.

Satan is our enemy. He is a counterfeiter and "masquerades as an angel of light" (2 Cor 11:14). He has his "deceitful workmen" (2 Cor 11:13) at work in this world, blinding the lost and seeking to lead believers astray. But more than that, Satan likes to use an inside attack. It's much easier for us to identify the lion when he's roaring than to detect the serpent when he's slithering into our lives.[68]

## The Flesh's Attack

The Gibeonites told lie after lie. Instead of consulting the Lord, Joshua and all Israel relied on their good wits. Satan's ambassadors can lie so convincingly.[69] We can't afford to "lean to our own understanding" (Prov 3:5-6) in any situation. Satan is a liar and the father of lies (Jn 8:44), and he will use your flesh to keep you in bondage. You are free from the power of the flesh if you are a child of God. You see, it's impossible to serve God in with the fleshly, self-centered mindset.

> For the mind that is set on the flesh is hostile to God, for it does not submit to God's law; indeed, it cannot. —Romans 8:7

If our mind is not set on Christ in faith, we are going to make bad decisions, even if we have a ton of good theology. The people of Israel

---

[68] Wiersbe. *Be Strong*, 107.
[69] Ibid., 108

had just read God's law, the entire Pentateuch, in Shechem, between two mountains: Ebal and Gerizim. They had the Word. What was their problem? They "did not ask counsel from the Lord" (9:14). We must never act on mere instinct. The flesh always leads us down the wrong path.

Beware of the flesh's attack. It's an inside job. Your own heart can deceive you and turn against you. Like the Gibeonites, the flesh is very subtle. In your flesh, you may be worried or angry or just plain apathetic. And you tell yourself:

- "Everything's ok."
- "I'll just worry more, and I'll feel better."
- "I'll just stew and fuss a bit more and I'll feel better."
- "I'll ignore it and it will go away."

It's a lie. It never works. You can't *worry* yourself to happiness. You can't *ignore* the pain of your sins and get happiness. You can't *fuss* about your life and it get better. It's all the flesh. It's all a lie.

The Christian must have the direct guidance of God by the Holy Spirit through the Word. You cannot lean to your own understanding. Our own flesh will deceive us. Through pride and self-righteousness, we can think, "I got this." Your desires of the flesh will deceive you every time. Remember the godly counsel from Proverbs.

> Trust in the Lord with all your heart, and do not lean on your own understanding. [6] In all your ways acknowledge him, and he will make straight your paths. —Proverbs 3:5-6

Leaning to your own understanding is leaning into the schemes of the enemy. Stay alert!

> Be sober-minded; be watchful. Your adversary the devil prowls around like a roaring lion, seeking someone to devour. —1 Peter 5:8

You've got to constantly be renewing your mind, walking in the Spirit, putting on the Word of God. Our fellowship with God and worship is the very center of all good fruit and wise choices in our lives. Spirit-guidance brings fullness of joy (Psa 16:11). Check your misery level to see if you have fallen for the schemes of the enemy. He's a trickster. You can't trust him.

## The Enemy's Defeat

Now we are going to see that in spite of the Gibeonites' craftiness, God still defeated them. Instead of being put to death, they were raised to life. They became servants for the Tabernacle. They were wood cutters and water carriers for the worship of Yahweh. Praise God, the Lord defeated me, not by putting me to death, but by raising me to life. But still, Joshua and the leaders of Israel did wrong, because they did not seek the Lord.

## THE POWER OF PRAYER (9:14-16)

Now we see the power of prayer, and the devastation of prayerlessness. If you are not praying as a believer, walking in the Spirit, praying without ceasing, you may suddenly find yourself in the trap of the enemy.

Joshua and his men were completely taken by surprise by the Gibeonites. This was likely the most powerful of all seven-nation alliance in Canaan. They looked and sounded reasonable. So Joshua 'made peace with them and made a covenant with them, to let them live' (9:15).

**Joshua 9:14-16** | So the men took some of their provisions, but did not ask counsel from the Lord. **15** And Joshua made peace with them and made a covenant with them, to let them live, and the leaders of the congregation swore to them. **16** At the end of three days after they had made a covenant with them, they heard that they were their neighbors and that they lived among them.

## Take Time to Pray

Had they taken time to "ask counsel from the Lord" they would have had a covering over them. Prayer is a covering.

He who dwells in the shelter of the Most High will abide in the shadow of the Almighty. —Psalm 91:1

Joshua made peace with the enemy because he didn't have that covering of prayer. For some reason, it did not occur to Joshua and the leaders of Israel to "ask counsel of the Lord" (9:14). The Lord's direction was available but was ignored. It was not that they were sloppy in their investigation, but they were alone in their decision. It wasn't that they didn't think but that they didn't pray. They did not have because they did not ask (Jas 4:2).[70]

Why did the enemy succeed (9:14-15)? The reason is simple: Joshua and the leaders of Israel were hasty and didn't take time to consult the Lord. They walked by sight and not by faith. After listening to the Gibeonites' speech and examining the evidence, Joshua and his leaders concluded that the men were telling the truth. The leaders of Israel took the "scientific approach" instead of the "spiritual approach." They depended on their own senses, examined the "facts," discussed the matter, and agreed in their conclusion. It was all very logical and convincing, but it was all wrong.

How we need to take time and consult the Lord. Had Joshua and his leaders paused to think and pray about what they saw, they would have concluded that the whole thing was a trick.

> If any of you lacks wisdom, let him ask of God, who gives to all liberally and without reproach, and it will be given to him. —James 1:5

## Consult the Word of God

Joshua made peace with the enemy because he didn't consult the Lord. They had just read the entire Pentateuch at Shechem between Mount Ebal and Mount Gerizim. But that's not enough. They needed to consult the Lord again. That's what we need to do, over and over, day after day. You know the Word, but you need to consult him again and again. We need to seek him in his Word experiencing one level of glory to another level of glory. Daily, we need God's wisdom. Yesterday's power is not sufficient for this hour.

God's Word will show you the way! "Your word is a lamp to my feet and a light to my path" (Psa 119:105). The Word of God is more important than food. Job and Jesus agree. Said Job: "I have not departed from his commands, but have treasured his words more than daily food" (Job 23:12). Jesus said, "Man shall not live by bread alone, but by every word that comes from the mouth of God" (Mt 4:4; cf Deut 8:3).

God's Word cleanses us. That's what Jesus said, "Already you are clean because of the word that I have spoken to you" (John 15:3). "Sanctify them in the truth; your word is truth" (John 17:17).

---

[70] Ellsworth, *Joshua*, 85.

God's Word can convert your heart. "You have been born again, not of perishable seed but of imperishable, through the living and abiding word of God" (1 Pet 1:23).

God's Word cuts. "For the word of God is living and active, sharper than any two-edged sword, piercing to the division of soul and of spirit, of joints and of marrow, and discerning the thoughts and intentions of the heart" (Heb 4:12).

God's Word grows us. "All Scripture is breathed out by God and profitable for teaching, for reproof, for correction, and for training in righteousness" (2 Tim 3:16).

God's Word succeeds. It will not return void. "So shall my word be that goes out from my mouth; it shall not return to me empty, but it shall accomplish that which I purpose, and shall succeed in the thing for which I sent it" (Isa 55:11).

God's Word judges. You will never get away with rejecting God's Word. "The one who rejects me and does not receive my words has a judge; the word that I have spoken will judge him on the last day" (Jn 12:48).

God's Word sanctifies. It will keep us from sin. "I have treasured your word in my heart, that I might not sin against you" (Psa 119:11). You can't risk not consulting the Lord. Look what happened to Joshua.

> The blessed man's "delight is in the law of the Lord, and on his law he meditates day and night. [3] He is like a tree planted by streams of water that yields its fruit in its season, and its leaf does not wither. In all that he does, he prospers. —Psalm 1:2-3

Joshua would have been blessed had he consulted the Lord!

## Be Sure to Obey

Of course, when we seek God's will from God's Word, we have to be ready to obey. When Joshua consulted the Lord at Jericho, they were given some strange commands, to walk around the city and then the city walls would fall. But they obeyed, and God blessed. God's Word is not just for our mental acuity, but for to be put into action in our life.

> Your word is a lamp to my feet and a light to my path. —Psalm 119:105

When God shows you the way, you have to take courage and put God's Word to practice. Prayer is not enough. Often, we pray, and keep on praying when we need to obey. Some of you are begging God for something, and you need to quit begging and rest in the Lord. You need to walk in faith.

Bible knowledge is not enough. We may think because we've renewed our mind with God's Word, that is enough. It's not enough to merely know the Word, we have to walk in the Word. We have to do the Word. The essence of obedience is walking in the Word by the Spirit. If you don't do that, you fail, like Joshua did. Get into the Word and walk in it.

> But be doers of the word, and not hearers only, deceiving yourselves. [23] For if anyone is a hearer of the word and not a doer, he is like a man who looks intently at his natural face in a mirror. [24] For he looks at himself and goes away and at once forgets what he was like. [25] But the one who looks into the perfect law, the law of liberty, and perseveres, being no hearer who forgets but a doer who acts, he will be blessed in his doing. —James 1:22-25

Are you blessed in your doing of the Word? Are you living it out? Or is it all stuck and stored up in the attic of your mind? Get the Word into your life. Live it out. Walk in the Spirit and in the Word. Oh, had Joshua consulted the Lord, he could have avoided such a great failure. Instead, he compromised with the enemy! What could he do now? Well what can any of us do with our failures?

## THE POWER OF REDEMPTION (9:17-27)

The people of Israel had made a huge mistake. Three days later, the leaders of Israel realized their folly. The Gibeonites were not from a far country at all! They were rather 'their neighbors who dwelt near' to Israel (9:16). As such, they were under the same sentence of death as the rest of the Canaanites! So Joshua was in a dilemma! How could he carry out the sentence against the Gibeonites and also keep his word to spare them? Let's read about it.

**Joshua 9:17-27** | And the people of Israel set out and reached their cities on the third day. Now their cities were Gibeon, Chephirah, Beeroth, and Kiriath-jearim. [18] But the people of Israel did not attack them, because the leaders of the congregation had sworn to them by the Lord, the God of Israel. Then all the congregation murmured against the leaders.[19] But all the leaders said to all the congregation, "We have sworn to them by the Lord, the God of Israel, and now we may not touch them. [20] This we will do to them: let them live, lest wrath be upon us, because of the oath that we swore to them." **21** And the leaders said to them, "Let them live." So they became cutters of wood and drawers of water for all the congregation, just as the leaders had said of them. **22** Joshua summoned them, and he said to them, "Why did you deceive us, saying, 'We are very far from you,' when you dwell among us? **23** Now therefore you are cursed, and some of you shall never be anything but servants, cutters of wood and drawers of water for the house of my God." **24** They answered Joshua, "Because it was told to your servants for a certainty that the Lord your God had commanded his servant Moses to give you all the land and to destroy all the inhabitants of the land from before you—so we feared greatly for our lives because of you and did this thing. **25** And now, behold, we are in your hand. Whatever seems good and right in your sight to do to us, do it." **26** So he did this to them and delivered them out of the hand of the people of Israel, and they did not kill them. **27** But Joshua made them that day cutters of wood and drawers of water for the congregation and for the altar of the Lord, to this day, in the place that he should choose.

We see, that even in a great failure, God can redeem. He promises to "work all things together for good for those who love God" (Rom 8:28).

## God Blessed Joshua

Joshua acted with integrity. He repented. He honored his covenant with the Gibeonites, even though his own people complained (9:18). Joshua knew that to break the oath would dishonor the name of Yahweh before the pagan Gibeonites. Remember, they had sworn "by Yahweh the God of Israel" and any breach of such oath implies that Yahweh cannot be trusted (9:19-20). Hence the Gibeonites are to become woodcutters and water carriers for Israel's sanctuary (9:21).[71] God turned this failure of Israel into a blessing. What a blessing for Joshua, but an even greater blessing for the Gibeonites!

## God Blessed the Gibeonites

Think about how God could redeem this. God blessed the Gibeonites. The Gibeonites left the coalition of seven nations and essentially

---

[71] Davis, *Joshua*, 77.

surrendered to the God of Israel. The Gibeonites now get to come under the teaching and worship of Yahweh. Praise God.

Joshua did not let the Gibeonites continue as an independent nation, but rather made them servants (wood-cutters and water carriers) for the Tabernacle (9:23).[72] Instead of destroying them, God gave Joshua wisdom to make them servants of Israel at the house of worship. In a pretty amazing way, the Gibeonites surrendered to the God of Israel by surrendering to Joshua. They deceived Joshua, but they didn't deceive the God "who is not willing that any should perish, but that all should come to repentance" (2 Pet 3:9).

## God Blesses Us

It's incredible that God can turn this entire thing to Joshua's good and God's glory. And so it is with the believer today. You are "predestined to be conformed to the image of God's dear Son" (Rom 8:29). Predestined. God will not waste your failure. You will not be conformed to this world, child of God, but you will be transformed. So remember to get up and keep going when you fall. Do as Joshua did, and walk in integrity. Confess and forsake your sins. And going forward in the future, stay on guard so that you don't commit the same sins again. Let me give you some spiritual warfare advice.

### You are Redeemed for Victory

You've got to be ready for satanic attack. You will win. You just have to put on the armor of God and walk in victory.

> Put on the whole armor of God, that you may be able to stand against the schemes of the devil. [12] For we do not wrestle against flesh and blood, but against the rulers, against the authorities, against the cosmic powers over this present darkness, against the spiritual forces of evil in the heavenly places. —Ephesians 6:11-12

For one thing, it reminds us that Christians are in a spiritual war and that deceptiveness is the primary tactic of our enemy, the devil. Satan has his strategies and plans (Eph 6:11). He is able to transform himself into "an angel of light" (2 Cor 11:14). Know this: once you declare your allegiance to the Lord, you have a target on your back. You can't afford to not consult with the Lord. And if you choose to serve the

---

[72] Ellsworth, *Joshua*, 85–86.

Lord and walk with him each day, you will most certainly walk in victory!

### You are Redeemed for Wisdom

Dear child of God, you are also redeemed for wisdom. Joshua didn't consult the Lord, and he missed out. It led him to failure. Listen saint, you are the Temple of the Holy Spirit. In the Spirit you have incredible wisdom and revelation. Jesus said to Peter:

> Flesh and blood has not revealed this to you, but my Father in heaven. —Matthew 16:17

This passage reminds us of the importance of the people of God continually seeking the mind of God. There is nothing in this life that is so clear to your heart and mind that it precludes you from seeking the mind and face of God.

> Seek the LORD and his strength; seek his presence continually! —1 Chronicles 16:11

Human logic is not enough to make good decisions. We need to seek the wisdom of God. James says if you lack wisdom, consult the Lord, and the Lord will give you wisdom generously without reprimanding you (Jas 1:5). He loves to give his children wisdom. You will not see your situation correctly without wisdom and revelation from the Lord.

> Paul prayed, "that the God of our Lord Jesus Christ, the Father of glory, may give you the Spirit of wisdom and of revelation in the knowledge of him, [18] having the eyes of your hearts enlightened. — Ephesians 1:17-18

### You are Redeemed to Persevere

A final lesson for us has to do with living with our sins. Joshua failed, but God redeemed the situation. The Gibeonites went on to know and serve the Lord in the worship of the Tabernacle. Joshua learned a great lesson and showed his integrity by keeping his oath. God redeems us, and that means when we fall down, we get right back up and persevere. The devil would have us believe that sin disqualifies us from doing anything for the Lord! He uses this argument because he knows the effectiveness of putting as many Christians as possible on the sidelines. None of us would serve the Lord if the standard were to be completely glorified. The truth is, when we fall we get back up again.

The steps of a good man are ordered by the Lord, And He delights in his way. [24] Though he fall, he shall not be utterly cast down; for the Lord upholds him with His hand. —Psalm 37:23-24, NKJV

God's got you! We are weak, but God is strong, and he's got you. You may fall, but you will not be utterly cast down. He has brought you out of the horrible pit and set your feet on the Rock, Christ Jesus (Psa 40:2).

## Conclusion

God's people were double crossed. They didn't know recognize their enemy because they didn't seek the Lord. Yet, God brought good things out of it! You may have failed but keep looking to Jesus. We can all say, "God came to save sinners, of whom I am chief" (1 Tim 1:15). Jesus didn't come to save the righteous, but to call sinners to repentance (Lk 5:32). I love your testimonies, dear saints. There have been times, we've been tricked and deceived by sin, but we learn from it. Don't stay down when you've sinned. Get up and because God has great exploits for you. He wants you to expand his kingdom. He wants to use you in a mighty way!

# 11 | JOSHUA 10
## SUN STAND STILL

*"Sun, stand still at Gibeon, and moon, in the Valley of Ai-jalon." And the sun stood still, and the moon stopped, until the nation took vengeance on their enemies. Is this not written in the Book of Jashar? The sun stopped in the midst of heaven and did not hurry to set for about a whole day.*

JOSHUA 10:13

Surrender to God gives him freedom to do God-size things in your life. Sometimes God breaks through the normal happenings of history and science and does a miracle. Chapter 10 of the book of Joshua celebrates a divine intervention unparalleled in world history. There was "no day like it" (10:14).

So many Christians are living out a crippled and paralyzed faith. Joshua 10 calls us to live out a courageous faith. This is the chapter where God gave Joshua the power to command the sun to stand still. When God asks us to do something uncomfortable, it's usually because he wants to do something remarkable. Are you uncomfortable in some area of your life? You've got to surrender, or you will lose it all. You might be so worried about your health. Why would God want to heal you if you have made your health an idol? Same with our finances, our treasures. If the love of money is controlling you, why would God bless you so that you? He wants you to be generous, not a hoarder. Maybe you are uncomfortable in your marriage. You will not see real joy in marriage until you surrender. Maybe it's your time. You will always be exhausted and incredibly discouraged until you have just given up your rights to everything! The Christian life is one of cross bearing. You have to take up your cross, deny yourself, and follow Christ.

Our call today is to surrender in full obedience as followers of Christ and leave the consequences up to God. Joshua is brought to an impossible situation. He's to face the five remaining nations of the Canaanite Coalition. Bad experiences or the disappointments from our past or present can turn our courageous faith into the dead weight of concrete. God doesn't just want you to survive another day. He wants you to believe God for what only he can do.

> What is impossible with man is possible with God. —Luke 18:17

We can't let hurts or misunderstandings hold us back. God has no Plan B. The Bible throws down the gauntlet in Hebrews 11:6: "Without faith it is impossible to please God." It doesn't get any plainer than that. Faith isn't just a Get Out of Hell Free card. It's the most vital building block of your relationship with God. And it's the only real foundation worth establishing your life on.

## THE MESS (10:1-5)

### The Mess Described

Here we have the Gibeonites being attacked by five Canaanite kings, led by Adoni-zedek (king of righteousness), king of Jerusalem. This is the first mention of Jerusalem in the Bible. These are not great empires, but city states. They are like kings of great cities, more like war lords. Now it seems like Joshua and Israel's army were in a bad spot because of an unwise decision to make a union with the Gibeonites. So now, the Canaanite kings feel like if Gibeon falls, they'll all fall. They need to get Gibeon back!

**Joshua 10:1-5** | As soon as Adoni-zedek, king of Jerusalem, heard how Joshua had captured Ai and had devoted it to destruction, doing to Ai and its king as he had done to Jericho and its king, and how the inhabitants of Gibeon had made peace with Israel and were among them, [2] he feared greatly, because Gibeon was a great city, like one of the royal cities, and because it was greater than Ai, and all its men were warriors. [3] So Adoni-zedek king of Jerusalem sent to Hoham king of Hebron, to Piram king of Jarmuth, to Japhia king of Lachish, and to Debir king of Eglon, saying, **4** "Come up to me and help me, and let us strike Gibeon. For it has made peace with Joshua and with the people of Israel." **5** Then the five kings of the Amorites, the king of Jerusalem, the king of Hebron, the king of Jarmuth, the king of Lachish, and the king of Eglon, gathered their forces and went up with all their armies and encamped against Gibeon and made war against it.

If a great city like Gibeon capitulated to the Jews, then one more barrier was removed against the advancement of Israel in the land. It was important for the Canaanites to recover that key city, even if they had to take it by force. Four other Canaanite kings allied with Adoni-zedek (King of Jerusalem), and their combined armies encamped before Gibeon. The poor Gibeonites had made peace with the invaders and were now at war with their former allies![73] What a mess! God has a plan, but it sure doesn't look like anything more than a mess. But God has a plan for your mess. He wants to make your mess a masterpiece. God says,

> For my thoughts are not your thoughts, neither are your ways my ways, declares the Lord. For as the heavens are higher than the earth, so are my ways higher than your ways and my thoughts than your thoughts. —Isaiah 55:8-9

## My Mess is God's Masterpiece

Have you ever seen a great artist turn a mess into a masterpiece? A big pile of sand becomes fantastic castle. A useless, discarded piece of wood with a few strokes of a chainsaw becomes a glorious eagle. That's how it is with God. He takes a mess and makes it a masterpiece. The mistakes we make embarrass us, especially those mistakes that are caused by our running ahead of the Lord and not seeking his will. But we need to remember that no mistake is final for the dedicated Christian. God can use even our blunders to accomplish his purposes. Warren Wiersbe said, "Somebody defined success as 'the art of making your mistakes when nobody's looking'; but a better definition would be 'the art of seeing victory where other people see only defeat.'" [74] He was using these events to accomplish His own purposes. Instead of having to

---

[73] Wiersbe. *Be Strong*, 112.
[74] Ibid., 113.

defeat these five city-states one by one, the LORD would help Joshua conquer them all at one time! [75]

### Joshua's Mess

You have to remember, Joshua had seen this before. He had seen God turn a mess into a masterpiece. Joshua was born into Egyptian slavery as had everyone in his generation. Through God's call he became Moses' assistant. All was going according to plan at the border of the Promised Land when disaster struck.

The 12 spies were sent into the Promised land and brought back the produce: a single cluster of grapes took two men to carry on a pole between them. They enjoyed pomegranates and figs (Num 13:23). The unbelieving spies announced to all the people that there were armies of giants so that "we seemed to ourselves like grasshoppers" (Num 13:33).

When the people heard that giants stood between them and taking possession of their destiny, they panicked. Everyone wanted to turn back and give up. Everyone, that is, except Joshua and his friend Caleb. You probably know the story. Unlike the other spies, Joshua and Caleb returned from scouting out the Promised Land with a message of faith, not fear. They had great faith in a big God. Listen to their words:

> The land, which we passed through to spy it out, is an exceedingly good land. [8] If the Lord delights in us, he will bring us into this land and give it to us, a land that flows with milk and honey. [9] Only do not rebel against the Lord. And do not fear the people of the land, for they are bread for us. Their protection is removed from them, and the Lord is with us; do not fear them. —Numbers 14:7-9

Sadly, fear won out that day. Ten spies were put to death by order of the Lord. The line had been crossed. The people had no faith. Forty wasted years followed. We have to feel for Joshua and Caleb. They have to bear the consequences of his nation's faithlessness. What a mess!

### Joshua's Masterpiece

When Moses died, Joshua became his successor, and eighty-year-old Joshua was ready with courageous faith. He launched a campaign of enthusiastic faith in God's goodness and power. What a masterpiece! They were so weak, but God is so strong.

---

[75] Ibid.

I will boast all the more gladly of my weaknesses, so that the power of Christ may rest upon me... For when I am weak, then I am strong.
—2 Corinthians 12:9-10

## THE MISSION (10:6-11)

## The Mission Described

As the chapter opens, we read that five opposing Amorite armies were planning to attack. The Gibeonites plea for Joshua's help, and Joshua delivers. It's an impossible mission! Having decided to strike first, Joshua led his entire army toward the Amorites on an all-night march. Sometime during that march, God spoke to Joshua. He told him: "Do not fear them, for I have given them into your hands. Not a man of them shall stand before you" (10:8).

**Joshua 10:6-11** | And the men of Gibeon sent to Joshua at the camp in Gilgal, saying, "Do not relax your hand from your servants. Come up to us quickly and save us and help us, for all the kings of the Amorites who dwell in the hill country are gathered against us." [7] So Joshua went up from Gilgal, he and all the people of war with him, and all the mighty men of valor. [8] And the Lord said to Joshua, "Do not fear them, for I have given them into your hands. Not a man of them shall stand before you." [9] So Joshua came upon them suddenly, having marched up all night from Gilgal. [10] And the Lord threw them into a panic before Israel, who struck them with a great blow at Gibeon and chased them by the way of the ascent of Beth-horon and struck them as far as Azekah and Makkedah. [11] And as they fled before Israel, while they were going down the ascent of Beth-horon, the Lord threw down large stones from heaven on them as far as Azekah, and they died. There were more who died because of the hailstones than the sons of Israel killed with the sword.

It's an impossible mission. The five remaining Canaanite Coalition are getting ready to attack, but God says: you give them a surprise attack! Joshua stayed on mission. God said to Joshua, "Don't fear," and Joshua obeyed and trusted the Lord. That's the foundation of faith. Don't fear; have faith in the Lord. He marched all night long, about 15 miles from Gilgal to Beth-horon. What happened? At dawn, the Israelites unleashed a surprise attack, and right from the beginning the battle went well. When the enemy lines broke, and the Amorites started to flee into the valley, Joshua's men chased them down. And God got personally involved. "As they fled before Israel," the account reads, "the Lord threw down large stones from heaven on them... and they died" (10:11). We'll find that more Canaanites died from the hail stones than from the fighting! Consider this vital principle: God can do far more than you can ever ask for.

> Now to him who is able to do far more abundantly than all that we ask or think, according to the power at work within us, [21] to him be glory in the church and in Christ Jesus throughout all generations, forever and ever. Amen. —Ephesians 3:20-21

## The Mission Demonstrated

I want to emphasize that before God got involved, the soldiers of Israel were on task. They were doing what God asked them to do. They were fighting. They were battling. This teaches us a very important lesson. Faith is not an excuse for laziness. We need to be carrying out the responsibilities God has given us and then by faith know that God will step in and put his fingerprints on the details. We are called to stay on task, expecting God to work.

> Work out your own salvation with fear and trembling, [13] for it is God who works in you, both to will and to work for his good pleasure. — Philippians 2:12-13

Are you expecting God to work? We are to be faithful in seeking God, striving after him, walking in the Spirit. Revivals occur as we carry out the ordinary, "instituted means of grace—preaching, pastoring, worship, prayer."[76] We must be diligent in living out the normal Christian life in the Spirit's fullness. This is where God manifests himself. As we work out the Spirit-filled life, God works in and through us. With Joshua, he was obeying God's command and call on his life. In the midst of obedience there was a miracle. This is how God normally works.

---

[76] William B. Sprague. *Lectures on Revivals of Religion* (London: Simpkin and Marshall, 1832), 133.

## THE MIRACLE (10:12-15)

### Joshua's Miracle Described

God is going to grant a miracle to Joshua, but that miracle begins in verse 10, which says, "Joshua spoke to the Lord" (10:12a).

**Joshua 10:12-13a** | At that time Joshua spoke to the Lord in the day when the Lord gave the Amorites over to the sons of Israel, and he said in the sight of Israel, "Sun, stand still at Gibeon, and moon, in the Valley of Aijalon." <sup>13</sup> And the sun stood still, and the moon stopped, until the nation took vengeance on their enemies...

### God's Promise

As the sun sank toward the horizon, Joshua faced a decision. The victory wasn't complete, and once it got dark, the rest of the Amorites would slip away. But Joshua was determined to fight on. Perhaps he realized that if he didn't destroy the enemy now, Israel's conquest of Canaan would grind to a halt. Maybe he knew that anything less than total victory would conceal God's presence and glory. Besides, he remembered God's promise in the night: "Not one of them will be able to withstand you" (10:8b). Most of us—even really good Christian people—would have called it a day. I've done all I can do. I've exhausted every option. I've given it all I've got. But Joshua wasn't most people. He refused to go out like that. That wasn't the way it was supposed to end. This was where his audacious faith began. Where your strength ends, is where God's miraculous power begins.

### Joshua's Prayer

Joshua sized up the situation, summoned all his available courage, and delivered one of the most gloriously courageous prayers in the entire Bible:

**Joshua 10:12b** | "Sun, stand still at Gibeon, and moon, in the Valley of Aijalon."

I know this proposition seems impossible to us. But according to Scripture, God gave Joshua exactly what he ordered. Just when the Amorites were hanging on for the cover of darkness, darkness never came. Just when they thought the curtains were about to drop on their day from hell, God came out for an encore. Sometimes, God crushes us through a trial or a failure, like when Israel compromised and made a covenant with the Gibeonites. They didn't say, I'm done. No, the best was yet to come. Think about Peter. He said, "I go a fishing" after his great failure of denying the Lord. But no, his best was yet to come. Where your strength ends, God's miraculous power begins.

He resists the proud, but gives grace to the humble. —1 Peter 5:5

### God's Preservation

God answered Joshua's prayer.

**Joshua 10:13-14** | And the sun stood still, and the moon stopped, until the nation took vengeance on their enemies. Is this not written in the Book of Jashar? The sun stopped in the midst of heaven and did not hurry to set for about a whole day. [14] There has been no day like it before or since, when the Lord heeded the voice of a man, for the Lord fought for Israel.

Why did the sun stand still? How could that happen? Anything can happen when God is in the equation! We read clearly that "the LORD fought for Israel" (10:14b). Did God actually stop the earth on its axis? Did he create some kind of substitute sun to extend daylight? In other words, what really went down here? I don't know the answers to those questions. There are other books written by much smarter people that address the practical implications of this event. But my faith is pretty simple. I choose to believe that the same God who intervened to bring his Son back to life intervened on this day in history to help his people. God chose to answer Joshua's courageous prayer.

This is the last miracle recorded in Joshua and certainly the greatest. Joshua prayed for God's help, and the Lord answered in a remarkable way. This event is questioned by those who deny the reality of miracles and look only to science for truth. "How could God stop the rotation of the earth and extend the length of a day," they ask, "without creating chaos all over the planet?" They seem to forget the fact that days are *normally* of different lengths in various parts of the world without the planet experiencing chaos. At 2 o'clock in the morning, you can read a book by sunlight at various times of the year in Alaska.

But how do you explain a miracle, *any* miracle? Of course, the simplest answer is the answer of faith: The Lord is God and nothing is too hard for him (Jer 32:17, 27). Day and night belong to God (Psa 74:16), and everything he has made is his servant. If God can't perform the

GROWING AND CHANGING COMMENTARY: JOSHUA

miracle described in Joshua 10, then he can't perform *any* miracle.[77] Never be content with a little victory, because God wants you to live in the fullness of his complete victory.

So on the Israelites fought from sun up one day and into the next day with full daylight. Why did they need an extra day? This an especially interesting question since the Bible says,

**Joshua 10:11** | The Lord threw down large stones from heaven on them as far as Azekah, and they died. There were more who died because of the hailstones than the sons of Israel killed with the sword.

If God killed most of the Canaanite soldiers himself, why did the soldiers of Israel need an extra day to destroy them? Likely it is because the Canaanite soldiers were hiding in caves to protect themselves from the hailstones. The army of Israel had to do a search and destroy mission until every last one of the Canaanites were killed. God preserved his earthly army on this amazing day. What a miracle. God turns messes into miracles!

### Israel's Peace

As a result, Joshua and all Israel returned home to Gilgal.

**Joshua 10:15** | So Joshua returned, and all Israel with him, to the camp at Gilgal.

There is a peace that comes when we rest by courageous faith in a miracle working God. When God intervenes in your life, you have "peace that passes understanding" and "joy unspeakable and full of glory."

## Your Miracle

Jesus said we should pray this way. Our God is a big God, so go big or go home. What is a miracle but expecting God to act like God in your life. Give him control and watch him work mightily. See his supernatural hand in the natural events of your life.

### Big Messes

Here are some of the most common things I've seen people pray courageous "Sun Stand Still" prayers about:

- broken relationships

---

[77] Wiersbe. *Be Strong*, 114–115.

- financial provision
- career aspirations
- spiritual breakthroughs at work, in the community, or elsewhere in the world
- physical and emotional healing
- loved ones who are far from God
- standing strong against temptation
- achieving important life goals
- finding and embracing purpose
- ministry resources and momentum

### Big Miracles

Jesus wants us to have a big faith in a big God. Remember the Lord's instructions to us in the book of Mark.

> Have faith in God. [23] Truly, I say to you, whoever says to this mountain, 'Be taken up and thrown into the sea,' and does not doubt in his heart, but believes that what he says will come to pass, it will be done for him. [24] Therefore I tell you, whatever you ask in prayer, believe that you have received it, and it will be yours." —Mark 11:22-24

Jesus is likely on the Mount of Olives when he says this from which vantage point, he can see Herod the Great's underground palace (the Herodium). Herod took one mountain, cut it down, and piled it upon the mountain where he had his palace, so he had a kind of James Bond 007 secret palace that is still there to this day. When I visited there, there were piles and piles of rocks from the work that Herod's workers did. They were actually restoring his palace under the ground when I visited there (January 2018). He had a sauna and shower area (bathhouse). He had a place to entertain guests, a theater, a synagogue, and a gigantic freshwater swimming pool with water piped from Bethlehem. As exquisite as it was at the time, it all would come to nothing. The kingdom of this world will fail and will become the kingdom of our God and of his King, Jesus. It's so simple, as Jesus said, "Without me you can do nothing" (Jn 15:5). Jesus says, essentially, pray to me, and Herod's kingdom will be cast into the sea. No matter how great the request, if it is according to God's will, God wants us to pray in faith believing, nothing wavering.

Big messes give way to big miracles, when there is a true surrender. God's often got a completely different idea in answering your prayer.

He's the God who answers "exceedingly, abundantly above all that we could ask or imagine" (Eph 3:20-21). God wants to do something so great that you can't even imagine it.

Consider these applications. [78]
1. Nothing is too hard for the Lord.
2. We should expect days of great personal victory in our walk with God.
3. Joshua prayed with full faith to God, but he was not slack in his own responsibility. He battled, and he believed!
4. Big messes often precede big miracles. Don't get down about any mess in your life. God is the God of redemption. He loves to turn messes into miracles.

### Conclusion

Remember, when God asks us to do something uncomfortable, it's usually because he wants to do something remarkable. What's the lesson? The uncomfortable thing he wants you to do always requires surrender. What it takes to see God work is your surrender. If you are worried about your health, why should God heal you. You've got to be ok with God controlling your life, including your health. You want God to work in your marriage, stop demanding what you want your spouse to be and start serving God by serving your spouse. No expectations. Give up your rights. Be crucified. That's the Christian life. Do you want to become a generous giver? You've got to surrender your treasure to God. It's not yours. It's his. Maybe you have no time for your family or for God. You'll never get the time you need till you surrender all your time to God. If you surrender to God, he'll give you those "sun stand still" moments!

---

[78] Boice. *Joshua*, 83.

# 12 | JOSHUA 11:1-9

## SOME TRUST IN CHARIOTS

*And the Lord said to Joshua, "Do not be afraid of them, for tomorrow at this time I will give over all of them, slain, to Israel. You shall hamstring their horses and burn their chariots with fire."*

JOSHUA 11:6

If we live in fear, we are not taking God at his Word, and we can't receive God's blessings. When we live by faith, God enlarges our heart so we can receive more blessing.

Sometimes God breaks through the normal happenings of history and science and does a miracle. Chapter 10 of the book of Joshua celebrates a divine intervention unparalleled in world history. There was "no day like it" (10:14). So that's like high school graduation. They've seen some amazing things, but now they are going to get a course in college level sanctification. Joshua 10 records the defeat of the southern nations of Canaan. Joshua 11 now records the defeat of Northern Canaan. And it's going to be way harder. This group is far more equipped than the south. They have chariots of iron.

We come to a theme in Joshua 11 about walking in faith instead of fear. The final phase of the conquest of Canaan was in the north, and again it followed the actions of the kings of the land. Jabin, king of Hazor, was the leader of a northern coalition, just as Adoni-Zedek, king of Jerusalem, had been the leader in the south. He was alarmed at the Jewish victories, as well he should have been, so he called the kings and armies of the northern cities together. These joined forces near the Waters of Merom, a lake a little north of the larger Sea of Galilee.

The new element in this battle was the use of chariots by the coalition. I do not know how accurate Josephus, the Jewish historian, is at this point, since he wrote so many hundreds of years later, but according to him, the combined forces of the Canaanites numbered 300,000 foot soldiers, 100,000 cavalry, and 20,000 chariots. If this was so (or even if it is only an approximation of the size of the army), this must have been the greatest engagement of Joshua's distinguished career. The numbers themselves are daunting, but in addition, there were the chariots, against which Israel had never before fought.[79]

## THE ENEMY MAY BE GREAT (11:1-5)

The enemy may be great, but we must never allow any fear to be magnified as greater than God. This is why worry and fear are such a great sin.

### The Temptation to Forget God

We read a very detailed summary of the enemy's expanse. Why so much detail? The writer is helping us to see the almost hopeless situation Israel faces.[80] When we see the greatness of what is against us, we are tempted to forget God. We must always remember that God is greater than any enemy that tries to distract or discourage us.

**Joshua 11:1-5** | When Jabin, king of Hazor, heard of this, he sent to Jobab king of Madon, and to the king of Shimron, and to the king of Achshaph, [2] and to the kings who were in the northern hill country, and in the Arabah south of Chinneroth, and in the lowland, and in Naphoth-dor on the west, [3] to the Canaanites in the east and the west, the Amorites, the Hittites, the Perizzites, and the Jebusites in the hill country, and the Hivites under Hermon in the land of Mizpah. [4] And they came out with all their troops, a great horde, in number like the sand that is on the seashore, with very many horses and chariots. [5] And all these kings joined their forces and came and encamped together at the waters of Merom to fight against Israel.

---

[79] Boice. *Joshua*, 87–88.
[80] Davis, *Joshua*, 90.

To impress the reader (and Israel) with the massive resources available to the enemies of God makes the power of God shine more brightly in delivering his people from their hands. The new element in this battle was the use of chariots by the coalition. I do not know how accurate Josephus, the Jewish historian, is at this point, since he wrote so many hundreds of years later, but according to him, the combined forces of the Canaanites numbered 300,000 foot soldiers, 100,000 cavalry, and 20,000 chariots. If this was so (or even if it is only an approximation of the size of the army), this must have been the greatest engagement of Joshua's distinguished career.[81]

## The Temptation to Worry

When we clearly see both Canaan's numerical (11:4a) and technological (11:4b) edge, we realize that however big our fears might be, God is infinitely greater than anything that might bring us fear.[82] Yet we still struggle with worry. God commanded them not to commit the sin of fear and worry when it came to the Canaanites. And these are good words for us.

> When you go out to war against your enemies, and see horses and chariots and an army larger than your own, you shall not be afraid of them, for the Lord your God is with you, who brought you up out of the land of Egypt. —Deuteronomy 20:1

Why is worry sinful? Three reasons: (1) because it expresses heart idolatry (Mt 6:19-24), (2) because it expresses heart unbelief (Mt 6:25-34), and (3) because it expresses heart idolatry (Mt 6:19-24). We magnify something as a fear that God cannot handle. So it begins to eat at us. But we are not taking God at his Word. Fear comes when we treasure something or someone too much, and we fear that security, health, comfort, or relationship being taken away. Here is a good question to consider: what do you sometimes tend to treasure or magnify more than the Lord? The Lord gives us three pictures to illustrate the atheism of worry: competing treasures (Mt 6:19-21), competing eyes (Mt 6:22-23), and competing masters (Mt 6:24) security, health, comfort. Worry is sinful because when you worry, you are saying:

♦ I am afraid God will not take care of me.
♦ I am treasuring comfort more than God.

---

[81] Boice. *Joshua*, 88.
[82] Ibid.

What's the remedy? Identify, repent of, and uproot your heart idols. Question: What earthly treasures—good things (people, possessions, circumstances, identities, etc.)—do you sometimes tend to treasure more than the Lord and his heavenly treasures?

Worry is especially sinful because expresses unbelief (Mt 6:25-34). Worry is an unbelief in the love of God. It's not the total unbelief of a pagan, but the remnant unbelief of a true believer. Jesus gives us reasons why we never need to worry: (1) because the God who provides for birds and flowers is your Father, and he values you much more than he values them (Mt 6:25-30), (2) because worrying characterizes pagans, not those who belong to and who are known by God your Father (Mt 6:31-32), and (3) because worrying can't improve your future, and it instead diverts you from your present responsibilities (Mt 6:34).

What should you do instead of worry? You should seek God's kingdom (Mt 6:33).

> Seek first the kingdom of God and his righteousness, and all these things will be added to you. —Matthew 6:33

## GOD IS GREATER THAN THE ENEMY (11:6-9)

> Greater is he that is in you, than he that is in the world. —1 John 4:4, KJV

### Put Away Fear

Faith focuses on the certainty of greatness of God and his love for me, not on the possibilities of fear. Do you have a good theology of worry? You should never magnify anything as greater than God. The moment you sense worry, cut it off.

> Cast all your anxiety on him because he cares for you. —1 Peter 5:7

> Do not be anxious about anything, but in everything by prayer and supplication with thanksgiving let your requests be made known to God. [7] And the peace of God, which surpasses all understanding, will guard your hearts and your minds in Christ Jesus. —Philippians 4:6-7

We are called to magnify the power and love of our great God. Never should we be guilty of yielding to a double mindedness that worry creates. We must cut off all remnants of unbelief and learn to fully trust and surrender to our loving God. This is what the Lord told Joshua.

**Joshua 11:6|** And the LORD said to Joshua, "Do not be afraid of them, for tomorrow at this time I will give over all of them, slain, to Israel. You shall hamstring their horses and burn their chariots with fire."

Hamstringing a horse made the animal militarily useless; it involved cutting the large tendon at the back of the knee on the hind legs. It did not kill them or permanently injure them. It merely made them not able to be as quick, so they were no good for war. Some hold that the Israelites did this because they were untrained in the machinery of Canaanite hi-tech warfare and, not knowing how to use horses and chariots themselves, simply disabled and destroyed them. However, the command probably stems more from God's divine intention which was to teach Israel not to depend on such modes of assistance but to repose in God's help alone. [83]

> Some trust in chariots and some in horses, but we trust in the name of the LORD our God. —Psalm 20:7

What is a chariot compared to the infinite God? God wants Israel to understand his infinite power. By prohibiting such means of normal human security, The Lord is looking for them to depend on him alone. They can't give glory to their weapons or their wisdom. It's all God.

## Put on Faith

God doesn't want us to sit back in fear, but to walk in faith. Faith is complete trust or confidence in someone or something. Jesus said faith is always accompanied by obedience.

> If you love me, you will keep my commandments. —John 14:15

> Work out your own salvation with fear and trembling; [13] for it is God who works in you both to will and to do for his good pleasure. —Philippians 2:12-13, NKJV

Joshua 11:6–7 contain an implicit recognition of our God's sovereignty enables our courage and conviction to face the enemy.

**Joshua 11:6-7|** And the Lord said to Joshua, "Do not be afraid of them, for tomorrow at this time I will give over all of them, slain, to Israel. You shall hamstring their horses and burn their chariots with

---

[83] Boice. *Joshua*, 92

fire." **7** So Joshua and all his warriors came suddenly against them by the waters of Merom and fell upon them.

In verse 6 Yahweh gives his sovereign assurance, "I will give over all of them, slain, to Israel"; in verse 7 Joshua and Israel blast into the enemy camp in a surprise attack, "So Joshua and all his warriors came suddenly against them by the waters of Merom and fell upon them" (11:7). Isn't the sequence significant? Divine sovereignty does not negate human activity but stimulates it. Because God is sovereignly directing, we should act in faith and go forward, not "let go and let God." Joshua knew better. His view was not to let go but to grab hold of the divine power of God. Divine sovereignty creates confidence, which calls forth our effort even to the point of reckless abandon. God's sovereignty is not a doctrine that shackles us but a reality that liberates us.[84]

God doesn't want us to sit back in fear, but to walk in faith. Faith is complete trust or confidence in someone or something. Jesus said faith is always accompanied by obedience. He loves you.

> I have loved you with an everlasting love; therefore I have continued my faithfulness to you. —Jeremiah 31:3

That means... God my Father *knows* what is best for me. God my Father is more than *able* to bring what is best for me. God my Father deeply *wants* what is best for me. God my Father *will* always give me what is best for me. You worry because you are not taking God at his Word!

## Put God's Word to the Test
Trust God. He is faithful to his word.

**Joshua 11:8-9** | And the LORD gave them into the hand of Israel, who struck them and chased them as far as Great Sidon and Misrephoth-maim, and eastward as far as the Valley of Mizpeh. And they struck them until he left none remaining. **9** And Joshua did to them just as the Lord said to him: he hamstrung their horses and burned their chariots with fire.

Joshua obeyed, just as the Lord told him to do. He says something amazing later in the book of Joshua.

---

[84] Ibid, 90–91.

Not one of all the Lord's good promises to Israel failed; every one was fulfilled. —Joshua 21:45

God keeps his Word. You will see this if you walk in faithful obedience instead of fear. God will do what he says he will do.

My word... shall not return to me void, but it shall accomplish that which I purpose, and shall succeed in the thing for which I sent it. —Isaiah 55:11

You will not be disappointed when you obey God's Word. Our peace is different than the theocracy of Israel. Today's Israel, the church, sees the victory through the inner workings of the Holy Spirit with peace, love, and joy in the heart of the Christian. Are you at rest? Faith is not in any way faith in our ability, but trust in God's ability. remember when abraham was informed that Sarah would be pregnant. God said,

Is anything too hard for the Lord? At the appointed time I will return to you, about this time next year, and Sarah shall have a son. —Genesis 18:14

## Conclusion

Now look at the blessings that Joshua received because he and all Israel took God at his Word! Joshua closes the conquering of the land of Canaan, with a kind of celebration. a glorious celebration. Verses 1–6 speak of the conquest and settlement of the land east of the Jordan, which had happened under Moses, while verses 7–24 list the thirty-one kings that fell to Joshua from Jericho onward. Each king and kingdom represent the removal of an impossibly strong opposition by the hand of the living God and his limitless, sovereign power. So let us celebrate. To God be the glory. We have every spiritual blessing in Christ. We have the fullness of God dwelling in us in the Holy Spirit. We have the riches of his presence. We have power to live in the pure peace and love and righteousness in the Spirit. We no longer have to fuss and worry and despair.

If you are fussing and fearing, you are not taking God at his Word. As a Christian, you never have to live in the bondage of fearing and fussing. You have the kingdom. It's not a physical kingdom like Canaan.

For the kingdom of God is not meat and drink; but righteousness, and peace, and joy in the Holy Ghost. —Romans 14:17

What is left for the Christian is to lament this wicked world. We weep with those who weep. We come alongside the sufferers, but we never lose hope. We are still in a battle till we see Jesus, but the enemy is defeated. We don't ever have to worry or fear or fuss. That is not what we do. Fearing and fussing are indicators that you are not taking God at his Word. Whatever is in front of you, take God at his Word. When you see an impossible situation, count it all joy. Rejoice because you are going to do exploits as your your great God fights for you. Look at all those kings listed. They had no chance. And no sin has a change in your heart when the Spirit and the Word are reigning. Do fear. Don't fuss. Wal in the Word through worship and celebrate! Insist on living out the Word of God by faith. We are in the Promised Land; Christ is our inheritance. We are united to him, and he to us. Our great God and Savior Jesus Christ has rescued us from the domain of darkness and transferred us to his eternal kingdom (Col 1:13). [85] We are in the Promised Land! To him be the glory forever and ever!

Is your heart enlarged, or are you dealing with a tiny, tiny heart that relies on the horses and chariots of idolatry? We must trust God alone. He will enlarge our hearts to receive all his incredible blessings!

---

[85] Jackman, *Joshua*, 134.

# 13 | JOSHUA 11-12
## LIVING BY FAITH IN THE LAND

*So Joshua took the whole land, according to all that the Lord had spoken to Moses. And Joshua gave it for an inheritance to Israel according to their tribal allotments. And the land had rest from war.*

JOSHUA 11:23

When we live by faith, we will magnify God, live in peace, and celebrate victory after victory. In Joshua 11, we read of the conquest of northern Canaan, and in chapter 12 a record of a complete conquest of Canaan, their new home, the Promised Land of Israel.

The point of the land of Israel is not merely a piece of real estate, but that God would make his abode there and live there. His eventual home is on top of Mount Moriah in Jerusalem, where the Temple Mount is today.

You will bring them in and plant them on your own mountain, the place, O LORD, which you have made for your abode, the sanctuary, O Lord, which your hands have established. —Exodus 15:17

The point of God bringing them into the land was to abide with them. So understand, the main point of the inheritance for Israel and for us is not the land. The land is the wrapping paper. The gift is God's presence. We see this in the Abrahamic covenant in Genesis 17.

And I will establish my covenant between me and you and your offspring after you throughout their generations for an everlasting covenant, to be God to you and to your offspring after you. —Genesis 17:7

With that in mind, let's remember that we are on the same journey as Joshua and the children of Israel. Our enemy is different, but our inheritance is the same. And the pathway to claim that inheritance is the same: faith. You must have faith to follow God in your battles, and you are guaranteed victory. God will fight for you. You will see his mighty hand. You will continually experience his manifest presence, his Shekinah glory. This is what God promised to Abraham and to Joshua and to us. Shekinah means God's presence will manifest by "dwelling" or "settling" with us.

That's his promise. How do you get it? Well if you are a Christian, you have it. You are God's Temple. His Shekinah glory dwells in you. That's his promise: to dwell in his Temple, which is his people. It's not just a mountain in Israel. Mount Moriah in Jerusalem where the Temple Mount is built is not the permanent dwelling place of God. You are his permanent dwelling place.

So you say: how do I experience this incredible presence? That's what we are talking about today. God wants you to experience the fruit of his presence, which is the fruit of the Spirit. Are you experiencing and manifesting his glory today through peace, love and joy?

> For the kingdom of God is not a matter of eating and drinking but of righteousness and peace and joy in the Holy Spirit. —Romans 14:17

You see? We don't just get the land, we get more than the land. We get the Kingdom. We get God himself, ruling and reigning in us. How? By faith. We live by faith in the land. I want to teach you how to live by faith. Someone defined faith this way: Faith is trusting God by the work of Christ knowing the outcome is in his control for your good and his glory.

Biblical faith is a victorious faith. If you live a life submitted to God, you will win every single time.

## A VICTORIOUS FAITH (11:10-15)

Peace! Oh that the Christian might live with peace in his or her heart at all times. This is what victory looks like.

### Peace Reigned in Joshua's Victory

In order to have peace, there had to be a total destruction of the tribes of Northern Canaan. They destroyed the Anakim, except for those in the area of Gaza (vs 21-22). Remember that's where Goliath comes later. There has to be a total victory. These later became the kingdom of the Philistines. The emphasis here is total victory. That's what all God's people must expect and attain.

**Joshua 11:10-15** | And Joshua turned back at that time and captured Hazor and struck its king with the sword, for Hazor formerly was the head of all those kingdoms. [11] And they struck with the sword all who were in it, devoting them to destruction; there was none left that breathed. And he burned Hazor with fire. [12] And all the cities of those kings, and all their kings, Joshua captured, and struck them with the edge of the sword, devoting them to destruction, just as Moses the servant of the Lord had commanded. [13] But none of the cities that stood on mounds did Israel burn, except Hazor alone; that Joshua burned. [14] And all the spoil of these cities and the livestock, the people of Israel took for their plunder. But every person they struck with the edge of the sword until they had destroyed them, and they did not leave any who breathed. [15] Just as the Lord had commanded Moses his servant, so Moses commanded Joshua, and so Joshua did. He left nothing undone of all that the Lord had commanded Moses.

The commands in question are those in the Pentateuch that call Israel to utterly destroy the Canaanites (*cf* Num 27:18–23; Deut 3:21–22; 31:7–8, 23). Why destroy the Canaanites? Isn't that cruel? Listen to one commentator who helps us understand.

Obedience for Israel meant decimating and/or expelling the native population of Canaan (11:10–12, 14b). Naturally, we regard such commands as unnecessarily vicious, because we do not comprehend the contagious spiritual cancer that was throughout Canaan. We arrogantly pride ourselves on being kinder than God, but we only prove that we haven't a clue about what holiness is. [86] —Dr. Ralph Davis, Reformed Theological Seminary

## Peace in the Christian's Victory

Victory came for Joshua and Israel because of obedience to God. Joshua "left nothing undone of all that the Lord had commanded Moses" (11:15). Don't miss that. That sounds bland and nonthreatening enough, and commonplace. We are not called to trust our own hearts or our own judgment, but the Word of God alone.

Trust in the Lord with all your heart, and do not lean on your own understanding. [6] In all your ways acknowledge him, and he will make straight your paths. —Proverbs 3:5-6

---

[86] Davis, *Joshua*, 92–93.

Joshua had victory because of obedience. That means we are worshipping God both with our thoughts, our emotions, our words, and our actions. Every part of us is engaged in worship. There is no place for idolatry. Nothing can be magnified as greater than the pleasure and peace we get from Jesus. That's what Joshua was walking in. The only reason we don't have total victory is that we refuse to obey God and take him at his Word.

Fussing, frustration and fear fill the hearts of Christians. And then that's too much, so you swing over to apathy and foolishness. Some of you are feeling low level anxiety and guilt. This indicates the need for surrender. Your flesh is holding onto something. These fleshly emotions indicate a lack of victory because of obedience. What have you not surrendered? Where are you not taking God at his Word? Where are you not enjoying the Shekinah presence of God abiding and dwelling in you?

What does total victory look like for the Christian? It looks like peace and fellowship. This is worship. When we say "total victory" we are talking about 100% worship. Every day we are casting our crowns before the Lord. Every day we are like the 144,000 who go into all the earth and evangelize. We are worshippers. We are walkers in the Word. We are robed in the white robes of the righteousness of the saints: Jesus' perfections. We have hearts filled with the Holy Spirit. We are walking in victory! So, faith that enjoys the presence of God is a victorious faith. The victory comes from a total obedience and surrender to God. The indicators of obedience are the fruit of the Spirit.

## A PERSEVERING FAITH (11:16-20)

True biblical, robust faith is not only victorious, it's also persevering. It never, never, never, never gives up because God's mercy never, never, never gives up on us. You fall down, then you get up again. You've got to be looking into the eyes of your heavenly Father who is good and expect a good outcome for your good and his glory, no matter how long it takes.

Joshua did this. He made war a long time, probably five to seven years if we do the math. The next few verses are very brief, but they represent a long, long time. Waiting on God is no problem if you know there is a good outcome.

## Persevere in God's Timing

**Joshua 11:16-18** | So Joshua took all that land, the hill country and all the Negeb and all the land of Goshen and the lowland and the Arabah and the hill country of Israel and its lowland [17] from Mount Halak, which rises toward Seir, as far as Baal-gad in the Valley of Lebanon below Mount Hermon. And he captured all their kings and struck them and put them to death. [18] Joshua made war a long time with all those kings.

Joshua made war a long time because he took God at his Word. You see we often start off good in the Christian life, we are taking God at his Word, but then the pain increases, the trials mount, and we forget God's goodness. No, robust faith is always persevering, remembering that God has a good outcome (Rom 8:28-30).

For the LORD God is a sun and shield; the LORD bestows favor and honor. No good thing does he withhold from those who walk uprightly. —Psalm 84:11

It's not that we forget the Bible. We know it. But we refuse to walk in it because of unbelief, which is rooted in a suspicion of God. Is he really good? If you have that attitude you will not persevere. You will give into fear and frustration and despair instead of taking God at his Word. But if you know God is good, you will persevere. You will not be a forgetful hearer but a doer. We can persevere in God's timing, because we know he has a good outcome!

Be doers of the word, and not hearers only, deceiving yourselves. [23] For if anyone is a hearer of the word and not a doer, he is like a man who looks intently at his natural face in a mirror. [24] For he looks at himself and goes away and at once forgets what he was like. — James 1:22-23

## Persevere in God's Mercy

Now one thing that is powerful about faith is that it always comes from a tender, humble, childlike heart. God resists the proud and gives grace to the humble. So even though Joshua and Israel are just one nation, untrained in war, they are going to devastate the Canaanites in the north, just as they did in the south. Why? Because the Canaanites hearts are hard. You see our strength comes from trusting God in his mercy. Tender hearts bring powerful victories.

This is where we read about some very chilling verses about the hardening of the Canaanites hearts. These Canaanites heard of the great miracles from Israel, but they refused to surrender their lives to the Lord. Anytime you refuse to surrender to the Lord with a tender heart, you lose. So the Lord defeated the Canaanites through giving them what they wanted. They hardened their hearts, so the Lord let them remain in their hardness of heart.

**Joshua 11:19-20** | There was not a city that made peace with the people of Israel except the Hivites, the inhabitants of Gibeon. They took them all in battle. [20] For it was the Lord's doing to harden their hearts that they should come against Israel in battle, in order that they should be devoted to destruction and should receive no mercy but be destroyed, just as the Lord commanded Moses.

How do we explain God hardening people's hearts? Let's understand God is merciful, Amen?

The Lord is... is patient toward you, not wishing that any should perish, but that all should reach repentance. —2 Peter 3:9

So why does God harden some people's hearts? That's a good question! We find in the book of Genesis that Pharaoh hardened his heart 7 times, and God hardened his heart 3 times. When God hardens hearts, it is that he withdraws his common grace. We never want that to happen. But his mercy is always there for anyone who wants to come to him. He says:

Come to me, all who labor and are heavy laden, and I will give you rest. —Matthew 11:28

The Bible teaches that all human beings know God, but they suppress the truth in unrighteousness (Rom 1:18ff). Hardening then is God taking away his restraints and allowing them to do as they please.

As the Holy Spirit says, "Today, if you hear his voice, do not harden your hearts." —Hebrews 3:7-8

Remember God is not tempted to do evil, neither does he tempt any one of us (Jas 1:13). The only thing that holds sinners back from the Lord is their own stubborn wills. If they persist in turning against the Lord, God will harden their hearts. There comes a place of rejection for some, where their hearts are so hardened that God does not grant them repentance because they cut off they only way that have to God:

faith. They refuse to believe. If you have any conviction right now, any pangs of heart, then your heart is not hardened. But if you have been resisting Christ, come to him immediately. Stop hardening your heart, or there may come a time when God may judicially leave you where you are. God wants us to have a tender heart.

## A MAGNIFICENT FAITH (11:21-23)

When we talk about a magnificent faith, I'm talking about a faith that magnifies the Lord's greatness.

## Magnify the Lord's Greatness

Track with me here saints. God should be magnified over any of our fears. How great is our God compared to any giant, any army of giants? And that's what we have here: an army of giants: the Anakim.

**Joshua 11:21-22** | And Joshua came at that time and cut off the Anakim from the hill country, from Hebron, from Debir, from Anab, and from all the hill country of Judah, and from all the hill country of Israel. Joshua devoted them to destruction with their cities.[22] There was none of the Anakim left in the land of the people of Israel. Only in Gaza, in Gath, and in Ashdod did some remain.

How great is he compared to an innumerable army of Canaanites with chariots and horseman? And how small is our greatest enemies compared to our great God? Our trials, our sin, our greatest fears, our greatest hurts and frustrations disappear when we magnify the greatness of our God.

Oh, magnify the Lord with me, and let us exalt his name together! [4] I sought the Lord, and he answered me and delivered me from all my fears.  Psalm 34:3-4

Dear saints, we have *nothing to fear*. God is greater than anything you might try to magnify. Remember, these Canaanites had tens of thousands of chariots and horsemen. It was an impossible victory. But all the Christian life is impossible victory after impossible victory. Do you think God would do things that were explainable? Is there anything too hard for the Lord? Remember when the people of Israel were so afraid of the giants in the land in Numbers 13? They were afraid of the giants in the land, the Anakim. What a joy to read that Joshua and Caleb were not afraid of the giants back in Numbers. Well, they get their chance to finally destroy the Anakim. No matter how you magnify your trial or your enemy, God is greater! The Anakim were an army of Goliaths. God took them down. Remember what God promised Israel:

> Do not be afraid of them, for tomorrow at this time I will give over all of them, slain, to Israel. —Joshua 11:6

What do we have to be afraid of?

> Greater is he who is in you than he who is in the world. —1 John 4:4

What do we have to be afraid of? In Christ we should fear nothing. Anything in this life is infinitely small compared to the greatness of God.

> God gave us a spirit not of fear but of power and love and self-control. —2 Timothy 1:7

This kind of victory over the Canaanites is a foreshadowing of the Christian's victory. It's guaranteed. Think of the promises we have! The Christian is "set free from the law of sin and death."

> The law of the life-giving Spirit in Christ Jesus has set you free from the law of sin and death. —Romans 8:2

No giant of sin can dominate you.

> We are more than conquerors through him who loved us. —Romans 8:37

> Sin will have no dominion over you, since you are not under law but under grace. —Romans 6:14

Israel's greatest battle was never against the Canaanites, it was against sin. That's why they erected a Tabernacle. That's why they offered sacrifices. Our great God has done something greater than defeating all of Canaan. He's defeated sin and death. He sent the King of kings and Lord of lords, and can I say, Jesus got us the victory. Just as he gave Joshua the victory, he's given us the victory! Is there anyone greater than the Lord? Who could destroy sin and death? Who will open the Scroll of Redemption and save us? Weep not! We have a conqueror! We have a King! His name is Jesus. He gives us the victory!

Joshua magnified the Lord's greatness and took out the Anakim and all the 300,000 soldiers, 100 thousand horsemen, and 20,000 chariots (according to Josephus) of the armies of northern Canaan. [87] So we see we need to magnify the Lord's greatness. Is there anything too hard for the Lord? No! But also let's magnify his goodness.

## Magnify the Lord's Goodness

Joshua magnified the Lord's goodness, and oh, how good is our God! He gave Joshua the whole land.

**Joshua 11:23** | So Joshua took the whole land, according to all that the Lord had spoken to Moses. And Joshua gave it for an inheritance to Israel according to their tribal allotments. And the land had rest from war.

Look at what he gave Joshua. The whole land. Rest from war. Let's magnify the Lord. He's greater than any sin problem you have. He wants to take that from you if you will surrender to him. Oh the rest he wants to give you!

### What is our Inheritance?

God wants you to have the fullness of his inheritance, which is not the land of Israel, but Jesus himself. Oh, we will get the land.

Blessed are the meek, for they shall inherit the earth. —Matthew 5:5

The promise to Abraham and his offspring that he would be heir of the world... came through the righteousness of faith. —Romans 4:13

With Abraham, we will inherit the earth and the entire cosmos. We are heirs of God and joint-heirs with Christ (Rom 8:17). Ultimately God himself is our inheritance!

And you shall be my people, and I will be your God. —Jeremiah 30:22

### What is our Rest?

What is this rest? Their rest was not mainly getting the land, but having God as their God. We get a commentary on this from the author of Hebrews.

For if Joshua had given them rest, God would not have spoken of another day later on. [9] So then, there remains a Sabbath rest for the people of God, [10] for whoever has entered God's rest has also rested from his works as God did from his. —Hebrews 4:8-10

---

[87] Boice. *Joshua*, 87–88.

God wants us to live in the rest and comfort of the fruit of the Spirit at all times. He wants us to experience close communion and worship in him all day long, day and night. We rest in Jesus (Mt 11:28). We have the rest of joy unspeakable and full of glory. We have the rest of perfect peace because of the blood of Christ who settled our sin debt with his own blood. Rest! Glorious rest! Only through faith, surrender — total trust in Jesus.

## A CELEBRATORY FAITH (12:1-23)

Now look at the blessings that Joshua received because he and all Israel took God at his Word! We are not going to read it, but we have a list of all the conquered kings and kingdoms conquered by Moses and Joshua. Joshua closes the conquering of the land of Canaan, with a kind of celebration. Chapter 12 gives us a glorious celebration. Verses 1–6 speak of the conquest and settlement of the land east of the Jordan, which had happened under Moses, while verses 7–24 list the thirty-one kings that fell to Joshua from Jericho onward. Each king and kingdom represent the removal of an impossibly strong opponent by the hand of the living God and his limitless, sovereign power.

So let us celebrate. To God be the glory. We have every spiritual blessing in Christ (Eph 1:3). We have the fullness of God dwelling in us in the Holy Spirit (Eph 1:23; 3:19). We have the riches of his presence. We have power to live in the pure peace and love and righteousness in the Spirit. We no longer have to fuss and worry and despair.
If you are fussing and fearing, you are not taking God at his Word.

As a Christian, you never have to live in the bondage of fearing and fussing. Instead, you need to rest on his Word. There's nothing to fear. God is greater than anything you are facing. You never need to fuss and be bitter or angry. God is in control.

You have an inheritance that is greater than all of northern and southern Canaan! Rejoice that you have the kingdom. It's not a physical kingdom like Canaan.

> For the kingdom of God is not meat and drink; but righteousness, and peace, and joy in the Holy Ghost. —Romans 14:17

What is left for the Christian is to lament this wicked world. We weep with those who weep. We come alongside the sufferers, but we never lose hope. We are still in a battle till we see Jesus, but the enemy is defeated. We don't ever have to worry or fear or fuss. That is not what we do. Fearing and fussing are indicators that you are not taking God at his Word.

## Conclusion

Whatever is in front of you, take God at his Word. When you see an impossible situation, count it all joy. Rejoice because you are going to do exploits as your great God fights for you. Look at all those kings listed. They had no chance. And no sin has a change in your heart when the Spirit and the Word are reigning. Do fear. Don't fuss. Wal in the Word through worship and celebrate! Insist on living out the Word of God by faith. We are in the Promised Land. Christ is our inheritance. We are united to him, and he to us. Our great God and Savior Jesus Christ has rescued us from the domain of darkness and transferred us to his eternal kingdom (Col 1:13). We are in the Promised Land! To him be the glory forever and ever!

# 14 | JOSHUA 13
## OUR GLORIOUS INHERITANCE

*I myself will drive them out from before the people of Israel. Only allot the land to Israel for an inheritance, as I have commanded you.*
### JOSHUA 13:6

This is a chapter in God's Word for anyone here that might be tired. You are weary in this world. Things are spinning out of control in this world. Here's the message: This world is temporary. Don't put your hope in this world. We have an inheritance that is not from this world. My hope is that we will no longer be focused on this world, but that we will lay up treasure in heaven.

*This world is not my home.*
*I'm just a-passing through.*
*My treasures are laid up*
*somewhere beyond the blue.*

Israel was given an inheritance: a place to worship God. It had been promised to Abraham, and now they were finally going to take possession of it. For centuries, Israel had waited to receive its long-promised inheritance. And now, the day to inhabit the land had arrived. Joshua 13–19 explores the placement of God's people in the land. What was once promised to Abraham, is now coming to fulfillment in the days of Joshua.

For us today, this passage is equally exciting when we consider the inheritance promised to us in Christ—an inheritance we still look for in the new heavens and the new earth. Thus, these chapters should not bore us with their detail; they should stir excitement in our own hope of heaven—i.e., a heaven on earth when Christ returns. But there is something further. We have the down payment of our inheritance already, the promised Holy Spirit. We get to enjoy heaven now. I want to look at how to do that and what that means. Every child of God has a glorious inheritance that should be enjoyed right now.

In Joshua 13, there is a drama and an excitement. The day of inheritance has come. For Joshua and Israel, and for us, it's more than we can grasp and comprehend.

## OUR INHERITANCE IS INEXHAUSTIBLE (13:1-7)

### Leaders are Expendable

Leaders are expendable, but our inheritance is inexhaustible. We need to make sure the next generation is engaged, trained, and ready. God's plan is not bound to your lifetime but encompasses the coming generations. That means the next generation needs to be prepared. It is incumbent upon every believer to do everything you can to train up the next generation. We see this clearly in Joshua's life, as he nears the end.

**Joshua 13:1** | Now Joshua was old and advanced in years, and the Lord said to him, "You are old and advanced in years, and there remains yet very much land to possess."

Joshua was 80 years old when he began to conquer Canaan. He's nearing 110 when he dies. Ok now that's old. Joshua had conquered so much, but there is always more land to be conquered. A careful look at 'the land that remains' shows that it consists of Philistia and Lebanon.[88] In essence, these were the edges of Israel. They had conquered almost the entirety of the land that God had promised. In order to expand the land and hold it, they needed to raise up the next generation. The book

---

[88] Yohanan Aharoni. *The Land of the Bible: A Historical Geography*, rev. and enl. (Philadelphia: Westminster Press, 1979), 233–39, and Yohanan Aharoni and Michael Avi-Yonah, The Macmillan Bible Atlas, rev. ed. (New York: Macmillan, 1977), 50–51.

of Judges showed how leaving a vacuum in leadership can be such a great failure. Let's take heed to this.

### A Word on Discipleship

We are all called to make disciples. If you are not making disciples, you are missing a major part of your spiritual growth. You grow by helping others grow. The last command given by Jesus is to:

Go... and make disciples of all nations. —Matthew 28:20

Who are you discipling? This is the key to our spiritual growth as a church. I am praying that while the culture is having a break*down*, we will have a break*through* with God, so that each one of us will be mobilized to help another toward holiness. Discipleship entails a learner's spirit. It takes a humble, childlike attitude. If you are serious, you will begin to surrender and be free in ways that you never thought possible. Are you getting discipleship? If not, are you mature enough now so that you are making disciples? If you want discipleship, don't wait someone to come to you. Go after it. It's intense, but it will change your life. So, we have learned with Joshua's old age, that leaders are expendable, and each one of us needs to step into that vacuum and lead through discipleship.

## Land is Limited

And look at the land. There's still so much to conquer. And even if they conquered it all, God is not limited to one strip of land. The whole world is to worship him.

**Joshua 13:2-6a** | This is the land that yet remains: all the regions of the Philistines, and all those of the Geshurites [3] (from the Shihor, which is east of Egypt, northward to the boundary of Ekron, it is counted as Canaanite; there are five rulers of the Philistines, those of Gaza, Ashdod, Ashkelon, Gath, and Ekron), and those of the Avvim, [4] in the south, all the land of the Canaanites, and Mearah that belongs to the Sidonians, to Aphek, to the boundary of the Amorites, [5] and the land of the Gebalites, and all Lebanon, toward the sunrise, from Baal-gad below Mount Hermon to Lebo-hamath, [6] all the inhabitants of the hill country from Lebanon to Misrephoth-maim, even all the Sidonians.

In verses 2-5 we read about the land that remains. Land is limited. As I said, we see in the book of Judges that within one generation,

Israel's disobedience invites foreign oppressors. But even more devastating in the history of Israel is the expulsion of Israel from the land when the powers of Assyria and Babylon come and conquer God's obstinate people. What's the answer? You must choose to enter into the Lord's inheritance for yourself. Go and conquer. Even small sins are not ok. We are to be holy as the Lord is holy (1 Pet 1:16). How holy is God? How perfect is he?

We are to live life, experiencing God in the events and circumstances that the Lord gives us with victory! God guarantees the victory if we proceed in faith. In this inheritance, there are many trials, tests, and tribulations, but the Lord chooses these things for us. Enter into the inheritance God appoints for you and rejoice in it.

> He will choose our inheritance for us, the excellence of Jacob whom he loves. —Psalm 47:4, NKJV

## Our God is Inexhaustible

Joshua is near the end of his life. He's exhaustible. The land is limited. But I want you to see that the people have a weapon that is greater than chariots of iron or horses. We have the inexhaustible God! Listen to God's promise to defeat Israel's enemies.

**Joshua 13:6b-7** | I myself will drive them out from before the people of Israel. Only allot the land to Israel for an inheritance, as I have commanded you. 7 Now therefore divide this land for an inheritance to the nine tribes and half the tribe of Manasseh."

When we speak of Israel's earthly inheritance, we talk in terms of the land, and it's limited and can be taken away. It's just the wrapping paper for the real inheritance. The real inheritance is God who will drive out the enemies. For us that Person is the Holy Spirit. He is what, or better yet, who you are getting in heaven. He's the first installment of our glorious inheritance according to Ephesians 1 because we cannot encompass God fully.

> In him you also, when you heard the word of truth, the gospel of your salvation, and believed in him, were sealed with the promised Holy Spirit, [14] who is the guarantee of our inheritance until we acquire possession of it, to the praise of his glory. —Ephesians 1:13-14

We are limited and sinful. But God wants us to grow in our capacity to enjoy the fulness of his fellowship. The Holy Spirit is the first installment of our inheritance, and he is able to hold us, sustain us and satisfy us. You cannot exhaust the blessings you have in Christ right now.

> Blessed be the God and Father of our Lord Jesus Christ, who has blessed us in Christ with every spiritual blessing in the heavenly places. —Ephesians 1:3

He wants us to experience the unlimited fullness of God. The Lord wants you... "to know the love of Christ that surpasses knowledge, that you may be filled with all the fullness of God" (Eph 3:19). So when God says, "I'll fight for you...", he's saying you lack nothing. You have everything you need. This is a truth that is found constantly in the Word of God. You have everything you need in Jesus for perfect peace and holiness in your life right now. It's incredible what you have in your inheritance if you will just take hold of it. Paul says you need to open your eyes to the incredible riches of the inheritance you have.

> Having the eyes of your hearts enlightened, that you may know what is the hope to which he has called you, what are the riches of his glorious inheritance in the saints. —Ephesians 1:18

We have so much, but we need to know how to access the riches of our glorious inheritances as God's saints. You and I are like one of my favorite superheroes.

You are like Peter Parker. Remember how Peter Parker became Spiderman? He got bit by a radioactive spider. Understand that the moment he got bit, he had all the power of Spiderman, but not of the skills. He had no idea how to use his powers, but he still had the power. Remember the first time he touched his sink spickets, he ripped them off and water spurted everywhere? Remember he got scared and jumped to the ceiling and was stuck there because he didn't know how to release his adhesive hands? He had the power but not the skills.

God promises to give Israel all that they need. He will drive out the Canaanites. A major phase of our inheritance begins right now, where God drives out the sinful, selfish works of the flesh from us, and gives us the Kingdom of God right here and right now. Every Christian has all the power they need for holiness and perfect peace. Holiness only comes from a fully surrendered heart. That's what discipleship is all about: learning to walk in perfect harmony with God.

## We Have a Better Joshua

Israel's Joshua died. He couldn't train the people the way he might have wanted. You see Joshua was a great general, but he's just a black and white picture of redemption. The good news of the rest of the story is that another Joshua has come, and our Joshua, King Jesus, gives us an inheritance that is inexhaustible, and cannot be taken away from us. Our great God came to us to deliver our inheritance to us. The Son of God gave himself for us on a tree, that we might have the full inheritance.

## We Have Greater Promises

That promise looks a bit wild in light of the map, since it prods Israel to aim for dominance far north of Tyre and Sidon. But then the Lord's promises frequently are wild, as Abraham and a few others could attest.[89] We have greater promises than Joshua. Israel was promised the land of Israel, and we are promised the cosmos. What are some wild promises that you are looking to God for? Are they spiritual? Are they according to God's will? No matter how outlandish they are, you ought to expect them. God wants you mature. He wants you to leave a spiritual legacy. He wants you to make disciples. He wants to answer far more than anything you ask.

> Now to him who is able to do far more abundantly than all that we ask or think, according to the power at work within us, [21] to him be glory in the church and in Christ Jesus throughout all generations, forever and ever. Amen. —Ephesians 3:20-21

## OUR INHERITANCE IS ATTAINABLE (13:8-13)

Verses 8-33 discuss the inheritance of Manasseh, Gad, and Reuben and all the land East of the Jordan River which Moses conquered with the children of Israel before he died. It's quite impressive. There are so many rivers and mountains and landmarks that are named.

And while it is true that the Lord was their portion, God did not just give Joshua a magic wand to defeat the Canaanites. They had to work hard for it. They had to fight. And sadly, they didn't conquer everything they could have.

---

[89] Davis, *Joshua*, 109.

## Reach for the Attainable

**Joshua 13:13** | Yet the people of Israel did not drive out the Geshurites or the Maacathites, but Geshur and Maacath dwell in the midst of Israel to this day.

Israel's inheritance was for them. They were to enjoy it all. They were to attain it, but trusting God in battle. But sad thing is they fell short. As we look at the first three tribes, we see in verse 13 an incomplete obedience. It brings no immediate crisis. It seldom does. However, here is a testimony to all God's people from Theologian Dale R. Davis,

> We frequently and strangely prove faithful in the great crisis of faith, remain steadfast in severe storms, perhaps even relish the excitement of the heaviest assaults, yet lack the tenacity, the dogged endurance, the patient plodding often required in the prosaic affairs of believing life; we are often loath to be faithful in (what we regard as) little.[90]

What does Christ say about the little things?

> One who is faithful in a very little is also faithful in much, and one who is dishonest in a very little is also dishonest in much. —Luke 16:10

God wants us to attain the fullness of our salvation on earth, not just when he comes to get us in his Second Coming. We are promised the full power of the Spirit, the full love of Jesus, and all the fullness of God. He wants us to have "perfect peace" and to "be holy" as God himself is holy. Christ has attained our eternal salvation, but we are to "move into the land" and attain maturity in Christ, who is our inheritance.

Dear saints, Solomon said it's the "little foxes that spoil the vine" of our relationships (Song 2:15). It's the little angers and fears that cut off the vine of God's presence and drive us into unbelief. You don't have to put up with that. You can live a truly happy and contented life regardless of the difficulties and trials of your circumstances. You may think these little victories in your life are unattainable. I want to tell you that God wants you to live a life of holiness perhaps that you've not attained before or that you've attained, but only for short amounts of time.

---

[90] Ibid., 110.

Do you want that? It's possible through discipleship. That's the only way. Discipleship provides the Word of God with the presence of God and the encouragement and accountability of mature believers who love you and will care for you in the environment of the local church. I'm asking, do you want that?

### Remember What You Have Already Attained

In verse 8 through the end of the chapter, all this seems like so many lakes, rivers, valleys, plains, and towns all jumbled together. However, we must not miss the constant allusions and reminders of Israel's victories. What does this mean for us?

It means we need to remember the victory God has for you in Christ. You have everything you need for victory. You have been united to Christ in his death, his burial and his resurrection, as well as his victorious ascension where Christ sat down at the right hand of God. Now you too are seated in the heavenly places. In the Spirit, you have the power that raised Jesus from the dead. In the Word, you have the pathway and instruction for victory. In the Father, you have all the love and encouragement you could ever need. In Jesus, you have the right standing, and he wants your outward life to be conformed to your eternal standing with God. You've been saved. You've experienced the victory of Christ, now it's time to inhabit the land!

## OUR INHERITANCE IS PERSONAL (13:14-33)

Our final truth we want to understand is the very personal nature of our inheritance. In this section the writer points the people of God to their true inheritance. He does this in the two notes about the Levites. They were exceptional in that they did not receive a land allotment like the other tribes. Rather, Levi's inheritance consisted of the offerings by fire (or "food offerings" or "gifts"?) belonging to the Lord (13:14) or, quite plainly, of the Lord himself (13:33).

**Joshua 13:14** | To the tribe of Levi alone Moses gave no inheritance. The offerings by fire to the Lord God of Israel are their inheritance, as he said to him.

**Joshua 13:33** | But to the tribe of Levi Moses gave no inheritance; the Lord God of Israel is their inheritance, just as he said to them.

This was just as God had told Aaron, that the Levites would have no inheritance in the Land, but God would be the priests' inheritance.

And the LORD said to Aaron, "You shall have no inheritance in their land, neither shall you have any portion among them. I am your portion and your inheritance among the people of Israel. —Numbers 18:20

It doesn't get more personal than this.

## We Have a Personal God

Any believing Israelite could come to adopt this Levite perspective, realizing that, above all else, the Lord himself was his inheritance.

You are my refuge, my portion in the land of the living. —Psalm 142:5

Indeed God was the Old Testament believer's 'portion forever'.

God is the strength of my heart and my portion forever. —Psalm 73:26

The Israelites knew that the land wasn't the main inheritance. That's why we read so often about the Lord being our portion and inheritance. The Lord remained Israel's inheritance, even when the land was taken away as we read about in Lamentations. Jeremiah is writing while Babylon is destroying the Temple, enslaving the people, and occupying the land. So even when the land is taken away, the Lord, Jeremiah says, is his people's inheritance.[91]

The LORD is my inheritance; therefore, I will hope in him. —Lamentations 3:24

The Bible is full of references to the inheritance believers have in Christ.

In [Christ] we have obtained an inheritance, having been predestined according to the purpose of him who works all things according to the counsel of his will. —Ephesians 1:11

Our inheritance is, in a word, full fellowship with God himself. It is the sum total of all God has promised us in salvation. Look at these hopeful words in 1 Peter.

Blessed be the God and Father of our Lord Jesus Christ! According to his great mercy, he has caused us to be born again to a living hope through the resurrection of Jesus Christ from the dead, [4] to an

---

[91] Ibid., 111.

inheritance that is imperishable, undefiled, and unfading, kept in heaven for you, [5] who by God's power are being guarded through faith for a salvation ready to be revealed in the last time. —1 Peter 1:3-5

Consider four marks of our inheritance. It is *imperishable*: that means our inheritance in Christ won't decay, rust or fall apart. His love will never fail for you! It is *unspoiled*: this speaks of having no blemish, but being absolutely perfect. Christ is truly perfect. He is "holy, blameless, pure, set apart from sinners, exalted above the heavens" (Heb 7:26). It is *unfading*: it never loses its intensity or excitement. So it is with Christ! And it is *reserved*: Like Abraham, we are "looking forward to the city with foundations, whose architect and builder is God" (Heb 11:10). And it's just for you, guarded and kept. No one can take Christ from you. That city God has built is his people united to him!

So to answer the question in a different way.... What is our inheritance? The only thing that is imperishable, undefiled, and unfading is God himself. It's as the Psalmist wrote:

Whom have I in heaven but you? And there is nothing on earth that I desire besides you. —Psalm 73:25

## We Have a Personal Calling

We are not so focused on the things of this earth, the earths politics and earthly solutions. Our inheritance isn't ultimately on earth, though we will inherit the earth. It's just as we read in Philippians.

Our citizenship is in heaven, and from it we await a Savior, the Lord Jesus Christ. —Philippians 3:20

We are awaiting Jesus to return at his Second Coming when he will rule and reign over the entire earth. Heaven and earth will be joined in one. Of course, a good citizen of heaven will be a good citizen on earth, but our great mission is not the politics of this world. No. We are getting people ready for eternal life with Jesus. What good will it do if all the people of our nation have a good economy, but they lose their soul.

Go out and vote, go out and affect change. But that's way, way down on our list of priorities. My mission and goal, like my Lord, is to be a visible representative of the invisible God. We are ambassadors from another country. We are to recruit more citizens for the New Jerusalem, when heaven comes to earth. Get people ready for that. Just as the compass points north we should be pointing to heaven where our inheritance is.

So many of us are racked with fears and frustrations. You are so concerned about the things of this earth. How absurd that we who have tasted heaven would not be getting people ready for the world to come. Instead, we have become worried about making this world more comfortable. Listen, real eternal freedom and comfort comes from Christ alone. We are not here to lay up treasure on earth. We are not here to set up kingdoms on earth. We are here for the expansion of God's kingdom.

> Do not lay up for yourselves treasures on earth, where moth and rust destroy and where thieves break in and steal, [20] but lay up for yourselves treasures in heaven, where neither moth nor rust destroys and where thieves do not break in and steal. [21] For where your treasure is, there your heart will be also. —Matthew 6:19-21

Where is your heart? That's where you are going to spend your time and treasure. It's fine to give your kids an earthly inheritance, but what good is any of that if they don't have an eternal inheritance?

### Conclusion

In the ancient world, kings would mark their territory with images of themselves. They would put up statues. So instead of "Welcome to Babylon", you'd have a statue of Nebuchadnezzar. God has also marked his territory. It's not only Israel, but every tribe, language, people, family, and nation on the earth. And you are God's statue. You are his image. You are the visible image of the invisible God, being conformed each day, more and more to his likeness. And through you, God is saying, this earth is mine! It is so vitally important that you celebrate God's inheritance by living a that reflects Christ. You are his image to a dying world.

# 15 | JOSHUA 14
## GIVE ME THIS MOUNTAIN

*And now, behold, I am this day eighty-five years old. I am still as strong today as I was in the day that Moses sent me; my strength now is as my strength was then, for war and for going and coming. So now give me this mountain of which the Lord spoke on that day.... It may be that the Lord will be with me, and I shall drive them out just as the Lord said.*

JOSHUA 14:10-12

How vital it is to learn how to grow in faith and trust in God's promises. In Joshua 14 and 15, we see that Caleb finally gets to conquer the giants in the land and take some of the land of Judah, namely Hebron, for his family. Hebron is a land of fullness and fruitfulness, and it's a place of mountains and hills where he would fellowship with God. In fact, that's what the name Hebron means: "fellowship".

Here's the key thought for this chapter: If you will learn to conquer all enemies and idols in the heart by faith, you can live in joyful victory and uninterrupted fellowship with God.

You see, for the Christian, victory is uninterrupted fellowship with God. Did you know so many Christians today are earning a living while they're wasting and losing their lives? They are drawing their breath and drawing their salary, but they're living defeated lives because they have unsurrendered hearts. I want to ask you, are you living on the mountain of victory, or are you living in the wilderness of despair and frustration? Caleb is the prototype of the victorious believer. You ought to be that prototype as well. He didn't want to go halfway with God. He wanted the total victory that God promised. Do you want that?

The book of Joshua is more than history, it is an illustration of the victory that a New Testament Christian is to have. The Bible says of the Old Testament's record:

> Now these things happened to them as an example, but they were written down for our instruction. —1 Corinthians 10:11

> For whatever was written in former days was written for our instruction, that through endurance and through the encouragement of the Scriptures we might have hope. —Romans 15:4

## The Victorious Christian Life

What does the land of Canaan represent for the Christian? It represents the land of victory and rest for the Christian: a life of victory over sin. Let me illustrate that. Coming into Canaan meant release from slavery for them. Up until this time they'd been a nation of slaves. Aren't you tired of being the devil's slave? He says, "Jump" and you say, "How high?" Aren't you glad that "who the Son sets free is free indeed" (Jn 8:36)? For the Christians, that means we are no longer slaves to the impulses of sin. We've been set free! And it is said of every child of God:

> Sin shall not have dominion over you. —Romans 6:14

So there is a release from slavery and freedom. But there is also a rest that comes from living in victory and fellowship with God. Jesus said:

> Come to me, all who labor and are heavy laden, and I will give you rest. —Matthew 11:28

Up until this time God's people had been wandering round and round in the desert over the burning, blistering, broiling desert floor. And, now they enter into a land that the Bible says was a land of rest. They have to learn to defeat the enemy so they can have rest all around them. Oh, I see so many Christians who have everything but rest. They are so anxious; they are so frustrated and even angry; they are despairing and depressed. They don't know what to do. They are not living for the Kingdom, but for the world. God had said to Moses:

My presence will go with you, and I will give you rest. —Exodus 33:14

Up until this time God's people had been living in the wilderness, just heard sermons about Canaan and that was all, and now they see it for themselves. I want you to see the life of rest and peace, joy and righteousness in the Holy Spirit for you. There is a baptism, a filling of the Spirit with power that will not only bring you rest, but a new anointing for service. The Spirit will clothe you with power, but only if you want it more than you want to breathe.

My heart's desire is for God's people is to experience the genuine resurrection power that Christ has already won, bought and paid for. It would be wonderful. Oh, that you would hold of your inheritance in your spiritual Canaan, the victorious Christian life that God has for you. Are you living for the world to come?

## Joshua and Caleb Representations

Well, whom does Joshua represent? Joshua who led them in that day is an illustration and a type of Jesus. That is the Old Testament name for Jesus is Joshua, and Joshua represents Christ who leads us into the land of victory. And, Caleb, who does he represent? Well, we'll let Caleb represent you, all right? Caleb representing the Christian about to conquer his Canaan, about to possess his possessions, about to receive the promises that God has given to him. So let's discover the way to the Spirit-filled, power-endued Christian life. Is there any other kind of Christian life? How do we get there? Let's look at four marks of the victorious believer.

## GODLY CHARACTER (14:1-9, 14)

So many Christians are failing in the Christian life because they are aiming for behavior, when God aims for character deep down in the heart. We aim for the external, when God aims for the internal. We see this clearly in the life of Caleb. Caleb had such power because he walked with God in his heart.

Imagine what would happen if someone unplugged all your home appliances. Your refrigerator, microwave, and oven would be utterly useless. How long could you live that way, with no ability to make food? It wouldn't be long before you figured out the problem and plugged everything back in to the power source. Like those appliances, we too, are dependent on a power source. Jesus used the example of the vine and branches to illustrated it. He said:

Without me you can do nothing. —John 15:5

Are you connected to the Vine? Do you have a power source? That's what makes for godly character. It's to have a heart pulsating for Christ.

## The Place of Godly Character

Leaders are expendable, but our inheritance is inexhaustible. We need to make sure the next generation is engaged, trained, and ready. God's plan is not bound to your lifetime but encompasses the coming generations. That means the next generation needs to be prepared. It is incumbent upon every believer to do everything you can to train up the next generation. We see this clearly in Joshua's life, as he nears the end.

> **Joshua 14:6-9** | Then the people of Judah came to Joshua at Gilgal. And Caleb the son of Jephunneh the Kenizzite said to him, "You know what the Lord said to Moses the man of God in Kadesh-barnea concerning you and me. [7] I was forty years old when Moses the servant of the Lord sent me from Kadesh-barnea to spy out the land, and I brought him word again as it was in my heart. [8] But my brothers who went up with me made the heart of the people melt; yet I wholly followed the Lord my God. [9] And Moses swore on that day, saying, 'Surely the land on which your foot has trodden shall be an inheritance for you and your children forever, because you have wholly followed the Lord my God.'

> **Joshua 14:14** | Therefore Hebron became the inheritance of Caleb the son of Jephunneh the Kenizzite to this day, because he wholly followed the Lord, the God of Israel.

Three times God said it. Caleb was an unusual man who followed God's command to love God wholeheartedly. He followed the greatest commandment.

You shall love the Lord your God with all your heart, with all your soul, and with all your strength. —Deuteronomy 6:5

In verse 8 Caleb says: "I wholly followed the Lord my God." What was he saying? He was willing to die to follow God into the Promised Land. He wanted to please God more than he wanted to breathe. Literally. Caleb (along with Joshua) had the courage to stand alone and give a minority report (Num. 13:30) even though it nearly cost him his life (Num. 14:6–10). Everyone else said, "There are giants in the Land!" But Caleb and Joshua said, "We have a giant, infinite, almighty God in heaven! We can possess the land! The Lord is with us."[92]

Caleb was a man who gave God all that there was of him: every inch, every ounce, every nerve, every fiber. All there was of Caleb he gave to the Lord. He had completely given everything to his Lord. Do you see? Here is this 85-year-old man, and he doesn't say, "I'm tired. I've given my all, so I'm giving up." No. He wholly followed the Lord. He never forgot God's promises. He took God at his Word in the depths of his heart. That's where you will find victory. You can't white knuckle holiness in your behavior. It comes from a radical change of heart. Caleb refused to let frustration or fear rule him. A vision of the greatness and majesty of God chased the fear and frustration and unbelief right out of him!

## The Path to Godly Character

I wonder how many could say right now, "I have given everything to Jesus Christ. As far as I know, I want that total commitment to God." You say, "I'm serious. I refuse to be halfhearted." Amen. You see, the halfhearted will be the faint hearted and they will never conquer their Canaan.

You know about Dwight L. Moody, the great Chicago evangelist. He had a deeper experience with the Lord when some were praying for him. I want to tell you about an epic event in the life of Dwight L. Moody that he said was one of the turning points in his ministry. Moody first of all started out as a shoe salesman and then he became a Sunday school teacher. We know he later became a mighty evangelist. He went to England for the first time in 1867, and he met Charles H. Spurgeon, and George Muller and came back. But he didn't have the manifest power in his ministry that he was known for later in his ministry.

But something powerful happened the second time Moody was in England in 1870. He heard another evangelist preach in a field in an outdoor meeting. The evangelist's name was Henry Varley. He said, "The world has yet to see what God can do in and through and with and for a man wholly committed to him." Dwight L. Moody, responded, "By

---

[92] Davis, *Joshua*, 114.

the grace of God I will be that man. I want to be wholly, completely dedicated to him."[93]

Now God tested him and took everything from him. In the great Chicago fire, Moody lost his church the Illinois Street Church (later Moody Church) and his own home. But Moody was consecrated to God. And, God took this relatively unlettered, uncultured, untrained shoe clerk and used him to shake two continents for God. Like Caleb, Moody was wholly, completely dedicated to the Lord.

Listen, we need Bible knowledge. You need the local church. But without a heart saturated with Christ, it's all nothing. It's vain. Almighty God wants your heart, a total commitment to him. What part of the wilderness is God asking you to give up? What part of Egypt are you still hiding in your heart? Caleb said, "I don't want the wilderness. I want the Promised Land."

## The Pattern of Godly Character

There are many examples of this commitment to godly character. Ephesians tells us we need to put off the idolatry of the old life, renew your heart and mind, and put on the worship of the new life. I really appreciate how Galatians 5 puts it.

> But I say, walk by the Spirit, and you will not gratify the desires of the flesh. [24] And those who belong to Christ Jesus have crucified the flesh with its passions and desires. —Galatians 5:16, 24

As always, real change must happen in the heart. You can't just change the outward. Christ has to rule and reign in the depths of your heart. There is always a focus on Christ in all biblical change. "I want to be like Christ" is the believer's cry for repentance. "That Christ may increase, and I may decrease" as John the Baptist said.

You will not gratify the desires of the flesh that indicate idolatry: anger and fear, foolishness, and despair. Anger, rage, frustration: it's all murder. It's all unbelief. Anger says: "I am god". Fear says: "There is no God." Despair says: "God doesn't care." Foolishness says, "I don't care. I want to escape." One gaze of faith to Christ defeats them all. You have to turn your gaze and desire from the idol and look to Christ from the heart. For instance, what is it that makes you angry? What is it that

---

[93] R. A. Torrey. *Why God Used D.L. Moody* (Whitefish, MT: Kessinger Publishing, 2006), 10.

makes you fear? Do you fear losing the comfort of a relationship? Then you are worshipping the comfort of that relationship in place of your relationship with Christ. You'll never be happy in that relationship until you surrender it fully to Christ. Give Christ the reigns. Trust him. You'll know you have surrendered when you stop with the anger and pride, the foolishness and fear, the despair. You'll have the peace of God ruling in your heart no matter what happens.

What do you live for? What makes you truly happy? If it's not Christ, that's your idol. What do you get mad if you can't get it? Is it the peace that comes from financial stability or good health? You had better surrender those things, because the fear and anger and despair that comes from holding so tightly to those things is idolatrous. You've got to surrender everything in your heart to God. The only true pleasure comes from Christ. Everything else compared to Christ is "dung".

If your heart is attracted to anything else than Christ, you are going to be in for some real misery. No one compares to Christ. That's the first step in victorious living. You have to put off the old life and look to Christ. Renew your mind. Then you can start putting on the new life.

Caleb was a man of godly character. He loved God more than he wanted to breathe. But there was another mark of his victorious life we need to see.

## CONFIDENCE IN GOD'S WORD (14:6-12)

You've got to have clear vision if you are going to live victoriously in the land of your inheritance. Caleb's vision was so absolutely clear because of God's Word.

**Joshua 14:6-12** | ... Caleb the son of Jephunneh the Kenizzite said to him [JOSHUA], "You know what the Lord said to Moses the man of God in Kadesh-barnea concerning you and me. [7] I was forty years old when Moses the servant of the Lord sent me from Kadesh-barnea to spy out the land, and I brought him word again as it was in my heart. [8] But my brothers who went up with me made the heart of the people melt; yet I wholly followed the Lord my God. [9] And Moses swore on that day, saying, 'Surely the land on which your foot has trodden shall be an inheritance for you and your children forever, because you have wholly followed the Lord my God.' [10] And now, behold, the Lord has kept me alive, just as he said, these forty-five years since the time that

the Lord spoke this word to Moses, while Israel walked in the wilderness. And now, behold, I am this day eighty-five years old. [11] I
am still as strong today as I was in the day that Moses sent me;
my strength now is as my strength was then, for war and for going
and coming. [12] So now give me this hill country of which
the Lord spoke on that day, for you heard on that day how
the Anakim were there, with great fortified cities. It may be that
the Lord will be with me, and I shall drive them out just as
the Lord said."

David said:

Your word is a lamp to my feet and a light to my path. —Psalm 119:105

Caleb had the same lamp. He could see clearly. If you don't see the
clear path to victory, you are not consistently reading God's Word.
Caleb said, "I'm going to have this mountain. I'm going to have this victory over the giants, *just as the Lord said.*" Over and over, he's taking
God at his Word.

"You know what the Lord said to Moses" (14:6).

"Moses swore on that day, saying" (14:9).

"Now give me this hill country of which the Lord spoke on that day"
(14:12a).

"It may be that the Lord will be with me, and I shall drive them out
just as the Lord said" (14:12b).

Listen to Caleb. "God said, God said, God said!" He could see
clearly because he trusted in God's Word. He said, "I'm going to take
the land of Hebron, the land of fellowship, just as God said. Yes, I see
giants, but they look small compared to my great God. I'm banking on
what God said." Do you hear his confidence? He wasn't wearing the
glasses of the flesh. All he could see was his great God, because of the
Word of God. Caleb's battle-ax was the Word of God. Caleb had a
mountain he needed to conquer. His battle-ax, his tank, his weapon,
was the promises in God's Word. That's how he got connected to the
power of God. He walked in the Word.

Some of us are willing to memorize the Word. We are willing to
casually listen to the Word. But are we willing to *walk* in the Word and
obey it? Are you and I willing to risk your reputation, our relationships,
and our future like Caleb did? Caleb was willing to stand alone on the

Word of God. He did stand alone, with only Joshua by his side, for 40 years. He knew God's Word was true, and he sacrificed everything for that victory. He wasn't going to die in the wilderness. Where are you? Is there a clear pattern of walking in God's Word in your life, or is there wilderness wandering?

God had given Caleb that mountain and hill country of Hebron. Caleb went up that mountain with the sword of God's Word in his hand. With that light, the giants looked so tiny. They looked defeated. His confidence and his clear vision came out of the Word of God.

> Faith comes by hearing, and hearing by the word of Christ. —Romans 10:17

If you want to see clearly, you've got to walk by faith in the Scriptures. The Word will cut away any kind of cancer blocking your vision. The Bible says,

> For the word of God is living and active, sharper than any two-edged sword, piercing to the division of soul and of spirit, of joints and of marrow, and discerning the thoughts and intentions of the heart. [13] And no creature is hidden from his sight, but all are naked and exposed to the eyes of him to whom we must give account. — Hebrews 4:12-13

Caleb walked into victory by walking on the sure foundation of God's Word. How would you like it if you bought a house, and the builder says: it's brand new. It's in perfect condition. You walk in, and you don't get two feet in the house, and the floor caves in, and you are in the basement? That's what it's like to live your life for idols and lies. Idols always promise you so much, but they leave you angry, depressed, defeated, afraid, and lied to.

You better take God's Word, soak your soul in it, saturate yourself with it, hide God's Word in your heart so you can say, "God has said." The Word alone will expose the world's lies. Do you know what God has said in this book? Do you understand the great eternal rock-ribbed promises of this book? Do you know them? Do you know what made Caleb such a great man? Caleb believed the Word of God and refused to believe what his eyes told him. His eyes saw giants. God's Word gave him glasses to see those giants as defeated foes.

So Caleb shows us the prototype of the New Testament believer, living in victory. He had godly character: his heart was plugged in to

God. He had a confidence in God's Word. He could see clearly. But, thirdly, his feet moved, with the courage he had. He was willing to defeat the enemy.

## COURAGE AGAINST THE ENEMY (14:7-12)

Caleb's confidence in God's Word led to Caleb's courage. You see, you'll never be bold, you'll never have courage, you'll never do valiantly until you have a pure heart and you've hidden the Word of God in your heart. But, when that happens, then you're going to have the kind of a courage that God wants you to have.

What a glorious hill country Hebron was. Hebron is the richest place. You can see the vineyards today. It was that place where when Caleb and the spies went over they came carrying out of Hebron a bunch of grapes that took two to carry on a pole. Why, it was a land that flowed with milk and honey, corn and wine, grapes, figs, pomegranates, all of it there. It was a rich land, but there were some dangerous adversaries. You know nothing great is ever done in a rocking chair. If you're looking for a cheap way, an easy way, a lazy way to be victorious, forget it. Caleb had some opposition that he had to overcome, but I want you to know that the door to the room of opportunity swings on the hinges of opposition and God has planned it that way. There's a great effectual door opened unto us, but there are many adversaries.

### Courage to Overcome Grasshoppers

I want you to notice some of the adversaries that Caleb had to overcome through his courage. In the first place he had to overcome grasshoppers.

> **Joshua 14:7-8** | I was forty years old when Moses the servant of the Lord sent me from Kadesh-barnea to spy out the land, and I brought him word again as it was in my heart. **8** But my brothers who went up with me made the heart of the people melt; yet I wholly followed the Lord my God

How did they make the heart of the people melt? We find this in Numbers 13:33. Here's what the other ten men said when they came back. Remember what they said?

> There we saw the Nephilim (the sons of Anak, who come from the Nephilim), and we seemed to ourselves like grasshoppers, and so we seemed to them. —Numbers 13:33

Caleb's fellow soldiers had a grasshopper complex. Don't be a grasshopper. You say, "There are too many giants in that land, nobody could ever live that way." And, do you know before a church does anything good or great it has to overcome the grasshoppers? The grasshoppers, there are plenty of them. People who sit around and say, "It can't be done, it won't be done, it shouldn't be done." These people are content to retreat back and live in the comparative safety of the desert wilderness because there are no giants out there. No, there are no grapes out there either, but that's where most folks are living. They are failing to possess their possessions because they have a grasshopper complex. Thank God that Caleb didn't follow the majority. Caleb overcame grasshoppers before he overcame giants.

## Courage to Overcome Giants

It's one thing to face grasshoppers, but God also wants us to overcome giants.

**Joshua 14:12** | "Now give me this hill country of which the Lord spoke on that day, for you heard on that day how the Anakim were there, with great fortified cities. It may be that the Lord will be with me, and I shall drive them out just as the Lord said."

If you get up high enough and you look down, even the most giant of things look pretty small. Now, what are Anakims? That's not something you take for a headache, like an advanced Advil or Aspirin. No these giants would give you headaches. The dreadful Anakim with "great fortified cities" (14:12). The Anakims were giants. There were giants in those days. I mean, great, huge giants. Caleb said, "I shall drive them out just as the Lord said."

Not only did Caleb have to face the grasshoppers, Caleb had to face the giants. And, oh there are some giants. But, Caleb wasn't bothered by those giants. As a matter of fact, he was kind of excited they were there. Do you know what Caleb said he first saw those giants for the first time in Numbers 14, so many decades earlier when he was just 40 years old?

If the Lord delights in us, he will bring us into this land and give it to us, a land that flows with milk and honey. ⁹ Only do not rebel against the Lord. And do not fear the people of the land, for they are bread for us. Their protection is removed from them, and the Lord is with us; do not fear them. —Numbers 14:8-9

Did you hear that? They are bread for us. We are going to eat them for lunch. What Caleb says, "We're going to eat them alive. They are bread for us. Their protection is removed." Do you know what bread is? Bread is something you eat to strengthen you and to enlarge you. Caleb said, "These giants will not be the means of our defeat, they will be the means of our growth. We're going to feed upon them."

Do you know what God has to say to us? "Now, dear, eat your Anakim. Eat your Anakim." "I don't want to fight any giants." "Go ahead, it's good for you." "No, I'd just rather not." "Go ahead and eat them." I want to tell you, dear friend, Anakim is the breakfast of champions. Whatever sin comes against you, yield to the Lord, and you will have victory for breakfast, lunch and dinner.

### A Winning Perspective

Be willing to face the giants. We are all seated in the heavenlies with Jesus. That means we are moving forward from the place of highest victory. The heavenlies is another way of saying, where Jesus' throne is. I'm already fighting from a position of total victory and annihilation. Jesus hasn't just won a little: he's won it all, entirely. It is finished. The battle's over. The war is won!

Look, you've been trying to get out of difficulty. You've been saying, "I don't want to face any problems. I don't want any difficulty." Don't you know that the difficulties that God gives you are the very things that will make you strong? They are bread. Sit down. Gobble them up. Listen to Isaiah.

No weapon that is formed against you will prosper. —Isaiah 54:17

These are not difficulties to paralyze you, but opportunities to grow you. I heard about a man who went to Africa as a shoe salesman. He stayed over there a while and wired his company back, he said, "Get me out of here." They said, "Why?" He said, "The people over here don't wear shoes." So, they brought him home and sent another man. He stayed there a few weeks and he wrote back and he said, "Send me all the shoes you can get, I've never seen so many prospects."

You need to look at a giant from God's viewpoint. You need to stop saying, "Look how much bigger he is than I am." You need to start saying, "Look how much smaller he is than God is." We are seated with Jesus in the Heavenlies. We need to see the opposition from his viewpoint.

Greater is he that is in you, than he that is in the world. —1 John 4:4

And, there is not a giant of doubt, and a giant of distress, and a giant of fear, and a giant of sin that should not fall before a Christian filled with the Holy Spirit. We are to be living victoriously. We are to have the Word of God in our heart and we are to believe God for victory. We need to say, "I want that mountain. It belongs to me." You get that victory of perfect peace and joy in Christ.

## Courage to Overcome Grey Hairs

There was something else Caleb needed courage to overcome: his own grey hairs! Listen to Caleb in

**Joshua 14:10-11a** | And now, behold, the Lord has kept me alive, just as he said, these forty-five years since the time that the Lord spoke this word to Moses, while Israel walked in the wilderness. And now, behold, I am this day eighty-five years old. [11] I am still as strong today as I was in the day that Moses sent me...

Caleb says: I'm as strong now as I was when I was forty years old. Listen Caleb knew the ultimate statistic: 10 out of 10 people die. But he also knew that "the joy of the Lord" was his strength. God supernaturally preserved him. Now we ought never retire; we just retread. There may be a new ministry, a new calling, but there is never an end to your calling. God has called each one of us to a particular calling. You serve God in that calling. And when grey hairs come, you get excited. This is the most productive and fruitful time of your life. Our goal as Christians is not to retire and pick up seashells. How sad. We are called to make disciples. We are called to slay giants. Caleb was an 85-year-old giant slayer! Hallelujah!

## ENJOYMENT OF CONQUEST (14:12-15; 15:14)

There is great joy in the victorious Christian life. Our lives should not be all over the place, based on our trials, our circumstances, or our problems. Whether you are in a prison or in a palace, Jesus is King and Savior, and that should be enough for true contentment and happiness. What does this kind of joy in conquest look like? Let's get Caleb's vantage point here in Joshua 14 and 15.

## The Mountain's Fellowship

This hill country was the land of Hebron, which means "fellow-ship". This was not merely a physical inheritance, but a place where Caleb would walk in fellowship with God. Victory is God's plan for you. Do you know what the name Hebron means? It means "fellowship." That's what it means. And Caleb is saying, "I want that mountain called 'fellowship with God.'" Everything good comes out of your fellowship with God.

> What we have seen and heard we proclaim to you also, so that you too may have fellowship with us; and indeed our fellowship is with the Father, and with His Son Jesus Christ. [4] And these things we write to you that your joy may be full. —1 John 1:3-4

The followers of Jesus knew that true happiness could only come from constant fellowship with God.

## The Mountain's Fruitfulness

This was a land flowing with milk and honey, a place of rich fruit-fulness. Caleb had waited for this satisfaction and sustenance. But he had to enter in and claim it for his own. Here were grapes from the vineyards that took a group of men to carry them out. Isn't that where you want to live? Wouldn't you like to live on the mountaintop of fel-lowship with God? Wouldn't you like for your life to be like a vineyard full of fruitfulness?

Is your life fruitful? Look at your family around you. Are you reaching them, discipling them? Look at your co-workers. Look at your connections and friends. Are you bearing fruit? We are to bear fruit both personally and externally: in myself and in others. Do you have fruit in your own life? Jesus tells us how to bear fruit in John 15.

> I am the true vine, and my Father is the vinedresser. [2] Every branch in me that does not bear fruit he takes away, and every branch that does bear fruit he prunes, that it may bear more fruit. [3] Already you are clean because of the word that I have spoken to you. [4] Abide in me, and I in you. As the branch cannot bear fruit by itself, unless it abides in the vine, neither can you, unless you abide in me. [5] I am the vine; you are the branches. Whoever abides in me and I in him, he it is that bears much fruit, for apart from me you can do nothing. —John 15:1-5

In your heart, you have to constantly be putting off idols by living fruitfulness of a life connected and plugged in to Christ. Do you want the fruit of peace and joy and righteousness to affect your heart and the lives of others? Start bearing fruit. For some of you that means you need to take a step into a serious discipleship relationship where there is almost serious weekly encouragement and accountability. For a lot of you, fruit means you need to be that disciple maker. For all of us, that means we need to be connected and plugged in to our Vine!

## The Mountain's Fullness

Caleb was not experiencing the fullness of the mountain because of the Anakim, the giants. Do you know Caleb took the whole hill country of Hebron? Do you know what that stands for? Fullness. All that God had for him. That meant Caleb had no fear going against the giants in the land. We read about it in Joshua 15.

> According to the commandment of the Lord to Joshua, he gave to Caleb the son of Jephunneh a portion among the people of Judah, Kiriath-arba, that is, Hebron (Arba was the father of Anak). [14] And Caleb drove out from there the three sons of Anak, Sheshai and Ahiman and Talmai, the descendants of Anak. —Joshua 15:13-14

Arba was the father of the land of the giants. Caleb wasn't afraid of the Anakim. Caleb was willing to cast out the giants in the land. He wouldn't settle to live with them. He wanted them completely defeated, because he wanted the fullness of the land and the fullness of God. He wanted to fellowship with God in the hill country of the land of fellowship: Hebron. We must cast down every idol, cast out every foe if we are to have the fullness of the Spirit. The Spirit, and nothing else, must have full control.

> Do not get drunk with wine, for that is debauchery, but be filled with the Spirit. —Ephesians 5:18

This fullness is for believers. You must surrender all idols, all enemies of the soul, and be under the control of the Holy Spirit. You must want nothing less than the fullness of the Spirit. You must want nothing less than full surrender. The South African Pastor of the 1800s, Andrew Murray said it so clearly:

> We cannot be filled with the Spirit until we are prepared to yield ourselves to be led by the Lord Jesus—to forsake and sacrifice everything for this pearl of great price.

Here is another quote by Murray.

Why should a Christian be called upon always to deny himself, his
own feeling, and will, and pleasure? Why must he part with his life—
that life to maintain which a man is prepared to make any sacrifice?
Why should a man hate and lose his life? The answer is very simple. It
is because that life is so completely under the power of sin and death
that it has to be utterly denied and sacrificed. The self-life must be
wholly taken away to make room for the life of God. He that would
have the full, the overflowing life of God, must utterly deny and lose
his own life.[94]

Surrender your reputation, and you will be free from the praise of
man. Surrender what anyone thinks of you. You have to do that.

Surrender your peace and comfort and security based on circumstances. Stop fighting for that. Stop loving the world. You need to rest
in the peace and security you already have in Christ's kingdom.

Surrender your lust for more and more and more in possessions.
You don't need to buy another thing to be happy. Surrender those pur-
chases that will never make you happy and be content with the infinite
riches you have in Christ.

Surrender your need for pleasure and find that all pleasure flows
from the fountain of Christ, and until you have Christ ruling, you really
cannot truly enjoy anything.

Surrender your need to have power and be in control. Put off anger
and put on that meek and gentle spirit of Jesus. Learn to solve problems in kindness and not in hatred and anger, which is the spirit of
murder and destruction. Be kind and lay yourself down for others while
you solve problems.

Surrender all to Jesus, and he will give you "all the fullness of God"
and the "fullness of the Spirit." You will not lack anything.

Jesus said, "whoever drinks the water I give them will never thirst.
Indeed, the water I give them will become in them a spring of water
welling up to eternal life." —John 4:14

### Conclusion

Are you ready to stop being wilderness dwellers and start being
mountain climbers? I want that mountain called *Fellowship with God*.
Whatever you need to do to get that fountain is worth it. Whatever God
is asking you to forsake is 10,000 times worth it. Don't stop. Be like

---

[94] Andrew Murray. *Experiencing the Holy Spirit* (New York: Start Publishing,
2015), Kindle Locations 713-717.

Jacob and wrestle with God, and say, "I won't let you go until you bless me" (Gen 32:16). You take the Lord up on his promises. You say, "Lord, give me this mountain."

# 16 | JOSHUA 15-19
## MAXIMUM LIVING

*So Joshua said to the people of Israel, "How long will you*
*put off going in to take possession of the land, which the*
*Lord, the God of your fathers, has given you?"*
JOSHUA 18:3

Joshua records the distribution of the land of Israel. Let me mention that these are some of the most skipped chapters in the Bible. They are often forgotten. But we believe that the entire Bible, every word, is profitable for our growth. And there is an amazing lesson here. As we see all this land and all these details, we should remember something. God cares about details. Here we see a very important lesson: the kind of detailed concern that God has for his people, so detailed, where you're going to put the boundary line, and what family is going to inhabit this portion of land, down to the individuals named. God is concerned about everything. The Bible says:

God will perfect that which concerns me. —Psalm 138:8

All of those little details of your life that you think, "Oh, they're not important, it's just a little private, personal matter," God wants to stick his nose in. He wants to be the Lord of that. "Oh, I shouldn't pray about this. This is so insignificant. God is so big. He's running the universe making that thing spin on its axis. I couldn't bring this before him." Bring it before him. It's these kinds of chapters that bring out that kind of a lesson, the detailed concern that God has. David framed it beautifully when in Psalm 8, no doubt he was thinking of his shepherd days, as he looked up in the heavens and began to praise the Lord.

When I consider the heavens, the work of your hands, the moon and the stars, which you have ordained, what is man that you are mindful of him or the son of man that you visit him? —Psalm 8:3

That's a good perspective. It really goes along with the details in Joshua. God cares about every river, every mountain, but most of all God cares about every soul in Israel. David wrote about this in Psalm 8. The God of this great big universe cares about you. The one who flung the stars into space cares about every detail in your life. He's never anything but near you. He is not far away from any one of us. You may be distracted from God, but God is never distracted from you. Think of the magnitude of God's love for you. For me, it always helps sometimes to just walk outside and look up and think how small I am and how big God's creation is.

The earth is traveling at 45,000 MPH in orbit and spinning at 1,000 MPH on its axis. I am one of 7.6 billion other little people that inhabit this earth that's traveling in orbit at 45,000 miles per hour. Not only that, the earth is spinning on its axis at a thousand miles per hour. And then this earth itself is pretty small when you think of the universe that it's in. If you were to consider the sun, the sun is 93 million miles away from the earth and yet the energy that it exerts that we can feel 93 million miles away is pretty significant.

The sun is 860,000 miles in diameter. And if you were to put it in perspective, you could put 1,200,000 spheres the size of this earth inside of it. That's just the nearest star. There are other stars and there are other galaxies beyond that. And so the real question of David is, "In lieu of the fact we have such a grand universe, why would you think so intimately about us, so detailed about me?" Yet God does think of me. God is concerned, even down to how he thinks about you and me.

I know the thoughts that I think toward you, says the Lord, thoughts of good not of evil, to give you a future and a hope. — Jeremiah 29:11

And then Psalm 139, as David thinks about the majesty of God and praises him.

How precious to me are your thoughts, O God! How vast is the sum of them! [18] If I would count them, they are more than the sand. — Psalm 139:17-18

God wants your whole heart. That's what these chapters about the division of the land are all about. How God cares about us, everything about us. He cared about every detail of the land, because his is where Israel would serve God and worship him. Now this is the giving of the land to each of the tribes of Israel. It should be a record of celebration and worship. Sadly, it is a record mostly of compromise and worldliness of heart.

These chapters are the exact measurements of God's promise to Abraham in Genesis 12 and 15. These chapters record one of the greatest truths in the Bible: God keeps his promises. God wants to establish worship in the hearts of his people and in the land he gave them. But Israel fails, and sets themselves up for terrible failure. We see the warning signs. They all have to do with not coming to a place of full worship with God. What is it that keeps us from maximum worship?

The key thought for this section of Scripture is: The only way to enjoy life to its fullest is to be satisfied in God completely, forsaking all idols and defeating all enemies for his glory and your happiness.

Be careful not to have a worldly heart. Most of the tribes settled into the land thinking the land itself was the goal: the promised land, flowing with milk and honey. They were dead wrong. Since their goal was the land, they were worldly. No one can be satisfied by seeking what is on earth. If you seek the world, your heart will be small. If you seek the Lord, your heart will be big. Remember the warning from the apostle John:

Do not love the world or the things in the world. If anyone loves the world, the love of the Father is not in him. [16] For all that is in the world—the desires of the flesh and the desires of the eyes and pride of life—is not from the Father but is from the world. [17] And the world is passing away along with its desires, but whoever does the will of God abides forever. —1 John 2:15-17

## A Dangerous Pattern

We see a dangerous pattern. Israel loved the land too much. They had an incomplete obedience that eventually caught up with them. At first, they left some Canaanites. Then we see, they marry Canaanite women in Judges 1. Their paganism infected their hearts and grew like a cancer until there was a civil war, a divided kingdom, and eventually, they lost the land entirely. How sad it is to have a worldly heart. They could have enjoyed the land so much more had they had a heart for God.

The goal for Israel should have been worship. If you have any lesser goal in your life than the pure worship of the Almighty triune God, you will compromise with the world, and you will be miserable. This short history of the allotment of land to Israel, as well as the story of the book of Judges, proves that this is true. God is seeking worshippers to worship him in Spirit and in truth. Without worship, you are preparing yourself for misery. The children of Israel will teach us this this in our passage. They had a worldly heart. Do you? Consider the comparison of a worldly heart and a godly heart.

**WORLDLY HEART**
temporary peace
treasures
pleasures
man pleasing

**GODLY HEART**
heavenly peace
heavenly treasure
pleasure in God
God pleasing

## A WORLDLY HEART (15-19)

I want to show you three marks of worldliness that will keep you from the rich worship you so desire with the Lord: temporary peace, earthly security, and earthly ease. Some believers, they just want temporary peace instead of lasting obedience. They want earthly security. They give up everything, because they settle for compromising with the enemy. They are weary and just want peace. We can't settle for temporary peace. Our peace does not come from this world, but from God who never changes. Our joy and peace for maximum living comes from him alone. Don't have a worldly heart and seek your peace from things that can be shaken.

## Beware of Temporary Peace

Chapter 15 is the story of Judah. What an amazing tribe. Jesus comes from this tribe. This is a tribe that should be the location for worship. Part of Jerusalem is in Judah. But instead there is a compromise for temporary peace. Go along to get along. Temporary peace brings far more conflict in the long run.

The worldly heart loves temporary peace. It's too much work to really have real peace in the home. It's too much work to really do the hard work for peace, so instead I will isolate, I will cut people off. And so you do. Some of you cut off your spouse a long time ago. You are still married, but you don't have the peace of the Holy Spirit in your home. You won't do the hard work to get those Philistines out of your marriage, or out of your church, or out of your work relationships.

### Temporary Peace Brings Far More Conflict

We read about the Philistines in Joshua 15:33-60. And what we find is that making temporary peace brings far more conflict in the end to Israel. The Philistines live in the lowlands of Israel by the Mediterranean Sea. This is where they take root build a nation that is perpetually a thorn in the side of Israel. But because they want temporary peace, they leave some of these the Philistines (Ashdod, Gath, Gaza) in the land. And instead of worship, the tribe of Judah is unwilling to fight against the Philistines. Sadly, they leave some of the Jebusites in Jerusalem.

**Joshua 15:63** | But the Jebusites, the inhabitants of Jerusalem, the people of Judah could not drive out, so the Jebusites dwell with the people of Judah at Jerusalem to this day.

No big deal, right? Wrong! It's a big deal, because they Philistines and Jebusites come back and oppose Israel all during the time of the Judges. It's not until the time of King David that we see any sort of victory. Temporary peace today means misery for many days! Temporary peace gives the illusion that everything is ok when it is not. If you don't deal with problems in gentleness today, your bitterness will come to get you tomorrow.

As believers, we need to be willing to face conflict, not run from it. If you let bitterness dwell in your heart and you are ok with this temporary peace without really dealing with your love for yourself, your love for temporary peace more than real, heavenly peace and unity, you are walking in the flesh. Facing conflict with anger or irritation doesn't work. We face conflict with love and tenderness and kindness. But we can never, never find lasting peace if we refuse to deal with sin in our lives. Some of you have personal conflict in your life, and you are not really dealing with it. You are moving on without really getting things right. You are letting the Philistines live in your life and in your home!

If you leave the Philistine of fear or the Jebusite of anger in your home, and you just move on without really getting rid of these Canaanites, you set yourself up for future enslavement. If you put a band aid on cancer, it will come back bigger and more destructive in the future. On the other hand, we see someone in Joshua 15:16-19 that wasn't willing to compromise for temporary peace.

### Caleb Not Willing to Compromise

Caleb is from Judah which will eventually be the national location of worship for Israel. Farther south, we find the place that Caleb conquered. Hebron, Caleb's home is here, the mountain of fellowship. Caleb is from the tribe of Judah. Judah's allotment should go from the Dead Sea to the Mediterranean Sea. Caleb was to conquer the heartland of Israel between the Dead Sea and the Mediterranean Sea. And he does. He will not make temporary peace. He's willing to truly give all and sacrifice all. He's willing to give his daughter in marriage to the one who helps him conquer Hebron and the hill country.

**Joshua 15:16-19** | And Caleb said, "Whoever strikes Kiriath-sepher and captures it, to him will I give Achsah my daughter as wife." [17] And Othniel the son of Kenaz, the brother of Caleb, captured it. And he gave him Achsah his daughter as wife. [18] When she came to him, she urged him to ask her father for a field. And she got off her donkey, and Caleb said to her, "What do you want?" [19] She said to him, "Give me a blessing. Since you have given me the land of the Negeb, give me also springs of water." And he gave her the upper springs and the lower springs.

So Othniel wins Caleb's daughter Achsah (AK-sah) and becomes Israel's first judge after Joshua (Judges 1-3). He rules in Israel for 40 years, teaches Israel's next generation to war and worship, and brings peace for 40 years. There are some really powerful victories.

But not everyone is willing to sacrifice, and they leave off fighting the Jebusites and the Philistines in order to gain temporary peace. They give up Ashdod and Gath and Gaza to the Philistines. They want instant gratification. They tax the Philistines. No big deal, right? But yes, disobedience is a big deal. These are two groups, as I said, that later give David big problems. He has to deal with them later.

Now are you Christian willing to stop worshipping at the altar of temporary peace? You know things are not right. They are not dealt with. But you go on as if they are. God wants your heart to be a place of worship, but you have allowed the Philistines and Jebusites to live there. These are two of the most important places in Israel, but instead of worship there is weariness, bitterness, and fear. You haven't made things right. There's just this temporary peace. Perhaps it's a family member, or a spouse, or a child, and you are subjecting them to the Philistines of bitterness. Don't let these enemies dwell in your heart. They will torment you. They will keep you from worship.

## Beware of Earthly Security

In these chapters (Joshua 16-17) you have the allotments for the sons of Joseph, Ephraim and Manasseh. We find these two tribes have money trouble. The desire for money makes them compromise their faith. They keep Canaanites alive and enslave them instead of driving them out of the land. They'd rather profit from them than drive them out.

**Joshua 17:13** | And it happened, when the children of Israel grew strong, that they put the Canaanites to forced labor, but did not utterly drive them out.

These Canaanites come back to destroy them later. All because of money and earthly security. Possessions and *treasures* can be an idol keep us from our ultimate treasure. Christ Himself is our ultimate treasure. All else pales in comparison to him (Phil 3:7–11). Money is another incredible idol that is set up among Ephraim and Manasseh long before they compromise and go into captivity. Some people really hold on to possessions for their idol. This will come to bite Ephraim and Manasseh later on.

Ephraim and Manasseh were the mighty sons of Joseph, the great Prime Minister of Egypt. Don't rely on your previous accomplishments. Keep gaining new ground. Instead Ephraim and Manasseh made a deal with the Canaanites who had chariots of iron. They wanted extra money. Their heart got choked by riches. The love of money can choke out your worship. Jesus says that riches and the cares of this world can choke out the seed of the Gospel.

> Other seed fell among thorns, and the thorns grew up and choked it, and it yielded no grain. —Mark 4:7

### Trusting in Earthly Security

Trusting in earthly security will hurt your worship. Now Shiloh (16:6) is mentioned here in the hill country of Ephraim. This is where the Tabernacle will dwell for 369 years until the Philistines burn it down.

**Joshua 16:6** | Then on the east the boundary turns around toward Taanath-shiloh...

Just a few verses down, we read about their compromise. Even though this is the place of worship for 369 years, they are going to learn to live with earthly security instead of real peace. Look down at Joshua 16:10.

**Joshua 16:10** | However, they did not drive out the Canaanites who lived in Gezer, so the Canaanites have lived in the midst of Ephraim to this day but have been made to do forced labor.

This choice not to drive them out will hurt Israel's worship. Ephraim and Manasseh let the Canaanites live and make a little extra money by enslaving them. They've got the Canaanites under control, right? That's what we always think. I've got a little extra money in my pocket. You think you've captured sin, but instead of you capturing sin, sin captures and enslaves you.

Are you compromising like Ephraim and Manasseh in your finances? They kept them alive to get some extra money. Is earthly security keeping you from serving God? Are you always thinking about money so that you can't do what you want to for God? Do you get angry about money? Do you get stressed about finances? That is idolatry. The love of money will enslave you and keep you from serving the Lord. Be careful of this idol!

There's a twist in our story. The tribes of Joseph (Manasseh and Ephraim) believe because they are such a powerful people with such a history of greatness, that they should have preferred treatment. They fall into the trap of pleasing man and pride. Don't fall into the trap of pleasing man and pride. Manasseh and Ephraim get comfortable with the giants and the Canaanites with chariots of iron.

**Joshua 17:14-16** | Then the people of Joseph spoke to Joshua, saying, "Why have you given me but one lot and one portion as an inheritance, although I am a numerous people, since all along the Lord has blessed me?" [15] And Joshua said to them, "If you are a numerous people, go up by yourselves to the forest, and there clear ground for yourselves in the land of the Perizzites and the Rephaim, since the hill country of Ephraim is too narrow for you." [16] The people of Joseph said, "The hill country is not enough for us. Yet all the Canaanites who dwell in the plain have chariots of iron, both those in Beth-shean and its villages and those in the Valley of Jezreel."

Joshua is holding these two tribes of Joseph accountable. Though they are complaining they have very little, they actually have two large sections both east and west of the Jordan River. So Joshua says: "But you have so much." And Ephraim and Manasseh say: "Well, it's just not enough. You see, we're a great people." I don't think they mean merely in terms of numbers, but also, "We're awesome. We're amazing. Remember our heritage? Joseph, our father, was the prime minister of Egypt. That speaks volumes, Joshua. We are somebody. We are important." They fall into the sin of pride and entitlement. "We really don't want to go up against those Canaanites with chariots of iron." They are resting on the accolades of the flesh instead of humbling themselves before God.

One of the most dangerous things for a Christian is to be supremely gifted, but to have no character. These sons of Joseph rested on the accolades of men. We have a heritage. We are the big wigs. We are the important people. We are gifted, and we deserve the easy land. They have no character. They want some easy street. Dear saints, you may be gifted, but you can't coast in the Christian life with gifting. You will fall if you don't have character. There are some who are gifted who will ask: "How come I don't have a bigger ministry? How come I'm not seen and I'm not in the limelight? I want more exposure." They have no character. But they have plenty of pride. They want the accolades of men, and they don't want to work hard.

## Humble Yourself with Hard Work

"Can we have the land without conquering the Canaanites?" Look at Joshua's answer, verse 17. No you can't just skip the hard work. You have to do the hard work of conquest. You will conquer. You can't rely on the pride and accomplishments of your father. You have to make way to destroy the giants and Canaanite GI Joes yourself. You have to learn to lean on God's power yourself.

**Joshua 17:17-18** | Then Joshua said to the house of Joseph, to Ephraim and Manasseh, "You are a numerous people and have great power. You shall not have one allotment only, **¹⁸** but the hill country shall be yours, for though it is a forest, you shall clear it and possess it to its farthest borders. For you shall drive out the Canaanites, though they have chariots of iron, and though they are strong."

If they have some humility, the Lord will lift them up over the Canaanites.

Humble yourselves before the Lord, and he will exalt you. —James 4:10

He said in verse 15, since you are so great, you go and clear the land of the Perizzites and the Rephaim, i.e. the giants. Since you are so great and numerous, go after the giants and the Canaanites with chariots of iron. They had the land, but they hadn't taken title of it. They hadn't moved in on it yet. Why? Because this is spiritual inertia: "We just want to go so far. It's easier to settle here. It's a little harder to go up to the mountains." They didn't like giants and the GI Joes. They didn't like the chariots of iron.

## Beware of Earthly Ease

Are you living for earthly ease? Are you living for the pleasure of the moment? God wants us to get rid of the Canaanites in the land so that we can enjoy him and have a life of maximum living. One of these Canaanites is earthly ease.

**Joshua 18:2-4** | There remained among the people of Israel seven tribes whose inheritance had not yet been apportioned. ³ So Joshua said to the people of Israel, "How long will you put off going in to take possession of the land, which the Lord, the God of your fathers, has given you? ⁴ Provide three men from each tribe, and I will send them out that they may set out and go up and down the land.

Seven tribes were waiting to go and take possession of the land. They shouldn't have been waiting. There is a time to wait, and there is a time to obey. Sometimes we settle for less and sometimes we settle for that average, dull, kind of living, when God wants rivers of living water" to come from us. Jesus said, "Out of his innermost being will flow rivers of living water." There's a spiritual inheritance to be had for the church.

### The Danites and Leshem

Here is another illustration of the idol of ease and pleasure. The men of Dan couldn't conquer the land they were assigned, so they end up compromising for more lush land. The land of Dan was in the south. They were to conquer the land that is in Philistine territory as well. But it was too much for them.

**Joshua 19:47** | When the territory of the people of Dan was lost to them, the people of Dan went up and fought against Leshem, and after capturing it and striking it with the sword they took possession of it and settled in it, calling Leshem, Dan, after the name of Dan their ancestor.

Here we read about Dan who doesn't want to fight with the Philistines in Ekron. Dan has a portion of land a little bit on the sea, but it's down south between the tribe of Benjamin and the Mediterranean Sea. This is Philistine country in the Old Testament. As soon as this tribe settled in and Dan was putting down its roots and building its towns, the Philistines and the Amorites came and attacked them so repeatedly.

Judges and Samson the Danite. Well, look at the book of Judges sometime with Samson, Samson was a Danite from the tribe of Dan, and all the conflict that Samson and the children of Israel had with the Philistines. Goliath was the big Philistine, he was a giant. The pressure became so great that eventually the tribe of Dan migrated north to the very tip of Israel to a city called Leshem. The tribe of Dan chose to migrate to the very same beautiful city state called Leshem, and it's still there today. They got comfortable. And if you've been to Israel, there is a place called Tel Dan where the tribe of Dan migrated and there are altars up there.

The ruins of the ancient city of Leshem, which was the town that Abraham came to when he came to the land, is still there. In fact, there is the gate made of mud bricks, that dates from before the time of Abraham.

Now Laish was renamed "The city of Dan". Why is this important? They didn't want the land they were assigned, so they when up north among the trees and rivers. This is really some of the best land in Israel. So much water and trees! But later, this became the very site for golden calf worship. What's the point? If you choose to not deal with your sin and live for worldly ease, you are living for idols. Now the idols weren't there right away, but very soon, this became a place of terrible idol worship. If you want to have a life of maximum living for the Lord, you have to put off earthly ease and embrace suffering. You have to learn to get your joy from the Lord, not from earthly ease.

> If anyone would come after me, let him deny himself and take up his cross and follow me. [25] For whoever would save his life will lose it, but whoever loses his life for my sake will find it. —Matthew 16:24-25

Your maximum life is always in Jesus. It's not in earthly ease.

## THE GODLY HEART (19:49-51)

When they had made an end of the dividing of the land as an inheritance according to their borders, the children of Israel gave an inheritance among them to Joshua the son of Nun.

**Joshua 19:49-51** | When they had finished dividing the land into its allotted portions, the Israelites gave Joshua son of Nun an inheritance among them, [50] as the Lord had commanded. They gave him the town he asked for—Timnath Serah in the hill country of Ephraim. And he built up the town and settled there. [51] These are the territories that Eleazar the priest, Joshua son of Nun and the heads of the tribal clans of Israel assigned by lot at Shiloh in the presence of the Lord at the entrance to the tent of meeting. And so they finished dividing the land.

This is the place that Joshua got, a place called Timnath Serah. Joshua didn't ask for it first. He waited until everybody else got their inheritance.

## Put on Humility

Instead of saying, "Look here, I'm the general. I took over for Moses. I'm the big guy on the block. I get my inheritance first. Caleb got his; I get mine." No. He let everybody else go and at the very end he asked for his allotment. Joshua knew something in his heart that the New Testament apostles write about: humility.

> God opposes the proud but gives grace to the humble. —James 4:6

Without humility you cannot experience the fullness of God. God resists you. Joshua didn't need first dibs. He was last. What a beautiful display of trust in God.

## Put on Simplicity

There was something else about Joshua. He wasn't seeking his happiness from the land. This world was not his home. He chose the place that is most simple and rugged. Joshua knew his citizenship wasn't on earth. This land wasn't all there was.

> Our citizenship is in heaven, and from it we await a Savior, the Lord Jesus Christ. —Philippians 3:20

The place that he asked for, Timnath Serah, is a dive. It's rugged. It's mountainous. It's infertile. It's barren. Hardly anything grows there. And you look at it and you wonder, "Why would anyone want this?" It reminds me of Abraham and Lot. And Abram said, "Hey, Lot, you take whatever you want, take the best of the land, and I'll take what's left over. I trust the Lord." And so Joshua let them have the best and he didn't get, you know, a nice beach villa down by the Mediterranean. If we are going to serve God, we have to give up the idea of having the best of everything in this life. We need to trust that God is sovereignly guiding our lives to change our hearts, not make us comfortable in this life. Let's be like Jesus. Remember what he said?

> Foxes have holes, and birds of the air have nests, but the Son of Man has nowhere to lay his head. —Luke 9:58

Jesus left the security of heaven and dwelt on this earth in simplicity. Joshua had the same mentality.

## Put on Service

Joshua didn't serve himself. He served others. The life of maximum living is one of serving others.

The Son of Man came not to be served but to serve, and to give his life as a ransom for many. —Matthew 20:28

Joshua knew this. He didn't serve himself. He didn't get the beautiful highlands of the northern Galilee. He got this barren, desert, rocky, rugged place and he was a builder. One of the last glimpses we get of Joshua is this guy who takes the backseat. It reveals a lot about his character. It also reveals a lot about their character, the children of Israel, that they would say, "Yeah, great, you take the trashy parts, we just want the good parts." Jesus was like this. When his disciples were fighting about having the best place in the kingdom, Jesus got his towel out, put on a slave's garment, and he started washing their feet. This is the way of maturity. Are you willing to serve others?

## Put on Devotion

Joshua did it all at Shiloh. That tells you about his heart. He has a heart of rich worship. It's not about the land. It's about the Lord. In everything Joshua worshipped and glorified the Lord.

Whether you eat or drink or whatever you do, do it all for the glory of God. —1 Corinthians 10:31

Everything you do is an act of worship for the Lord. Nothing on this earth can make you happy. One of the church fathers expressed the Lord as the only one who could satisfy the human soul.

Thou hast made us for thyself, O Lord, and our heart is restless until it finds its rest in thee. —Augustine of Hippo, Pastor in North Africa

### Conclusion

Maximum living is not only possible. You already have all that you need to live this life. You have the inheritance. You are seated in the heavenlies with all the power of Christ. You have the glory cloud, the Holy Spirit living in you. God will fight for you. You can have the peace that is only from heaven, the pleasure that is only from heaven. You can have the fullness of joy. But you have to forsake all and rely only on Christ. Have you found your rest only in Christ?

# 17 | JOSHUA 20
## CHRIST OUR REFUGE

*These were the cities designated for all the people of Israel
and for the stranger sojourning among them, that anyone
who killed a person without intent could flee there, so that
he might not die by the hand of the avenger of blood, till he
stood before the congregation.*

JOSHUA 20:9

We're going to be in the Old Testament, but we're going to be talking about Jesus, our Lord and Savior. One of the things I've learned about the Bible is all of the Bible is about Jesus. Sometimes people say, "Have you read the four gospels?" Dear saint, I've read all sixty-six of the gospels. Every book in the Bible is all about the Lord Jesus Christ. Jesus is the hero of the Bible. Salvation is the theme of the Bible. And since Jesus is the hero of the Scriptures, we find Jesus standing somewhere in the shadows in all of the Old Testament if we study it carefully and look at it. Every page, every chapter, points to Jesus. So God has tucked away so many illustrations that point to Jesus in the Old Testament. Here we find Jesus in the cities of refuge in Joshua 20. Our key thought for this chapter is this: Only in Jesus can we find our perfect refuge, true happiness and a perfect government to guide our lives.

Today a lot of people are divided in our country, but the people of God do not need to be discouraged. We serve a God that has already set up a perfect government in Jesus! Let's look at how we get that perfect government in our own lives in Joshua 20. We find Jesus is our place of refuge.

**Joshua 20:1-3** | Then the Lord said to Joshua, [2] "Say to the people of Israel, 'Appoint the cities of refuge, of which I spoke to you through Moses, [3] that the manslayer who strikes any person without intent or unknowingly may flee there. They shall be for you a refuge from the avenger of blood.

Now what is this talking about? In Bible times, they did not have the court system that we have today. If a man were guilty of intentional manslaughter, or he was careless, or even somehow felt that what he did in killing another was justified in self-defense, there were cities of refuge. The cities of refuge were six cities allocated to the Levite tribe in the Old Testament that provided asylum for perpetrators of unintentional manslaughter. Divinely appointed and subject to Mosaic Law, the cities offered offenders refuge and protection from retribution of the avenging family until their case went to trial (cf Num 35:9–34; Deut 4:41–43; 19:1–13). The town must guarantee protection for the person who is found not guilty of murder, but if the person wanders from the town he may be killed by the avenger of blood.[95] This avenger, or redeemer of blood, was "a near relative of the slain person charged with maintaining family rights, might."[96]

The Levites were the mediators, or the highest-ranking judges in the land, in these cities. So the Levites established and maintained these cities. But they also presided as the judicial authorities over them. They taught the law of God, and they also adjudicated them (Deut 33:10). These are cities of protection, where justice can be carried out carefully, without vengeance. God appointed these six cities of refuge. We're going to say more about that in a moment, but just remember this: Jesus Christ is our city of refuge.

## THE SAVING NATURE OF THESE CITIES (20:1-6)

As we look at this passage, Jesus is unmistakable.

---

[95] Hess. *Joshua*, 305.
[96] Davis. *Joshua*, 148.

**Joshua 20:4-6** | He shall flee to one of these cities and shall stand at the entrance of the gate of the city and explain his case to the elders of that city. Then they shall take him into the city and give him a place, and he shall remain with them. **5** And if the avenger of blood pursues him, they shall not give up the manslayer into his hand, because he struck his neighbor unknowingly, and did not hate him in the past. **6** And he shall remain in that city until he has stood before the congregation for judgment, until the death of him who is high priest at the time. Then the manslayer may return to his own town and his own home, to the town from which he fled.

The passage teaches that the high priest's death is the only ransom for the manslayer, that the high priest's death, in some prophetic way, atones for the blood shed by the manslayer and satisfies the claims of justice. Only the high priest's death can release the offender from his banishment and bring him home again. What a remarkable picture of what our "merciful and faithful high priest" has done for us.[97] We see this language in the book of Hebrews a lot.

Christ is our "merciful and faithful high priest in the service of God, to make propitiation for the sins of the people." —Hebrews 2:17

None other than Jesus is our refuge. He's our safety, and we can flee to the Lord Jesus Christ for ultimate refuge from the wrath of God that we deserve. Jesus is our wrath-bearer. He is our justice satisfier. He's the propitiation for our sins.

We who have fled to him [Jesus] for refuge can have great confidence as we hold to the hope that lies before us. —Hebrews 6:18

Jesus is our refuge. We can delight in him. We can worship him.

The name of the LORD is a strong tower; the righteous man runs into it and is safe. —Proverbs 18:10

Those who find their refuge in Jesus will never be disappointed. Jesus is our city of refuge. We flee to him for refuge, for forgiveness. He is our propitiation.

---

[97] Ibid., 150.

## THE SIGNIFICANT NAMES OF THESE CITIES (20:7-8)

We see Jesus Christ even in the significant names of these cities. We read them here in verses 7-8.

**Joshua 20:7-8** | So they set apart Kedesh in Galilee in the hill country of Naphtali, and Shechem in the hill country of Ephraim, and Kiriath-arba (that is, Hebron) in the hill country of Judah. **8** And beyond the Jordan east of Jericho, they appointed Bezer in the wilderness on the tableland, from the tribe of Reuben, and Ramoth in Gilead, from the tribe of Gad, and Golan in Bashan, from the tribe of Manasseh.

In verses 7, 8, we are given the names of these cities. And the Holy Spirit has given us all Scripture by divine inspiration. The Holy Spirit of God has set out six names. So sweetly it is that the names of these six cities really describe the character of our Lord Jesus Christ.

### Kedesh: My Holy Place

In verse 7, you see "Kedesh in Galilee in the hill country of Naphtali." This is the land where the Lord Jesus would grow up, in Galilee. This is where he would have his ministry. The city "Kedesh" means "sanctuary" or "holiness." This city was representative of a place to flee that is a holy place. Every one of us need that holy place to flee to, and his name is Jesus. You see, Christ alone is our holiness. You can find cleansing and holiness in Jesus alone! Any real righteousness cannot come from ourselves, but through Jesus alone. Paul says:

> That I may "be found in him, not having a righteousness of my own that comes from the law, but that which comes through faith in Christ, the righteousness from God that depends on faith" —Philippians 3:8

We need a holiness, a righteousness that is not our own. That's why I flee to Christ. Christ is my city of refuge. He is my holy place. And when we go to him, our holiness is found in him because as you would be in the city of Kedesh, the city of holiness, you are in Christ, the place of holiness.

Christ was born of a virgin. He lived a holy life, a sinless life. He died a vicarious death. His death makes me holy. Holy means separated or dedicated to God. You can't make dirty clothes clean by washing dirty clothes in dirty water. We have a Savior who is absolutely, perfectly holy that has removed all our sin.

## Shechem: My Helpful Place

And then look at the next name in verse 7, "Shechem in the hill country of Ephraim." The word Shechem means "shoulder", and it has the idea of strength. Not only do we have in Christ a holy place, but we have a helpful place. You see, Christ is our strong Savior. Christ bears us upon his shoulder. You know over there in Isaiah 9:6, the Bible says what? The government shall be upon his shoulder.

> For to us a child is born, to us a son is given; and the government shall be upon his shoulder, and his name shall be called Wonderful Counselor, Mighty God, Everlasting Father, Prince of Peace. —Isaiah 9:6

You take over there in Luke 15 where the good shepherd went out after the sheep that was lost. And the Bible says when the good shepherd found that sheep, and I've always been blessed by this, he places it upon his shoulders.

> What man of you, having a hundred sheep, if he has lost one of them, does not leave the ninety-nine in the open country, and go after the one that is lost, until he finds it? [5] And when he has found it, he lays it on his shoulders, rejoicing. [6] And when he comes home, he calls together his friends and his neighbors, saying to them, 'Rejoice with me, for I have found my sheep that was lost.' —Luke 15:4-6

Now how did that sheep get home? That sheep did not come home on its own four legs. That sheep came home on two legs, the legs of the Savior. He put it on his shoulder. That's how I'm coming home. I'm going all the way to heaven on the shoulders of the Lord Jesus Christ because I have come into Christ, my city of refuge. I'm rejoicing that Christ carries me upon his shoulders. The government is upon Jesus' shoulders. He's the Head of his church. That's the government that ultimately matters.

Now I'm grieved, in the 2020 Presidential election, that we have 80 million people in our country that voted for an anti-God agenda. An agenda of baby murder. An agenda that is anti-family. An agenda that promotes that a 7-year-old can decide to change his gender. We are living in dark times. But let us understand that the solution is never government. Government is the fruit of our society; it is never where our hope lies. Our hope is in the Lord. The hope to change humanity is in the church of Jesus Christ. It's always been this way. Before God changes this country, he has to heal his church. We've had a legislative agenda of murdering babies since 1973 in this country. How can we be surprised that we are getting the government that we deserve? The way forward now is to pray for the government. Pray for the President, and what looks like the President Elect.

But let's get this straight. Our help never has come from human government. Our help comes from the Lord. We need a national revival in this land. We need people's hearts to get right with their Maker and Savior, Jesus Christ. The government that matters right now is the one who sets up kings and removes them. We are called to be responsible and pray for human government, but we are never called to trust in human government. My trust is in the Lord. Jesus is seated at the righthand of God, ruling and reigning. My eyes look to his Kingdom. Every knee will bow and every tongue confess that Jesus is Lord. I pray that we might run once again to the divine government of Jesus. Our trust and refuge is never human government. It is Jesus' government. And it's Jesus that will carry me home!

## Hebron: My Harmonious Place

The next city we find is "Kiriath-arba (that is, Hebron) in the hill country of Judah," and the word Hebron means "fellowship." This is a place of harmony, where I am called to real harmony and fellowship with God. When you come to the Lord Jesus Christ, you come to a place of "joy unspeakable and full of glory" in the Lord Jesus. That's the reason the apostle John said our fellowship and joy are connected.

> That which we have seen and heard we declare to you, that you also may have fellowship with us; and truly our fellowship *is* with the Father and with His Son Jesus Christ. [4] And these things we write to you that your joy may be full. —1 John 1:3-4

So many Christians have no real harmony and wholeness in their lives. Their lives are like a great big roller coaster. Their happiness is sometimes here and sometimes not. A lot of Christians are truly miserable a lot of days of their life, living in anxiety and anger a lot of the time. I have lived that way at times in my Christian life, I am sad to say. Now that I've discovered the abiding life, I'm not lonely anymore. I don't have to get irritated with any kind of mistreatment by people. The life of fellowship is one of rich friendship with the Lord. Do you have it? I can try to fill that lonely void with people. And don't get me wrong, people are a blessing. I want to be around people constantly. It's a joy. But I have found a better way: a place of harmony and peace that is never lacking. I have found a place where I am never lonely. I have found my Hebron. Jesus is my place of harmony and fellowship. He is the "friend of sinners". He is the "friend that sticks closer than a brother."

I am not taken aback by people's opinion and difficult events in my life. I have not founded my happiness on who's president or not. My joy is founded on my fellowship with Jesus. He loves me! He has prepared a place for me! When all of this world is shaken, then that which cannot be shaken will remain.

## Bezer: My Hiding Place

And then, look at the next one in verse 8, "Bezer in the wilderness on the tableland, from the tribe of Reuben." And the word Bezer means "stronghold." It means fortification. It's a place of security. The Lord Jesus is also my hiding place. He is my fortress. He is my security. You know, the Bible says,

> The name of the Lord is a high tower, and the, and the righteous run into it and are safe. —Proverbs 18:10

And there is a hiding place that keeps us safe until the storm passes over. Thank God that we can come to the Lord Jesus Christ in our Bezer and find that hiding place. Now Jesus is our hiding place. He's defeated our sin, our guilt, our shame.

> As far as the east is from the west, so far has he removed our transgressions from us. —Psalm 103:12

But let me be clear. Jesus is our refuge from the wrath of God. He's our refuge from our own sin, but we will suffer in this life. The assumption that God should give faithful believers a comfortable life, and certainly no more than one dose of sorrow, seems to be an American-made version of the Christian life that doesn't hold up to examination. And it certainly doesn't hold up to what we see in the lives of followers of Jesus in the Bible. We've mistakenly determined an appropriate and acceptable trajectory of the victorious Christian life, thinking if we declare our solid belief in Jesus, he somehow owes us a life of limited difficulty.[98] Don't be ashamed that you are weak. You need Jesus! He's your refuge!

> God is our refuge and strength, a very present help in trouble. [2] There-fore we will not fear though the earth gives way, though the moun-tains be moved into the heart of the sea, [3] though its waters roar and foam, though the mountains tremble at its swelling. *Selah* —Psalm 46:1-3

Selah! Think about it! Dive into it. Run to Christ your refuge. He is a very present help in trouble. That's why "we will not fear". His pres-ence is magnified greater than every fear. All fears disappear when Christ is near, and oh, he is nearer than ever, united to you, his beloved child.

## Ramoth: My High Place

And then look, if you will, at the name of the next city in verse 8: "Ramoth in Gilead, from the tribe of Gad." The name Ramoth means "exalted." It speaks of a lofty place; a place where I can run to in trouble, a place free from fear and frustration. Jesus is my high place. The Bible says:

> He makes my feet like the feet of deer and sets me on my high places. —Psalm 18:33 (NKJV)

When I came to know Jesus, I'm told in Ephesians that I'm seated with Christ in the most exalted place: in heavenly places—the realm of God.

> That you may know "what is the immeasurable greatness of his power toward us who believe, according to the working of his great might [20] that he worked in Christ when he raised him from the dead and seated him at his right hand in the heavenly places, [21] far above all rule and authority and power and dominion, and above every name that is named, not only in this age but also in the one to come. [22] And he put all things under his feet and gave him as head over all things to the church, [23] which is his body, the fullness of him who fills all in all." —Ephesians 1:19-23

No matter who is elected in our country, you want to know some-thing? God is going to use it to expand his kingdom. All authority and

---

[98] Nancy Guthrie. *Hearing Jesus Speak into Your Sorrow* (Carol Stream, IL: Tyndale House Publishers, Inc., 2009), 44.

power and dominion belong to Jesus, Name above all names! And he's controlling not only all things "in this age, but also in the age to come" for the expansion of his kingdom. Take heart dear saints. God is still on his throne in that high place. And you are united to him, where he is ruling and reigning! Listen, when Jesus gained the ultimate victory, there was only one vote that mattered: God the Father. And you know what God did when Jesus won the victory over sin, death, hell, Satan, and the grave? Let's see how God voted.

> Therefore God has highly exalted him and bestowed on him the name that is above every name, [10] so that at the name of Jesus every knee should bow, in heaven and on earth and under the earth, [11] and every tongue confess that Jesus Christ is Lord, to the glory of God the Father. —Philippians 2:9-11

Let's declare the victory today: we have a place of refuge, and it's in no political party; our refuge is in Jesus alone. He's won the victory. He is exalted above every politician, every candidate for office. All presidents and kings, senators and congressman. They will all bow their knees and confess with their tongues that Jesus Christ is Lord! To him alone be the glory and honor and dominion forever and ever and ever.

## Golan: My Happy Place

And then the last city of refuge named is in verse 8: "Golan in Bashan, from the tribe of Manasseh." And the word Golan means "a place of rejoicing."[99] And that speaks so much to me of the joy of the Lord.

> The joy of the Lord is your strength. —Nehemiah 8:10

The number one question I am asked in discipleship is: how do I get from knowledge of the Lord to real practice and experience of victory in my life? How do I put on meekness when I begin to experience anger? How do I put on forgiveness when I am hurt? I'll tell you: you've got to get over you. You've got to die to you. How do you do that? You have to experience the divine love and joy of God.

> The Lord is my strength and my shield; in him my heart trusts, and I am helped; my heart exults, and with my song I give thanks to him. — Psalm 28:7

---

[99] James Strong, *Enhanced Strong's Lexicon* (Woodside Bible Fellowship, 1995).

We've already said that Jesus is a harmonious place over there in Hebron. But here, again, He is a happy place. Why? Because we have this joy of being with him. Did you know that when we invite you to come to the Lord Jesus, we're not calling you to a funeral; it's actually a feast! The call to Christ is one to come out of a life of misery, and into a life of abundant joy. There is deep satisfaction in Christ, and in Christ alone. Regardless of the recklessness of our country, there is safety, security and satisfaction in Christ! There is clarity and not confusion in Christ.

The saddest day for God in the history of the world was the day when we as the human race grabbed hold of something outside of him in an attempt to find joy and satisfaction. We believed the lie that God was withholding something from us that would make us happy. And in our choice to seek satisfaction apart from him, a great cavern of separation came between us. No longer could we walk together with God without shame or pretense. No longer could we enjoy a life of fulfillment, free of frustration. We opened the door to sin that day, and confusion came rushing into every aspect of our existence, taking away our freedom and our unfettered enjoyment of God himself. Sin always poisons our happiness.[100] Fellowship with God is the exclusive place of true happiness and joy!

## THE STRATEGIC NEARNESS OF THESE CITIES (20:9)

These cities were to be places of refuge. People needed to be able to get to the city very quickly. I mean, if you're in danger, if somebody is coming after you to imprison you and to put you to death, you've got to have a hiding place, a place where you can find a friend, a holy place, and a high place.

**Joshua 20:9** | These were the cities designated for all the people of Israel and for the stranger sojourning among them, that anyone who killed a person without intent could flee there, so that he might not die by the hand of the avenger of blood, till he stood before the congregation.

### Near to Anyone

Notice, anyone and everyone should be able to go there. And it has to be near. You've got to have it in a hurry, and so these cities were put

---

[100] Guthrie. *Hearing Jesus Speak into Your Sorrow*, 29-30.

in the east and the west of the Jordan River. They were put in the south and up in the north. They were put in the center of the land of Israel so that it would be very near, no matter where you might be. Now that reminds us again of the Lord Jesus Christ, for the Bible proclaims the nearness of God to the person with a humble heart.

The LORD is near to all who call on him... —Psalm 145:18

If you look at this map of these six cities of refuge in Israel, you would find out how strategically near all of these cities were, because God in mercy wanted everybody to have an opportunity to come into the city of refuge. Now what does that tell me about the Lord Jesus Christ and you today?

## Nearer Than You Imagine

Suppose you're here today. You are guilty. You know you deserve punishment for your sin. The judgment that your sin requires is coming for you, and you need to come to the Lord Jesus Christ. Well, I've got wonderful news for you. Look at how near Christ is to you. Paul said:

God "made from one man every nation of mankind to live on all the face of the earth, having determined allotted periods and the bounda-ries of their dwelling place, [27] that they should seek God, and perhaps feel their way toward him and find him. Yet he is actually not far from each one of us, [28] for 'In him we live and move and have our being.'" — Acts 17:26-28

Turn to Christ. He is right there with you. He's not far from any one of us. In him we live and move and have our being. Turn to the one giving you breath right now. Turn to the one giving you the ability to move. Turn to the one giving you the ability to have your being and personality, sustaining your every movement. Turn to him dear sinner. You will not regret it.

## Near and Clear

The roads to these cities were always wide. Every obstruction was removed from these cities. If there were a river, there had to be a bridge over the river. The priests and elders would go out and inspect the roads and the bridges to make certain that the way was open. They would put signposts there: "This way—Refuge!" And there would be a sign pointing there. It was so clear. You couldn't miss it. Do you want to be saved today? It's not difficult to understand. Jesus is the only way.

I am the way, and the truth, and the life. No one comes to the Father except through me. —John 14:6

## So we get to God by Jesus. How does that work?

God made him who knew no sin to be sin for us, that we might become the righteousness of God in him. —2 Corinthians 5:21

So Jesus as our great High Priest gives you his perfect righteousness for your rags of sin. You get his robe of perfection, and he gets your robe of sin. You have to come by faith and repentance. Let me illustrate it. Spurgeon, a 19th century pastor in London, said, repentance and faith is like a man who lived in a dark room. He lived on a bed of snakes, but he had no idea they were snakes. They were perfectly comfortable to him for his whole life. But once the light came on, he could see the ugliness of the snakes. He could see how vile and dangerous they were. He ran out of the room in the broad and bright light, into the arms of Jesus. [101] That's faith. That's repentance. Turn from that life of sin and turn to Jesus.

### Conclusion

Suppose you were to see a house on fire, and in that house, you were to see a mother who has a little baby in a crib, and the flames are creeping closer and closer to that crib. But strangely, you see that mother down on her hands and knees, and her arms are full of box filled with computer tablets and jewelry, putting them in this box. And, you see her as she begins to take the curtains down off the wall, folding them, and putting them in the box. And the house is being engulfed in flames. Of course, you'd say, "She's mad. She's insane, because the most precious thing there is the baby."

For what is a man profited, if he shall gain the whole world, and lose his own soul? —Matthew 16:26

If you leave everything behind, you'll not regret it. Get the most important thing. Run to Christ as your refuge!

---

[101] Charles Haddon Spurgeon. *New Park Street Pulpit, Vol 2.* "Turn or Burn" preached December 7, 1856.

# 18 | JOSHUA 21
## PROMISE KEEPER

*And the Lord gave them rest on every side just as he had sworn to their fathers. Not one of all their enemies had withstood them, for the Lord had given all their enemies into their hands. Not one word of all the good promises that the Lord had made to the house of Israel had failed; all came to pass.*
JOSHUA 21:44-45

Confession time. I'm not always great in keeping my promises. I've made promises to Jill or my kids, and I mean to keep them. I do keep them most of the time. But sometimes I fail. The message of Joshua 21 is one of deep hope, because we are talking about God being our "promise keeper." Wow, he's faithful, isn't he? No one is like him. He promises so many things. God is a promise keeping God. What are some promises God has given us?

I will restore health to you, and your wounds I will heal, declares the Lord, because they have called you an outcast. —Jeremiah 30:17

Powerful! Right?

The Lord your God is in your midst, a mighty one who will save; he will rejoice over you with gladness; he will quiet you by his love. — Zephaniah 3:17

Or what about this one?

See, I have written your name on the palms of my hands. Always in my mind is a picture of Jerusalem's walls in ruins. —Isaiah 49:16

He feels our affliction. We are graven on his hands. Look at another amazing promise.

I will restore to you the years that the locust has eaten. —Joel 2:25

God is a good God, bursting with goodness! He's given you incredible promises.

I will put the fear of me in their hearts, that they may not turn from me. [41] I will rejoice in doing them good, and I will plant them in this land in faithfulness, with all my heart and all my soul. —Jeremiah 32:40-41

With all God's heart and soul, he rejoices in doing good to you child of God. So let's look at our key thought today. The key thought for this chapter is this: God is a good God, bursting with goodness and mercy to outcasts, lepers, sinners, and all those who are unclean. He wants to make us clean, and not only clean but holy, special, used for his glorious purposes.

You may be feeling despair, struggling with feeling at all worthy. You may feel like such a failure as a Christian. If you have ever felt blinded by your own despair, then this message is for you. The overall theme of Joshua 21 is that God knows we need help: massive help! We need the truth, but we need it given to us in love, a very gentle and compassionate way. I've not been good at that. I truly want you to pray that I can teach and preach with a divine love. You see, we are all weak and wounded sinners. We need Christ to gently hold us and care for us. That's why I love that the majority of Joshua 21 is about the cities for the Levites.

## 48 Cities of Priests (21:1-42)

In the first 42 verses of Joshua 21, we see something so vital and important: the Levitical cities.

**Joshua 21:1-3** | Then the heads of the fathers' houses of the Levites came to Eleazar the priest and to Joshua the son of Nun and to the heads of the fathers' houses of the tribes of the people of Israel. [2] And they said to them at Shiloh in the land of Canaan, "The Lord commanded through Moses that we be given cities to dwell in, along with their pasturelands for our livestock." [3] So by command of the Lord the people of Israel gave to the Levites the following cities and pasturelands out of their inheritance.

"By the command of the Lord" (21:3), the Levites were to scatter around Israel in 48 cities and minister to the people of Israel. The point we are going to see is that we desperately need God's help and encouragement. Priests are there to give encouragement and compassion to God's people. In Joshua 21:4-42, we have a list of 48 cities where the Levites were to live. They were scattered among all the people for a purpose. They were to pray for the people, teach them the practice of the Word and to fear and worship the Lord in all things. They are to carefully apply the Word of God to their lives, like Ezra.

The priests live in these cities. The tribe of Levi get no inheritance of land, but they get cities throughout Israel. Some notable Levites in the Bible include: Notable Levites: Moses, Aaron the high priest, Eli (the priest who raised the prophet Samuel), Ezra (the scribe who partnered with Nehemiah to resettle Jerusalem), and of course, John the Baptist.

Here's something important about the priests: they were never more than ten miles away from anybody living anywhere. They were to proclaim the excellencies of God to all the people. And that's what we are to be doing as well!

> But you are a chosen race, a royal priesthood, a holy nation, a people for his own possession, that you may proclaim the excellencies of him who called you out of darkness into his marvelous light. —1 Peter 2:9

The Levites are shadows of the New Testament Christian. This is a picture of our New Testament priesthood. We are to be discipling each other. We are to proclaim the excellencies of the beauty of God as infinitely superior to the idols and counterfeit pleasures and treasures of earth. The priests proclaimed the excellencies of God. That's what we do. And they had another important job: restoring people to God when they became unclean. Bringing them back to fellowship with the people and with God. So many Levitical laws were about clean and unclean, holy and unholy.

Here's another truth: we are all unclean, unfit, unacceptable. But God is making us clean, calling the outcast, calling us not just to be his guests, but his very own children. So let me repeat our key thought again: God is a good God, bursting with goodness and mercy to outcasts, lepers, sinners, and all those who are unclean. He keeps his promises to make us clean, holy, and special, fit (by his grace) for his glorious purposes.

So as priests to God, let's proclaim his excellencies. And that's exactly what our text does here in Joshua 21, the final verses 43-45. They are what we should be proclaiming as priests. Our God is a good God, a promise keeping God!

**Joshua 21:43-45** | Thus the Lord gave to Israel all the land that he swore to give to their fathers. And they took possession of it, and they settled there. **44** And the Lord gave them rest on every side just as he had sworn to their fathers. Not one of all their enemies had withstood them, for the Lord had given all their enemies into their hands. **45** Not one word of all the good promises that the Lord had made to the house of Israel had failed; all came to pass.

Here we see the beauty and generosity of God to undeserving sinners. How is God a promise keeper? He is generous. God refers to promises that he swore to keep.

## GOD IS GENEROUS (21:1-43A)

One thing you to understand is God is a generous God. One thing you to understand is: You are created to be a recipient of God's infinite generosity. In the biggest picture of the book, we see a word of promise and generosity the Lord gave Joshua back in chapter one.[102]

Be strong and courageous, for you shall cause this people to inherit the land that I swore to their fathers to give them. —Joshua 1:6

Now look at the glorious assertion of fulfillment of this very promise.

**Joshua 21:43a** | Thus the Lord gave to Israel all the land that he swore to give to their fathers.

---

[102] Jackman, *Joshua*, 166.

## Generous to Israel

God is a promise keeping God. He's so generous. He gives. That's his nature. He's bursting with goodness and generosity. God promised an inheritance to Abraham, Isaac, and Jacob: all of Canaan will be yours! Abraham or his offspring didn't get to experience the fullness of Canaan. It wasn't until the time of Joshua that they actually got to receive all the land of Israel. Isn't God good? Yet they wouldn't keep it very long. Quickly, they would lose it because, while God had given the land to them, they only took possession of it for a short amount of time.

## Generous to Us

The priests were to proclaim this to the rest of Israel, in the 48 strategically located cities. God is good! He's generous. He kept his promise. Let us as priests proclaim the goodness of the Lord. He has given you an abundant inheritance. You have abundant life! He is more than enough for your desires to be completely satisfied. So many of us, we can see our purpose, but we fail to see God's goodness, and that's why we cannot grow and change the way we would like. We see our purpose, but we cannot see God's beauty.

The point is not that God gave this amazing gift of land to Israel. They were given the land to gaze on the beauty of God. The purpose of the land was to have a place to enjoy God. And whenever they would get too focused on the land, and lose sight of God, they would turn to the land gods, the fertility gods, like Asherah and Baal and Chemoth. These were all the land fertility idols. And they would do just about anything to keep the land fertile, even giving the children in human sacrifice to the Baals and Chemoth gods. We'll see this in the book of Judges, the wicked influence of the surrounding nations upon them. But all they had to do was gaze on the beauty of God, and his goodness and generosity, and they would keep the land, their children, and all the blessings of God. Get ahold of the goodness of God. His goodness is not about his gifts and giving you a comfortable life. Actually, materialism and comfort will be your greatest temptations. You want abundant living? You will not find it in this world. You will find it in Christ alone.

> The thief comes only to steal and kill and destroy. I came that they may have **life and have it abundantly**. [11] I am the good shepherd. The good shepherd lays down his life for the sheep. —John 10:10-11

The god of this world wants you to build your happiness on false comfort: materialism or relationships or a comfortable life. You cannot build your happiness on that which can be quickly stripped away. That's building your house on the sand. Build your happiness on the Rock, Christ Jesus. He gives you the abundant life. Build your joy on his beauty. He is good, and you have everything you could ever need in him. He is generous!

> His divine power has granted to us all things that pertain to life and godliness. —2 Peter 1:3

God's given you everything you need for your inheritance. But in order to actually take hold of it, you have to see his beauty. You see... The best gift God could ever give you is himself.The people of Israel got to see the beauty of God in a superficial way. That glorious pillar of fire which displayed God's presence was outside of them. They gazed on his beauty wherever they were. We gaze on him through his Word, and we look upon him in a way that is beyond the glory cloud. We gaze upon the glory of his love in Jesus Christ, and all who do that are infinitely happy. John Piper put it this way:

> All who cast themselves on God find that they are carried into endless joy. —John Piper[103]

I believe he was describing what David expressed so clearly in Psalm 63.

> O God, you are my God; I earnestly search for you. My soul thirsts for you; my whole body longs for you in this parched and weary land where there is no water. [2] I have seen you in your sanctuary and gazed upon your power and glory. [3] Your unfailing love is better than life itself; how I praise you! [4] I will praise you as long as I live, lifting up my hands to you in prayer. [5] You satisfy me more than the richest feast. I will praise you with songs of joy. —Psalm 63:1-5 (NLT)

So my question to you is your focus on the land? Don't seek the things of this earth. That was Israel's problem and they ended up losing everything. Seek the Lord! And everything else will be added to you. Do you want a happy marriage? Don't seek a happy marriage! That's the quickest way to misery. Seek the Lord! Do you want food and clothes

---

[103] John Piper. *Desiring God, Revised Edition* (Colorado Springs, CO: Multnomah Books, 2011), 54.

and an income? Don't seek money or material things. Seek the Lord! We know what God says.

> Seek first the kingdom of God and his righteousness, and all these things will be added to you. —Matthew 6:33

God is so generous! He wants to give you so much! But first you must grow your heart with his presence so that you will worship only him, and not your stuff or relationships or lack thereof. Gaze on the beauty of the Lord. The best gift God can give you is himself. What a generous God! But I think Israel, and we can say that God is not only generous, but powerful. And you are here, and you are saying, "I want to live the abundant life, but I'm so weak. I want to gaze upon the beauty of God, but I don't see it. How do I get there?" I'm glad you asked, because our God is powerful to give you eyes to see his beauty.

## GOD IS POWERFUL (21:43B-44)

Whatever God promises, he is able to bring it to pass. He gave the children of Israel the land he promised Abraham, and they were to take full possession and settle there, and worship God on his holy mountain in Jerusalem. If they found their rest and worship in him, he would make sure they kept possession.

### Powerful to Give You Possession

God is powerful to give his people the inheritance he promised them.

**Joshua 21:43b** | And they took possession of it, and they settled there.

They were to take full possession of the land, and they did. And they would keep it as long as they worshipped God. The reason God gave his people the land was for a place to worship him. As long as they worshipped God with a pure heart, they would keep possession of the land. That land was for worshipping the Lord. That's why he took hold of Abraham and eventually all the nation of Israel: he wanted to give them a land where they could worship him unhindered from the enemy. Paul says clearly that he wants to take hold of knowing Christ, in the way that Christ took hold of him.

> I make every effort to take hold of it because I also have been taken hold of by Christ Jesus. —Philippians 3:12

Don't you want to take hold of Christ, the way he took hold of you? God was powerful let his people experience full possession of the promised land. Sometimes we look at a house, and we go house shopping online, on Zillow or Realtor.com. But it's a whole 'nother thing to buy it and pay for it, and move in! That's what the Bible says that Israel got to experience. They moved in to the promised land. They got the keys and the title deed! God gave it to them. Israel couldn't take long term possession of the land because they wouldn't allow God to take possession of them. And some of you are looking at the Christian life as a window shopper, and you are saying, it sure looks nice. I sure would like to live a life of holiness. I sure would like to experience the presence of God. I sure would like to experience the defeat of my enemies. But you don't know how to get there. You have plenty of faith and virtue and knowledge, but you don't know how to really experience the beauty of Christ. He's taken possession of you, and you need to take hold of him. How? First realize, he gives "every spiritual blessing in Christ" (Eph 1:3). He wants you to take full possession of him.

God wants you to take possession of all that he has for you. Remember, the people of Israel were to take possession of the land as a place to worship him. That's why they were to inhabit the land. Worship! Now, your life, your family, your church, your job, your money, the circumstances of your life, are to be a place of worship. God gave the land to Israel. He gives us all things. It is our responsibility to settle there and worship him in all that he gives us. Let me give you the most important principle of possession: the fear of the Lord.

The fear of the Lord is the beginning of knowledge; fools despise wisdom and instruction. — Proverbs 1:7

Do you want all the secrets of wisdom and knowledge? Worship the Lord! Fear him. Be teachable. Invite him into every situation in your life. That's the fear of God. Are you so angry that you're about to bust vein in your forehead? Invite God into the situation with a humble heart. It'll take away your anger. Are you despairing? About to give up? Focusing on your hurt? Repent by inviting the God of all hope and all grace into your situation. He loves the outcast. He adopts the orphan and the abandoned one. Start getting excited about what God's going to do in your mess. Are you about to check out in your foolishness and act as if God doesn't exist in your situation? Be wise and worship him. Fear him and invite him to teach your foolish heart. Are you troubled about many things? Filled with anxiety and anger? Are you checking out on God. Remember what the Lord said to Martha.

> Martha, Martha, you are anxious and troubled about many things, [42] but one thing is necessary. Mary has chosen the good portion, which will not be taken away from her. —Luke 10:41-42

Mary couldn't get away from listening to Jesus. Mary has chosen "the one thing," the only thing that's really "necessary" in life. Mary had a gravitationally pulled toward Jesus. How do we take possession of all God has for us? We have to let him take possession of us. You want that fullness from the Lord? You want perfect contentment? Choose the one thing that is necessary: the beauty of God in Christ.

## Powerful to Give You Rest

> Be still, and know that I am God. —Psalm 46:10

There is something else God wants to give you, not only full and lasting worship and possession of him, but also rest for your soul.

> **Joshua 21:44a** | And the Lord gave them **rest** on every side just as he had sworn to their fathers...

There is a great temptation for anxiety in our lives. We have to dig down and ask, why are we anxious? So much of it is because we don't have rest. At times, we are attempting to sanctify ourselves in the power of our own flesh. Listen to Paul—you can't get rest in your own power.

> O foolish Galatians! Who has bewitched you? ... [3] Are you so foolish? Having begun by the Spirit, are you now being perfected by the flesh? —Galatians 3:1, 3

The fool is willing to just escape and check out. He doesn't like pain, so he seeks pleasure to dull the pain. Christ alone can satisfy our desires.

> Proverbs 27:20 — Just as Death and Destruction are never satisfied, so human desire is never satisfied.

Everything in your flesh is enslaving, if you let it, but there is freedom and rest in Christ. There is joy in Christ that will crush your never-ending hunger. The flesh is never satisfied, but you can be satisfied in only one place. Jesus said:

Come to me, all who labor and are heavy laden, and I will give you rest. —Matthew 11:28

People are doing whatever they can in their own power and flesh to get some rest. Some are getting medicine from their doctor, and that's good, but you know that full peace doesn't come from a pill: it comes from Christ. Someone here is probably self-medicating in this congregation. Often I don't find out someone has a problem with drunkenness or self-medication while they are a member here. Sometimes it's years later when the person has victory. Maybe you are here today, and you are medicating yourself from pain through pornography. You are willing to have a cold heart toward God just to get a little fleshly rest now.

Let me tell you, there is freedom, there is cleansing, there is *rest*, sweet rest in Christ alone. Jesus, like the priests and Levites in those 48 towns around Israel, would call the outcasts. He would call the leper.

You can only get rest for your soul through the cleansing that only Christ can give. There may be some uncleanness in your soul. In your sin, you may feel the filth and shame of your sin. Come to Christ for full and complete cleansing. He calls the outcasts and rebels. He calls the unclean. The lepers that would cry out: "Unclean!" Jesus would touch. They never had rest until they felt the touch of Jesus. Jesus embraces you and gives you his promise:

> I will restore health to you, and your wounds I will heal, declares the Lord, because they have called you an outcast. [19] Out of them shall come songs of thanksgiving, and the voices of those who celebrate. ...I will make them honored... [21] ... I will make him draw near, and he shall approach me, for who would dare of himself to approach me? declares the Lord. [22] And you shall be my people, and I will be your God." —Jeremiah 30:17, 19, 21

Most sinners and outcasts would never dare to draw near to a holy and just God, but our Lord is so bursting with goodness, that he says, "I am your God, you are my child." God calls the lepers and outcasts to join him, not as his guests, but as his beloved children. You may be despairing, feeling powerless, and even worthless. Lift up your head child of God. Jesus came to welcome the outcast. He came to heal the leper. You are no longer unclean. You are cleansed. You are beyond cleansed. You are holy. Holy means special and set apart for the God's honored use. Rest in Christ, since you cannot find true rest anywhere else!

## Powerful to Give You Victory

God is powerful to give you victory in obtaining your inheritance. You might say, I would see God in the beauty of his holiness. That's what I want, but I can't. I'm enslaved. I have enemies. So did Israel. But with God we are more than conquerors.

> In all these things we are more than conquerors through him who loved us. —Romans 8:37

Let's read about Israel's victory.

**Joshua 21:44b** | Not one of all their enemies had withstood them, for the Lord had given all their enemies into their hands.

Victory meant God would defeat all enemies. For us as believers, that victory is one over our greatest enemy: sin.

> Sin will have no dominion over you, since you are not under law but under grace. —Romans 6:14

There is a high price for victory. You have to die to your own power and prestige. Jesus said, in order to gain your life, you have to lose it. In order to live to the Spirit you have to die to the flesh. Paul understood that price when he said he lived a crucified life, so that he could live the abundant life in Christ.

> I have been crucified with Christ. It is no longer I who live, but Christ who lives in me. And the life I now live in the flesh I live by faith in the Son of God, who loved me and gave himself for me. —Galatians 2:20

How do you get there? You have to purposely live by faith in the Son of God, in his love, worshipping him, moment by moment. Treasure Christ and you will have infinite power over sin. We can say with Nehemiah:

> The joy of the Lord is my strength. —Nehemiah 8:10

Let's consider one last thing to praise God for. He is faithful. He's a promise keeper!

## GOD IS FAITHFUL (21:45)

God is faithful to conform you to Christ. He often will not change your circumstances, but he will change you. God's goal in bringing Israel to the land was to transform their character, not simply transform their landscape. The conquering of the land was all about learning to trust God and having their hearts transformed. Battle after battle, their faith built as they saw God keep *every single one of his promises.*

**Joshua 21:45** | Not one word of all the good promises that the Lord had made to the house of Israel had failed; all came to pass.

Praise God for our promise keeping God! Ok, here is where we get really nearsighted in our lives. We are quite impatient when it comes to waiting on God. But remember The Lord made promises to Moses, when Joshua was 40, but here it is 40 years later until the promise is fulfilled. Whatever God promises, he will do!

The steadfast love of the Lord never ceases; his mercies never come to an end; 23 they are new every morning; great is your faithfulness. — Lamentations 3:22-23

## Faithful though We Grieve

Sometimes it doesn't seem God is faithful, because of grief and loss. David says,

Yeah though I walk *through* the valley of the shadow of death, I will fear no evil. —Psalm 23:4

In this life, we must walk through that valley. We can't go around it. God is faithful, precious saint. He is faithful to be there when you are grieving. Some of you have suffered great loss. It hurts so bad, you want to run the other way. Don't be afraid. God is with you. His promises have not at all failed. It's hard to see clearly through all the tears, but it will get better. There will be a day when God will wipe away all the tears.

And God has a purpose for the grief and the loss. He's humbling you. Remember what he told Paul: because of the greatness of the revelations, to keep you from pride, I've put a "thorn in the flesh" in your life to humble you. I know you are hurting. I know you are suffering loss. You will get through this. God is keeping you humble through suffering so he can draw you so near! God is using this grief to draw you near to his sorrow. Our dear heavenly Father suffered loss as well. His own Son was crucified. You are learning the sufferings of Christ. But don't ever think because of your pain, that God is not faithful. He is always faithful. There is coming a day, when you will have a much clearer view of all the promises of God fulfilled. God will wipe away all tears from your eyes, and you will see clearly.

## Faithful Though We Suffer Deeply

If anyone would come after me, let him deny himself and take up his cross daily and follow me. For whoever would save his life will lose it, but whoever loses his life for my sake will save it. —Luke 9:23–24

There is no true Christianity without cross-bearing and a daily dying—which sounds very much like Paul's "I die every day" (1 Cor 15:31). God is faithful to bring all his promises to pass for you, but it is through a veil of tears and a pathway of suffering. It is suffering that tests your faith.

Through many tribulations we must enter the kingdom of God. — Acts 14:22

God tells us what the purpose of suffering is for his dear precious child.

We do not want you to be ignorant, brothers, of the affliction we experienced in Asia. For we were so utterly burdened beyond our strength that we despaired even of life itself. Indeed, we felt that we had received the sentence of death. But that was to make us rely not on ourselves but on God who raises the dead. —2 Corinthians 1:8–9

His purpose is to make us not rely on ourselves, but on the resurrection power of God. Samuel Rutherford said that when he was cast into the cellars of affliction, he remembered that the great King always kept his wine there.

## Worship God! He is Faithful!

How is God a promise keeper? He is faithful.

Great is your faithfulness. —Lamentations 3:23

**Joshua 21:45** | Not one word of all the good promises that the Lord had made to the house of Israel had failed; all came to pass.

Ok, here is where we get really nearsighted in our lives. We are quite impatient when it comes to waiting on God. But remember The Lord made promises to Moses, when Joshua was 40, but here it is 40 years later until the promise is fulfilled. No matter how long you've waited, God is faithful. No matter how weak you feel, God is faithful. Don't give up, for God will not fail in even "one word of all the good promises" he has made to you. For Israel it was the land. For you, there are so many! Peter says that we have so many "precious and very great promises" (2 Pet 1:4). What are God's promises for you? *He is faithful to cleanse you.* Jesus will touch you and cleanse you. When the leper came to him and knelt before Jesus, and said, "Oh Jesus, will you cleanse me?"

> Jesus stretched out his hand and touched [the leper], saying, 'I will; be clean.' —Matthew 8:3

He promises to touch you, cleanse you and bring you in to his arms. He restores the outcast. He adopts you and brings you into his family. *He is faithful to conform you to Christ.*

> Those whom he foreknew he also predestined to be conformed to the image of his Son. —Romans 8:29

> Now to him who is able to keep you from stumbling and to present you blameless before the presence of his glory with great joy, to the only God, our Savior, through Jesus Christ our Lord, be glory, majesty, dominion, and authority, before all time and now and forever. Amen. —Jude 24-25

> He who calls you is faithful; he will surely do it —1 Thessalonians 5:24

> And I am sure of this, that he who began a good work in you will bring it to completion at the day of Jesus Christ. —Philippians 1:6

## Conclusion
### What do we say to these things?

> If God is for us, who can be against us? [32] He who did not spare his own Son but gave him up for us all, how will he not also with him graciously give us all things? —Romans 8:31-32

God is a promise keeping God. Let's take hold of all that God wants to do in our lives. No more wasting time. Let's give our whole hearts to worship him. He is worthy saints! He is a promise keeping God!

# 19 | JOSHUA 22
## THE DANGER AND DELIGHT OF GOD

*Thus says the whole congregation of the Lord, 'What is this breach of faith that you have committed against the God of Israel in turning away this day from following the Lord by building yourselves an altar this day in rebellion against the Lord?*
JOSHUA 22:16

There are some things in life that are fascinating to study but terrifying up close. So many times, I've been fascinated by sharks on the Nat Geo channel or some ocean documentary. But I've learned that you don't want to see a shark up close! Which brings me to my son William's national football tournament of 2020, which happened to be in the shark attack capital of the world. We were minding our own business, enjoying the white sands and clear ocean waters of Panama City Beach. It was barely dusk when Jill and the kids came running into the shoreline, pale and frightened. It seemed as if they had seen a shark. That's because they had seen a shark!

It was a beautiful black tip shark, who, as we found out, come out to the sand bars at dusk to catch their prey. They don't like people, but they do like the little fish that congregate on the sandbars at dusk. We had no idea! Sharks are fascinating to look at in photographs and aquariums, but not so much up close. It's great to talk about sharks, look at shark documentaries, and study sharks. But no one wants to be 2 feet away from a shark (as Jill and the kids were). Why? As *glorious* as sharks are, they are *dangerous*. My wife's first reaction wasn't to stand still, mesmerized by the shark's beauty. No: it was to *run!* And the glory of God's creation is just a small little glimpse into our great and majestic God. We study the incredible power of hurricanes or tsunamis, but we don't want to be in one.

I think of Aslan, the Lion in the Chronicles of Narnia. There's a wonderful scene in that story where Mr. Beaver first tells the children about Aslan, the King of the wood.

Susan asks, "Is he a man?"

"Most certainly not," Mr. Beaver replies. "Aslan is a lion — the Lion, the great Lion." "Ooh!" says Susan. "Is he quite safe? I shall feel rather nervous about meeting a lion."

Mr. Beaver tells Lucy that Aslan, the true King of Narnia is a Lion. To which Lucy asks, trembling: "Is Aslan (the Lion) safe?" His reply: "Safe? Who said anything about safe? 'Course he isn't safe. But he's good. He's the King." Peter interrupts! "I'm longing to see him," said Peter, "even if I do feel frightened when it comes to the point." [104]

That's how it is with us. We know our Jesus is not just the Lamb of God, but the Lion of the tribe of Judah that takes vengeance on the earth. Jesus is not safe, but he is good! That's what we are going to learn today. This is the theme of Joshua 22, the passage for our study. The key thought for our passage today is theis: Our greatest happiness and safety is enjoyed as we live under the blessing of God's glory and presence, and our greatest sorrow, misery and danger is inflicted any time we choose to depart from God and his glory.

So let me ask you as we take a look at ancient Israel, who so often ran away from the blessing of God. Are you experiencing the ultimate happiness and comfort from God regardless of your circumstances? Are you enjoying his perfect peace, joy as you walk with him in paths of righteousness? The righteous path is the path where God is most glorified and pleased. Are you satisfied with his sweet presence, resting? Waiting on him? Enjoying him. Few Christians find this to be true, but God wants all Christians to experience it. This is the normal Christian

---

[104] C.S. Lewis. *The Lion the Witch and the Wardrobe* (New York: Macmillan, 1950), 43.

life. Once you understand this, it will bring an immovable foundation and an undefeatable joy that cannot fade to your life.

## The Situation

We come to a passage early in the existence of Israel, where you have a serious crisis that almost leads to civil war in Israel, just about the time the entire land is settled. The story is plainly shocking. This is the end of the book. You'd think it might end with a revival and celebration of the presence of God, but instead, Israel is on the brink of civil war. What? Yep, civil war before they hardly even begin as a nation. Let's consider what happens.

## The Commendation

Joshua commends the people!

**Joshua 22:3, 5-6** | You have not forsaken your brothers these many days, down to this day, but have been careful to keep the charge of the Lord your God... **5** Only be very careful to observe the commandment and the law that Moses the servant of the Lord commanded you, to love the Lord your God, and to walk in all his ways and to keep his commandments and to cling to him and to serve him with all your heart and with all your soul." **6** So Joshua blessed them and sent them away, and they went to their tents.

So Joshua sends the people of Israel off into two groups: those on the west side of Jordan, where Israel is today, and then you had the two and a half tribes on the east side of Jordan: Gad, Reuben and the half tribe of Manasseh. We see here that all the land is distributed from the western side of the Jordan to the eastern shore of the Mediterranean Sea. Joshua thanks them (21:1–9). All is well. The land is finally settled. Time to celebrate! They go home. End of story, right? Wrong.

## The Shock

The eastern Israelites have erected an altar, which is a complete departure from God. Remember their parents had erected an altar to Baal. It looks like a repeat. So the good western tribes get ready to go to war with the what looks like the "bad" eastern tribes. Let's read about it.

**Joshua 22:10-12** | And when they came to the region of the Jordan that is in the land of Canaan, the people of Reuben and the people of

Gad and the half-tribe of Manasseh built there an altar by the Jordan, an altar of imposing size. [11] And the people of Israel heard it said, "Behold, the people of Reuben and the people of Gad and the half-tribe of Manasseh have built the altar at the frontier of the land of Canaan, in the region about the Jordan, on the side that belongs to the people of Israel." [12] And when the people of Israel heard of it, the whole assembly of the people of Israel gathered at Shiloh to make war against them.

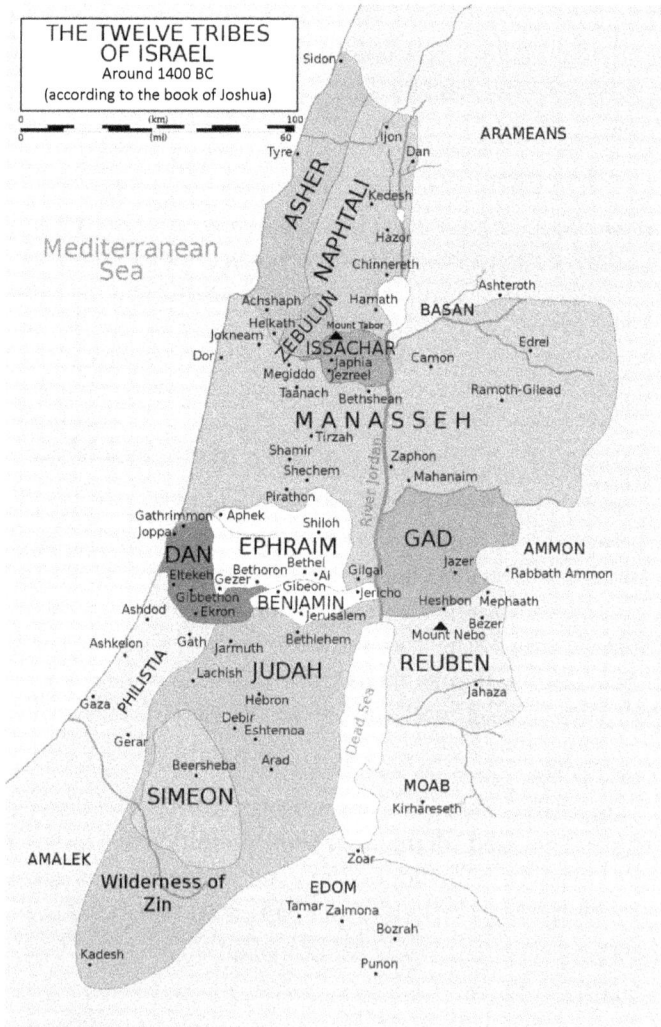

THE TWELVE TRIBES OF ISRAEL
Around 1400 BC
(according to the book of Joshua)

What would make western Israel go against eastern Israel (east of the Jordan)? I'll tell you what it was: idolatry. The children of Israel understood that to be blessed by the LORD, you had to worship him alone. There could be no other. That's actually the meaning of life. That's what Joshua commended everyone for! You love God alone! You will be blessed and supremely happy in him! They were to love the Lord (22:5-6)! Once back in their land, these tribes did a shocking thing. They built a very large and impressive altar (21:10). Nice, right? Wrong. The law of Moses clearly spelled out that there was to be only one altar for sacrificing to the Lord, and that was in Shiloh (Deut 12:5–7). This was an act of flagrant rebellion and must be quashed! The rest of Israel was shocked and enraged. They knew what this meant. Any idolatry of a tribe, in this manner, was to be dealt with through capital punishment. They were to treat their brothers as if they had been pagans. They cannot risk an infection of idolatry. When they heard of what looked like idolatry, they prepared for war (22:12).

## Why War?

What would make these who were ready to celebrate, not get ready to conquer the other remaining two and a half tribes east of Jordan? Seriously, why war? *Because living with the blessing of God over you is everything.* Love God. That's the command. Outside of loving God, you get counterfeits, misery, agony, emptiness. War is necessary. They were willing at this time to do whatever it took to remain under the blessing of God. It's dangerous to live outside of the blessing of God.

## OUR GOD IS A DANGEROUS GOD (22:1-20)

Our God is a dangerous God. It's dangerous to live for self. He's not safe, but he is good. We read this in so many places.

It is a fearful thing to fall into the hands of the living God. —Hebrews 10:31

Israel was to live out the fear (worship) of the Lord and be blessed. Without that worship, there is only death. It's dangerous to live a life outside of the glory and blessing of God. God wants to bless his people. But you have to choose to stay under that blessing.

The fear of the Lord is a fountain of life, that one may turn away from the snares of death. — Proverbs 14:27

Sadly, we find later on, much of the time, the Israel goes running recklessly towards death. And these people are a picture of all of us. We must see ourselves in them and learn from their failure to rightly fear God. Fear the Lord! He's a dangerous God. His glory is frightening in a sense. This is a warning that the western tribes and Joshua want to give to those who erected this altar.

## Idolatry is Dangerous

In verses 13 and following, Phinehas, the son of Eleazar the priest and a group of the ten chiefs of the tribes on the west side of the Jordan, met with those on the east side who erected the altar. He mentions two incidents of idolatry: one was national idolatry at Baal-Peor (22:17) where the people of Israel were introduced to the golden calf Baal worship when Moses was still alive. The Baal-Peor fiasco (Num. 25) brought Yahweh's plague against the congregation.[105] The other incident wasn't national idolatry, but the personal idolatry of Achan at Jericho (22:20). In both incidents, there were severe consequences. People died. Misery ensued. Idolatry will always bring you misery.

Now thankfully, Israel didn't have to descend into a civil war, because the altar, we'll find out is actually just a memorial and reminder for the eastern tribes to remember to go to Shiloh once a year to bring the Passover, so that they never forget they are part of Israel, though they are separated by the Jordan River. Needless to say, this was so serious that the tribes of mainland Israel met at Shiloh to 'go to war' against the east-side tribes (21:12). What would bring the tribes west of the Jordan to eliminate the eastern tribes? To be certain, this wasn't vengeance. These were brothers. But you have to understand, they saw the glory of God in so many ways. That is why Joshua 22 is a fitting conclusion as we wind down the book of Joshua. God's people understood the majesty of God's glory.

## Moses' Experience of God's Dangerous Glory

Moses brings the Israelites out of Egypt to meet with God at Mount Sinai. God wraps the glory cloud around Mount Sinai, and there is smoke, lightening, thunder, and a trumpet sound. God had revealed himself to Moses at the burning bush, but now he reveals himself to an

---

[105] Davis, *Joshua*, 166–167.

entire nation (Ex 19), and the people tremble with fear. They can't even go near the holy mountain, upon punishment of death.

When Moses was confronted with the glory of God, he feared he trembled and took his shoes off. Do you have a reverence for the presence of God that is in you? Moses goes up on the mountain. People are told if they touch the mountain, they will die. Moses has a heart that the Lord can see is completely devoted to God and his glory. Moses comes down with his face shining, so much so that he had to wear a veil over his face. The people are now afraid of Moses, because God's glory shines on him. You know those who like to play around with idols often don't want to be around those who walk with God.

## The Corinthians Experience of God's Dangerous Glory

God wants his people to live under his blessing. But if you won't live under his blessing, you are subject to sickness and death. Paul had to teach the Corinthian church about the danger of the glory of God. Paul says because you don't take the glory of God seriously "some of you are sick and some of you have fallen asleep [died]".

Mainland Israel got it. They understood. It was holiness or death for them. Death for their brothers was better than living without the glory of God. They treated idolatry like the beginning stage of cancer. They knew that idolatry had to be cut out no matter what the cost. Are you willing to say I want holiness so bad that I invite the chastening of God into my life if I don't go that way. "I want God to cut me and prune the dead parts of my life!"

> Every branch in me that does not bear fruit he takes away, and every branch that does bear fruit he prunes, that it may bear more fruit. — John 15:2

Now God's glory is dangerous, but it doesn't have to be. His glory is his person. We will all stand before the judgment seat of Christ. We will all give an account. We will all have to reckon with this holy God, the scrutiny of the living God. I could never stand before him in my own merit. I have the merit of another. Now that I know the delight of God's glory in Christ, why would I ever live under the danger of an unblessed life?

> He who dwells in the shelter of the Most High will abide in the shadow of the Almighty. [2] I will say to the Lord, "My refuge and my fortress, my God, in whom I trust. —Psalm 91:1-2

I don't want to live without the blessing of God's shadow and presence in my life. That's dangerous! Look at this tension in John 3.

> For God so loved the world, that he gave his only Son, that whoever believes in him should not perish but have eternal life. [17] For God did not send his Son into the world to condemn the world, but in order that the world might be saved through him. —John 3:16-17

Wonderful, right? Delightful, right? Right. But keep reading.

> Whoever believes in the Son has eternal life; whoever does not obey the Son shall not see life, but the wrath of God remains on him. —John 3:36

That's frightening. Our great God is not safe! But he is good! Listen to what one great theologian and pastor said.

> No one stands under the wrath of God except those who choose to do so. —J. I. Packer[106]

So what do we say? Why would Joshua and Israel be willing to fight against their own brothers? Let me say: it's a good thing. They treated idolatry like the beginning stage of cancer. They knew that idolatry had to be cut out no matter what the cost.

What is your attitude toward idolatry in your own life? Do you rationalize? Do you make excuses? That's dangerous. You will experience the glory of God. Will it be dangerous for you? God yearns jealously over your heart. For the child of God, there is no wrath. There is no danger like that. But there is a fierce love for you. There is a fierce jealousy for your soul.

> You adulterous people! Do you not know that friendship with the world is enmity with God? Therefore whoever wishes to be a friend of the world makes himself an enemy of God. [5] Or do you suppose it is to no purpose that the Scripture says, "He yearns jealously over the spirit that he has made to dwell in us"? [6] But he gives more grace. Therefore it says, "God opposes the proud but gives grace to the humble." [7] Submit yourselves therefore to God. Resist the devil, and he will flee from you. [8] Draw near to God, and he will draw near to you. Cleanse your hands, you sinners, and purify your hearts, you

---

[106] J. I. Packer. *Knowing God* (Downers Grove, IL: InterVarsity Press, 1993), 153.

double-minded. [9] Be wretched and mourn and weep. Let your laughter be turned to mourning and your joy to gloom. [10] Humble yourselves before the Lord, and he will exalt you. —James 4:4-10

When you commit idolatry against God, he jealously years over your spirit and heart, like a husband who's been betrayed by an adulterous wife. That's a dangerous jealousy. You are not in danger of damnation. You will never be condemned. But God is going to deal with your adultery. You can either humble yourself, or God will humble you.

Ok, so far this is heavy, as it should be. Glory has the idea of weightiness. But God wants us to enter into his glory, not be decimated by it. He wants us to delight in it.

## OUR GOD IS A DELIGHTFUL GOD (22:21-34)

The glory of God is the most beautiful and delightful thing ever. There is no overstating it. God is first and foremost a merciful God. The very reason he displays the fierceness of his glory to us is that he might humble us to receive his mercy.

Consider our key thought again for this passage: Our greatest happiness and safety is enjoyed as we live under the blessing of God's glory and presence, and our greatest sorrow, misery and danger is inflicted any time we choose to depart from God and his glory.

Now let's understand why this is an incredibly good story, and why we need it. What does it teach us about God? This story teaches us that God is both a dangerous and at the same time a delightful God. Before we go back to Joshua and their willingness to destroy their brothers in order to wipe out idolatry from Israel, I want to consider a lesson from Moses.

### A Witness of God's Glory

Moses says: Show me your glory! And Moses had seen God's glory at the burning bush. He also saw God's glory, Hebrews 12 says, at Mount Sinai, and he said, "I tremble with fear." Moses was afraid. He trembled. Israel was to shown God's glory, and it was absolutely frightening. God's wraps his glory around Mount Sinai, and there's smoke and fire and lightening and incredible thunder. The people are trembling. Moses is trembling.

For you have not come to what may be touched, a blazing fire and darkness and gloom and a tempest [19] and the sound of a trumpet and a voice whose words made the hearers beg that no further messages be spoken to them. [20] For they could not endure the order that was given, "If even a beast touches the mountain, it shall be stoned." [21] Indeed, so terrifying was the sight that Moses said, "I tremble with fear." [22] But you have come to Mount Zion and to the city of the living God, the heavenly Jerusalem, and to innumerable angels in festal gathering, [23] and to the assembly of the firstborn who are enrolled in heaven, and to God, the judge of all, and to the spirits of the righteous made perfect, [24] and to Jesus, the mediator of a new covenant... —Hebrews 12:18-24

How can we say God's glory is delightful? Moses was given access to the mountain. He came down with his face shining. He came down with joy. He says to God, "Show me your glory!" He's introduced to the delightful glory of God." And remember when God's glory passed before Moses, that glory was described as God's goodness!

Moses said, "Please show me your glory." [19] And he said, "I will make all my goodness pass before you and will proclaim before you my name 'The Lord.' And I will be gracious to whom I will be gracious, and will show mercy on whom I will show mercy. [20] But," he said, "you cannot see my face, for man shall not see me and live." [21] And the Lord said, "Behold, there is a place by me where you shall stand on the rock, [22] and while my glory passes by I will put you in a cleft of the rock, and I will cover you with my hand until I have passed by. —Exodus 33:18-22

Do you see? God's glory is the only thing worth living for! It's the only thing that is worth anything. To be outside the glory of God as a sinner, is dangerous. But to be accepted in Christ, it's a delight! The eastern tribes of Israel testify to this!

## A Witness of Praise

**Joshua 22:21-29** | Then the people of Reuben, the people of Gad, and the half-tribe of Manasseh said in answer to the heads of the families of Israel, [22] "The Mighty One, God, the Lord! The Mighty One, God, the Lord! He knows; and let Israel itself know! If it was in rebellion or in breach of faith against the Lord, do not spare us today [23] for building an altar to turn away from following the Lord. Or if we did so to offer burnt offerings or grain offerings or peace offerings on it, may the Lord himself take vengeance. [24] No, but we did it from fear that in time to come your children might say to our children, 'What have you to do with the Lord, the God of

Israel? **25** For the Lord has made the Jordan a boundary between us and you, you people of Reuben and people of Gad. You have no portion in the Lord.' So your children might make our children cease to worship the Lord. **26** Therefore we said, 'Let us now build an altar, not for burnt offering, nor for sacrifice, **27** but to be a witness between us and you, and between our generations after us, that we do perform the service of the Lord in his presence with our burnt offerings and sacrifices and peace offerings, so your children will not say to our children in time to come, "You have no portion in the Lord."' **28** And we thought, 'If this should be said to us or to our descendants in time to come, we should say, "Behold, the copy of the altar of the Lord, which our fathers made, not for burnt offerings, nor for sacrifice, but to be a witness between us and you."' **29** Far be it from us that we should rebel against the Lord and turn away this day from following the Lord by building an altar for burnt offering, grain offering, or sacrifice, other than the altar of the Lord our God that stands before his tabernacle!"

Phinehas and his delegation were tremendously relieved. All of Israel 'blessed God' and 'spoke no more of going against them in battle' (21:33). They found out that this was not an idol altar, it was a memorial of praise to God!

**Joshua 22:30-34** | When Phinehas the priest and the chiefs of the congregation, the heads of the families of Israel who were with him, heard the words that the people of Reuben and the people of Gad and the people of Manasseh spoke, It was good in their eyes. **31** And Phinehas the son of Eleazar the priest said to the people of Reuben and the people of Gad and the people of Manasseh, "Today we know that the Lord is in our midst, because you have not committed this breach of faith against the Lord. Now you have delivered the people of Israel from the hand of the Lord." **32** Then Phinehas the son of Eleazar the priest, and the chiefs, returned from the people of Reuben and the people of Gad in the land of Gilead to the land of Canaan, to the people of Israel, and brought back word to them. **33** And the report was good in the eyes of the people of Israel. And the people of Israel blessed God and spoke no more of making war against them to destroy the land where the people of Reuben and the people of Gad were settled. **34** The people of Reuben and the people of Gad called the

altar Witness, "For," they said, "it is a witness between us that
the Lord is God."

Instead of this altar being a witness of idolatry, it was a witness
of praise! You see this is how God's glory is a protection to us. We dwell
in the shadow of the Almighty (Psa 91:1) and we are protected. Praise
will protect you from all harm to your soul. Now it may not protect you
from harm in your body or in your circumstances. You will suffer in this
life. Jesus said,

> I have said these things to you, that in me you may have peace. In the
> world you will have tribulation. But take heart; I have overcome the
> world." —John 16:33

Can you say that "in Jesus I have peace"? Can you say with Christ,
"I have overcome the world" in spite of the tribulation you face? The
more you praise, the more you will see God's protection in your life.
The more you delight in Jesus, you are protected from the misery of
idolatry. Let me illustrate it with King Jehoshaphat.

### King Jehoshaphat's Protection of Praise

Remember in 2 Chronicles 20, a great multitude was coming
against King Jehoshaphat. When he sought the Lord, he was told to
send out the singers of Israel. God says to them:

> Do not be afraid and do not be dismayed. Tomorrow go out against
> them, and the Lord will be with you." [18] Then Jehoshaphat bowed his
> head with his face to the ground, and all Judah and the inhabitants of
> Jerusalem fell down before the Lord, worshiping the Lord. [19] And the
> Levites, of the Kohathites and the Korahites, stood up to praise
> the Lord, the God of Israel, with a very loud voice... [22] And when they
> began to sing and praise, the Lord set an ambush against the men
> of Ammon, Moab, and Mount Seir, who had come against Judah, so
> that they were routed. —2 Chronicles 20:17-20, 22

The tribes east of Jordan understood the power of praise. How
easy it is to forget the Lord. Praise is a protection for your soul.

## A Witness to Commitment

The altar had not been built for offering sacrifices, but rather as
a visible reminder that these two and a half tribes were part of Israel
(vv. 21–29). S. G. DeGraaf writes of the two and a half tribes:

They had been afraid that the two communities, separated by the Jordan, might become estranged from each other, and that the tribes to the west of the river might someday refuse to allow the eastern tribes to participate in the service of the Lord at Shiloh.[107]

We are family. We are on the same pathway. We are going to the same destination. We are going to spend the next billion years together. This is especially a challenge for those living in close quarters: brothers and sisters, husbands and wives, parents and children. You are family. This is also for the church. We are God's forever family. Connect on an eternal level. We can't just have commonalities around sports and politics or hobbies. Fine and well, but that is not the substance of Christianity. Our fellowship is around Christ. We are connected through the Holy Spirit.

## A Witness to Incarnation

Not only are we family, but we are to incarnate Jesus to our forever family, and to the world. Jesus came first in the incarnation. We celebrate Christmastime because the Word became flesh. We are to incarnate him to those around us. This is the essence of holiness. To be holy is to be separated unto God for his use and purposes. We are not called to the comfortable life but to the incarnational life. Jesus was obedient to God even if it meant crucifixion. That's us. Our focus can never be on my own comfort, my rights, my worthiness of respect.

There has been so much pride in my heart that I've been repenting of. Whenever there is anger or anxiety, I have to chase it down to the idol of pride. I'm worried that people don't respect me. I'm angry that I don't get the respect or love I think I deserve. I track it down, and I have to confess my pride until the anger and anxiety go away. The anger and anxiety are trying to rip the unconquerable God off his throne. So we are to incarnate the divine love of Christ to those around us.

### Incarnation Requires Humility

Joshua 22 serves as something of a handbook for God's people of all ages on the matter of dealing with misunderstandings. Don't assume! How often we think we know the motives of our brothers and

---

[107] S. G. DeGraaf. *Promise and Deliverance*, Volume 4 (Ontario, Canada: Paideia Press, 1977), 416.

sisters in Christ, and how often we are wrong! Instead of passing judgement on others' motives, we would do well openly and honestly to speak to them about any of their acts that concern us. A little honest talking often prevents a lot of heartache! Peter Jeffery perceptively writes,

> Innocent actions can be misconstrued, exaggerated and blown up out of all proportion. Sometimes we misrepresent the action of a fellow believer because we do not like that person and are only too glad for an opportunity to criticize. That is evil and wicked. Sometimes we misrepresent an action because we disagree with it. That is dishonest because the motives can be right even when the action is wrong. The Israelites were too quick to misconstrue and much too quick to be ready to fight, but we must pay tribute to them that before they did anything, they sent representatives to talk with their brethren. When they came face to face and talked the whole business through the problems were resolved. [108]

### Incarnation Requires the Spirit's Peace

We are not naturally people of peace. We come into this world with a sinful nature that puts us at odds with God and often at odds with others. But our God is a God of peace. Through the redeeming work of his Son, the Lord Jesus, God brings us into a state of peace with himself. He also gives us peace within. The people of God are, therefore, to be people of peace, and any failure in that area is a denial of the gospel we profess to revere. Nothing so hinders the progress of the gospel as lack of peace among God's people, and nothing so promotes it as warm-hearted unity.[109]

### Incarnation Requires a Willingness to Fight

In order to gain peace, we have to be willing to fight. I don't mean fight against your spouse or a church member. I mean fighting for your family and your church and your culture. Stand up and be counted!

### Conclusion

You are either under God's shalom or under his curse. The children of Israel wanted to remain under God's shalom—his blessing. After all the conquering of the Canaanite nations, Joshua 22 might seem like a strange way to wind down the book, but it's not. It's perfect. They

---

[108] Peter Jeffery. *Overcoming Life's Difficulties: Learning from the Book of Joshua* (Wyoming, MI: Evangelical Press, 2007).

[109] Ellsworth. *Joshua*, 105–108.

were to literally be willing to die for the glory of God and his blessing. That's how important it is. Life is miserable without God's blessing! Can you say with David that having God's blessing on your life, knowing his love and peace and righteousness, is better than the best that life can give me?

Your steadfast love is better than life..." —Psalm 63:3

What else can we say? He is worthy! There is nothing better than the blessing of God's presence, and nothing worse than to be outside of his blessing.

# 20 | JOSHUA 23-24
## LOOKING FOR A GREATER JOSHUA

*Joshua summoned all Israel, its elders and heads, its judges and officers, and said to them, "I am now old and well advanced in years. And you have seen all that the Lord your God has done to all these nations for your sake, for it is the Lord your God who has fought for you.*

JOSHUA 23:2-3

Joshua in the last two chapters gives his final parting words to Israel. He tells us of the importance of taking a stand in your own generation, and in doing so, he is pointing to the greater Joshua, the Lord Jesus Christ. At the end of the book, we want Joshua to stay but he has to go. "It is appointed unto men once to die…" In the end, we are left waiting for a greater Joshua.

After Joshua's death, we see that Israel quickly turns away from the Lord, and this seems to be the story for the rest of Israel's history. A leader comes on the scene, the people turn to the Lord, but as soon as that leader is gone, they turn away from God. They need a leader that won't die! This is that reminds us every day is a good day to celebrate Christmas. We are all reminded of the centuries of waiting for Someone greater than Joshua. We all cry out: O come, o come, Emmanuel, God with us, our Lord Jesus Christ.

## All Judges and Kings Mortal

Judges and kings would come, but all would be so sinful, so weak, and so mortal. As each judge or king arrives on the scene, we have such hope. In each one we see a glimpse of Jesus, but all the earthly leaders are imperfect, fallible and mortal. All are taken by death, suddenly off the scene and we are left waiting once again. When will the true leader, Messiah come?

Thankfully, there is a greater Joshua who is coming who will not only conquer the Promised Land but will conquer sin and death. It's not until the Christ child is born, and Jesus arrives on the scene that things begin to radically change. Jesus' birth changes the world! In his ministry, and through his miracles, disease is literally banished from Israel wherever Jesus is present.

Most importantly Jesus goes to a death for us! But he doesn't stay dead! He rises from the dead, conquering death by death! God's people till this point have never really have that international power and influence until Jesus comes and sends his Holy Spirit. Finally, the true Israel is seen in its full power under our true Joshua the Lord Jesus Christ. Here's the key thought for the end of the book of Joshua: For a legacy that changes a generation, you need to have a life that points to the greater Joshua, the Lord Jesus Christ.

Let's see these glimpses of our true King, the Lord Jesus Christ in Joshua's farewell speech. First, we see in this farewell speech, Joshua has a legacy that points to Jesus.

## A LEGACY THAT POINTS TO JESUS (23:1-13)

Joshua is old. He's about to die, but he gives his stirring farewell speech. His outlining his legacy: a legacy that points to Jesus. Let's read it.

**Joshua 23:1-13** | A long time afterward, when the Lord had given rest to Israel from all their surrounding enemies, and Joshua was old and well advanced in years, ² Joshua summoned all Israel, its elders and heads, its judges and officers, and said to them, "I am now old and well advanced in years. ³ And you have seen all that the Lord your God has done to all these nations for your sake, for it is the Lord your God who has fought for you. ⁴ Behold, I have allotted to you as an inheritance for your tribes those nations that remain, along with all the nations that I have already cut off, from the Jordan to the Great Sea in the west. [5] The Lord your God will push them back before you and drive them out of your sight. And you shall possess their land, just as the Lord your God promised you. [6] Therefore, be very strong to keep and to do all that is written in the Book of the Law of Moses, turning aside from it neither to the right hand nor to the left, [7] that you may not mix with these nations remaining among you or make mention of the names of their gods or swear by them or serve them or bow down to them, [8] but you shall cling to the Lord your God just as you have done to this day. [9] For the Lord has driven out before you great and strong nations. And as for you, no man has been able to stand before you to this day. [10] One man of you puts to flight a thousand, since it is the Lord your God who fights for you, just as he promised you. [11] Be very careful, therefore, to love the Lord your God. [12] For if you turn back and cling to the remnant of these nations remaining among you and make marriages with them, so that you associate with them and they with you, [13] know for certain that the Lord your God will no longer drive out these nations before you, but they shall be a snare and a trap for you, a whip on your sides and thorns in your eyes, until you perish from off this good ground that the Lord your God has given you.

Here was Joshua, and what a legacy he had. He had this divine influence over an entire nation, and then he would pass it off to Othniel (in the book of Judges), who would rule as a judge among them for 40 years, but then it is downhill from there. Joshua had a legacy that pointed to Jesus, but it fell short. Joshua is just a human savior. We are left waiting for a divine Savior. I want you to note several things that point us to Jesus in the legacy of Joshua.

## The Power of a Surrendered Life

Look at the power of a surrendered life.

**Joshua 23:3** | "I am now old and well advanced in years. [3] And you have seen all that the Lord your God has done to all these nations for your sake, for it is the Lord your God who has fought for you."

Joshua was God's human instrument to bring his message and power to Israel. He points to the greater Joshua, our Lord Jesus Christ. It's Christ who fights for us! Amen? The price is paid! The war is won! Christ has conquered sin and death. What a fight! What a victory.

Joshua lived a consistent, sincere life of a believer before all Israel. He was a shepherd and a general to Israel. He was from the tribe of Ephraim, a descendent of the great Prince of Egypt, Joseph. But there is a greater Prince, the Prince of peace! The King of kings and Lord of lords! Joshua lived that surrendered life, pointing to Jesus.

### What's a Surrendered Life Look Like?

What does a surrendered life look like? As Joshua goes through his farewell speech, we see this life and legacy that points to Christ. What is a surrendered, sold-out life and legacy? Jesus describes it in the book of Matthew. This total, radical commitment is taken on by every sincere Christian. Jesus says:

> Whoever does not take his cross and follow me is not worthy of me. [39] Whoever finds his life will lose it, and whoever loses his life for my sake will find it. —Matthew 10:38-39

For Joshua, he says several things here that show us what a surrendered life looks like.

## A Promise Believing Heart

Joshua didn't live for this world. He lived by faith for another world. He believed the promises of God when they seemed impossible. Joshua trusted God to defeat Israel's enemies and fight for them. Joshua says to Israel:

> **Joshua 23:5** | The Lord your God will push them [your enemies] back before you and drive them out of your sight. And you shall possess their land, just as the Lord your God promised you.

Do you believe that God can conquer all your enemies? ...Enslavement to sin, the devil and the world. Christ can defeat every enslavement.

> You will know the truth, and the truth will set you free. —John 8:32

How many of us can testify that this is true?

> If the Son sets you free, you will be free indeed. —John 8:36

Are you free from the choking fruit of a worldly heart: selfish anger and slavish anxiety? Are you totally free? Are these things quickly conquered in your heart? These are feelings, right? But what are feelings? Sometimes we don't think feelings can be sinful, but every feeling is merely a disposition of the heart. What kind of heart disposition, feelings if you will, should we have?

> But the fruit of the Spirit is love, joy, peace, patience, kindness, goodness, faithfulness, [23] gentleness, self-control; against such things there is no law. —Galatians 5:22-23

We are called to have the fruit of the Spirit. Love, joy, peace, patience... All of these are states of your heart that show you are resting in the promises of God. If you have a heart that is bitter and angry or anxious you are living with the enemy in control of your heart. You know that's a wrong state of heart. Joshua was not brought down by the power of his flesh. He was set free by the promises of God. It was the promises of God that brought down all Israel's enemies. Don't get to the end of your life with a wasted legacy.

How about you? Are you leaving a legacy that points to Jesus? Are you sniffing those enemies out? Do you even understand the sin beneath the sin in your heart? You may shout in anger, but have you dealt with the sinful anger in your heart? You say something unkind in fear, but have you dealt with the anxiety in your heart. Are you living in bitterness? God says you can be delivered from all your enemies! Are you experiencing "all the fullness of God?" Do you know the "peace that passes understanding?" Are you "filled with the Spirit" so that you are "not giving in to the desires of the flesh"?

## A Scripture Examined Heart

So many people live without victory, because they have an unexamined heart. A lot of Christians live in idolatry because they will not do the "heart homework" necessary to get to the roots of idolatry. The only way to have know where your heart is going wrong is the light of Scripture. Your heart should be examined always by the Scripture.

**Joshua 23:6** | Therefore, be very strong to keep and to do all that is written in the Book of the Law of Moses, turning aside from it neither to the right hand nor to the left.

> Your word is a lamp to my feet and a light to my path. —Psalm 110:105

We dare not live life through our own fallen hearts. We have to examine the disposition of our heart by Scripture. This is why Joshua tells the children of Israel to "be strong" to go to the Scripture. It's easy to go through our own fallen hearts. I'll tell you God would have you to have a heart that is "filled with all the fullness of God". Are you experiencing the "peace that passes all understanding"? Are you? Take a moment. Examine your heart. Chase down the emotions of your heart that are forbidden by God. Please hear me, Christians can lose years of peace and joy in their lives by living in the deceit of forbidden dispositions of the heart, what we call feelings. Consider four categories of fleshly heart dispositions, fleshly emotions. We might call these the "sin beneath the sin."

*Anger*: bitterness, wrath, rage, slander, angry shouting, malice, unforgiveness, blowing up, clamming up, disruption, filibustering, etc.

*Fear*: anxiety, phobias, terror, hyper scrupulousness, angst, morbid concern, unbelief, doubt, dread, horror, jitters, panic, scared, morbidly suspicious, terror, unease, uneasiness, worry, agitation, aversion, consternation, cowardice, discomposure, disquietude, faintheartedness, foreboding, frightened, trembling, trepidation, cold sweat

*Despair*: hopelessness, desperation, dejection, depression, despondency, gloom, melancholy, self-loathing. disheartenment, discouragement, resignedness, forlornness, defeatism, pessimism, etc.

*Foolishness*: I feel I need to escape. I feel God doesn't understand and so I dismiss him from my thoughts to relieve the pressure or pain or situation. The desires and feeling like I need to use alcohol, drugs, pornography, abuse of food, or any turning anything to an idol of escape that leads to an enslaving affection.

Is your heart filled with the noise of fleshly desires? Examine your heart with the Word. How do I get rid of this noise? I have to apply God's Word to my heart.

Your word I have hidden in my heart, That I might not sin against You. —Psalm 119:11 (NKJV)

Are you experiencing the "peace that passes all understanding"? Are you? Take a moment. Examine your heart. Chase down the emotions of your heart that are forbidden by God. Please hear me, Christians can lose years of peace and joy in their lives by living in the deceit of forbidden dispositions of the heart, what we call feelings. Renew your heart and mind through the Scriptures.

The blessed man's delight is in the law of the Lord, and on his law he meditates day and night. —Psalm 1:2

Oh that you might have a heart like Joshua that believed the promises of God.

## A Heart that Clings to the Lord

Yet ultimately you can know the Scripture but not know the Lord. So that's the biggest part of Joshua's legacy. He knew the Lord. He taught God's people to cling to the Lord.

**Joshua 23:8** | ...you shall cling to the Lord your God just as you have done to this day.

Do you have that kind of heart? Are you experiencing God and clinging to him? There's not a thousand things, or 12 steps you need to do. There is one step: love the Lord!

## A Heart that Expects Miracles

Joshua saw miracles occur constantly. What is a miracle? It is when the divine intersects the normal realm. Not just having the sun stand still. He taught the people of Israel to expect miracles where God became personal and cherished to them. Like one man putting a thousand Canaanite soldiers to flight. Look at this.

**Joshua 23:9-10** | ...For the Lord has driven out before you great and strong nations. And as for you, no man has been able to stand before you to this day. [10] One man of you puts to flight a thousand, since it is the Lord your God who fights for you, just as he promised you. [11] Be very careful, therefore, to love the Lord your God.

I want to testify of what it looks like to expect miracles in your life. Yesterday evening I was praying with a family in our church who was in dire financial need. I didn't know how, but I knew God would provide. I prayed diligently with this dear family for a "Christmas miracle". Within the hour, I got a call from a man. He's not even a member of our church. He's not even a professing Christian. But he called me and said, "I want to give a Christmas miracle to someone in your church."

See God has control of all people on the earth. He can provide in any way that he wants to. This was the kind of faith Joshua had. Are you seeing the miracle power of Jesus in your life? How are you different from the world? Is there a great influence and aroma for Christ in your life? If not, surrender to the Lord right now. A generation of lost souls is depending on you. What a legacy Joshua had. What kind of

legacy are you leaving behind when God takes you home? So Joshua
had a legacy that pointed to Jesus. He also had a testimony that pointed
to Jesus.

## A TESTIMONY THAT POINTS TO JESUS (23:14-24:13)

Dear saints, Joshua was constantly talking and testifying about
God. It's not enough to know him and cling to him. That's everything
to us, but if you keep Jesus all to yourself, "how will they hear without
a preacher?" (Rom 10:14).

## A Faithful Testimony (23:14-24)

Joshua had a faithful testimony.

**Joshua 23:14** | "And now I am about to go the way of all the earth, and
you know in your hearts and souls, all of you, that not one word
has failed of all the good things that the Lord your God promised
concerning you. All have come to pass for you; not one of them
has failed.

This is what Joshua said all his life. God is faithful! God's promises
are true! You need to believe and trust in the Lord.

Taste and see that the Lord is good! —Psalm 34:8

But part of Joshua's testimony was a warning.

**Joshua 23:15-16** | But just as all the good things that the Lord your God
promised concerning you have been fulfilled for you, so
the Lord will bring upon you all the evil things, until he has destroyed you from off this good land that the Lord your God has
given you, ¹⁶ if you transgress the covenant of the Lord your God,
which he commanded you, and go and serve other gods and bow
down to them. Then the anger of the Lord will be kindled against
you, and you shall perish quickly from off the good land that he
has given to you.

Do you see that he's warning these families in Israel: "I'm leaving
to depart to be with the Lord. When I'm off the scene, you need to follow the Lord or you might lose everything." Parents, do your kids see a
testimony that loves Jesus? So many parents fail, and then they feel like
they can't testify to their kids. Listen, if you messed up, testify to them
about Jesus' forgiveness. Repent before your kids. Let them see your

love for Christ. More importantly, get some accountability and rich discipleship so you can have a consistent walk with Christ. You should be saying:

Be imitators of me, as I am of Christ. —1 Corinthians 11:1

## A Personal Testimony (24:1-13)

Our testimony is not just bold and faithful, but personal. We need to be able to testify of our personal experience with the Lord. The first thirteen verses of Joshua 24 are Joshua reciting the history of Israel. Joshua was an eye-witness to the grace and glory of God. God says:

**Joshua 24:6** | I brought your fathers out of Egypt, and you came to the sea. And the Egyptians pursued your fathers with chariots and horsemen to the Red Sea.

Joshua is testifying, not only of the Word of God, but of what he experienced. A believer has firsthand experience of the living God. God says to Israel: You saw my miracles. You enjoyed my presence.

God not only mentions the Red Sea, but the crossing of the Jordan, where the Jordan River parted for twenty miles! God says:

**Joshua 24:11** | You went over the Jordan and came to Jericho, and the leaders of Jericho fought against you, and also the Amorites, the Perizzites, the Canaanites, the Hittites, the Girgashites, the Hivites, and the Jebusites. And I gave them into your hand.

God says, "I gave you victory after victory." This is the personal testimonies we ought to have. You remember when God did this for me last week? Remember what God did for so and so this week? There ought to be the fresh manna of God's miracle presence every day. It's a *personal* testimony. Can you testify of God's activity in your life?

## A WORSHIP THAT POINTS TO JESUS (24:14-33)

The last and most important thing Joshua is he points to the coming king's worship. The Old Testament motif or expression of worship is: "the fear of the Lord". Joshua says, that's the most important. Joshua defines worship in a wonderful way. Worship is not just singing or praying to the Lord. It's not just reading the Word. You can do that and still be serving two masters. Worship demands that we put anything that might compete with the living God away from our lives. Look at how Joshua defines the worship God desires in these farewell words.

## A Sincere Worship

**Joshua 24:1-15** | Now therefore fear the Lord and serve him in sincer-
ity and in faithfulness. Put away the gods that your fathers served
beyond the River and in Egypt, and serve the Lord. [15] And if it is
evil in your eyes to serve the Lord, choose this day whom you will
serve, whether the gods your fathers served in the region beyond
the River, or the gods of the Amorites in whose land you
dwell. But as for me and my house, we will serve the Lord.

Joshua says, here's the point of my life: "fear the Lord and serve
him"—worship the Lord! I want to worship him in every part of my life.
What kind of fear are we talking about? It's not a superstitious fear. It's
the fear of worship and reverence and adoration of God in all things.

The fear of the LORD is the beginning of wisdom, and the knowledge
of the Holy One is insight. —Proverbs 9:10

You will know all you need to know as you worship the Lord in all
things. You have to invite God into all your thoughts, words and deeds.
This is the abundant life that Joshua chose! Joshua says:

Choose this day whom you will serve! ... But as for me and my house,
we will serve the Lord. —Joshua 24:15

Joshua was pointing forward to Jesus. Joshua didn't know

## A Serious Worship

The people respond to Joshua.

**Joshua 24:16**| Then the people answered, "Far be it from us that we
should forsake the Lord to serve other gods...

Joshua says:

**Joshua 24:19-20**| But Joshua said to the people, "You are not able to
serve the Lord, for he is a holy God. He is a jealous God; he will
not forgive your transgressions or your sins. [20] If you forsake
the Lord and serve foreign gods, then he will turn and do you
harm and consume you, after having done you good.

This is serious. So many among us have turned from the Lord after
they've come from a Christian home or knowing so much of the Lord,
but they turn away without truly being born again. There is no hope for

any of us if we have a superficial worship that doesn't change us. It has to be a serious worship.

**Joshua 24:21-23** | And the people said to Joshua, "No, but we will serve the Lord." [22] Then Joshua said to the people, "You are witnesses against yourselves that you have chosen the Lord, to serve him." And they said, "We are witnesses." [23] He said, "Then put away the foreign gods that are among you, and incline your heart to the Lord, the God of Israel."

Serious worship begins when we start putting our idols away. So the question is: do you have just superficial worship? Or are you a serious worshipper of the Lord. This worship of the Lord was *serious*. They were to seriously take a reckoning of their lives and destroy all idols. That's what the Christian life is. We cannot have two masters. We cannot worship God and money or anything else. That was Joshua's legacy, testimony and worship. That's what I want to leave behind. We learn that...

After these things Joshua the son of Nun, the servant of the Lord, died, being 110 years old. —Joshua 24:29

What a glorious life!

## Conclusion

What legacy will you leave? Who will take a stand? How among us will be hot in a cold-hearted generation? The churches are growing colder and colder. Are you moving our church to become hotter and hotter? The only way forward is rich discipleship and fellowship and worship. The only way I can leave that legacy is by looking unto that greater Joshua!

Looking unto Jesus the author and finisher of our faith... —Hebrews 2:2a

Let's do that saints, let's look unto Jesus. Let's be intentional about drawing near to him in worship and testifying about him to the world. I'll leave you with the challenge Joshua gave dear saints:

Choose this day whom you will serve! ... But as for me and my house, we will serve the Lord. —Joshua 24:15

You may obtain this and many other fine resources made available by Proclaim Publishers by contacting us:

**Web**:
proclaimpublishers.com

**Email**:
contact@proclaimpublishers.com

**Postal Mail**:
Proclaim Publishers
PO Box 2082
Wenatchee, WA 98807

www.ingramcontent.com/pod-product-compliance
Lightning Source LLC
Chambersburg PA
CBHW030820090426

42737CB00009B/805